D1597389

KINGS OF THE JUNGLE

KINGS OF THE JUNGLE

An Illustrated Reference to "Tarzan" on Screen and Television

by DAVID FURY

McFarland & Company, Inc., Publishers
Jefferson, North Carolina, and London

Frontispiece: Johnny Weissmuller and Maureen O'Sullivan on the set of *Tarzan, the Ape Man* (1932).

British Library Cataloguing-in-Publication data are available

Library of Congress Cataloguing-in-Publication Data

Fury, David.
Kings of the jungle : an illlustrated reference to "Tarzan" on
screen and television / by David Fury.
p.   cm.
Includes bibliographical references and index. ∞
ISBN 0-89950-771-9 (lib. bdg. : 50# alk. paper)
1. Tarzan films—History and criticism.   2. Tarzan (Fictitious
character)   I. Title.
PN1995.9.T3F87   1994
791.43'651—dc20   92-56644
CIP

Manufactured in the United States of America

McFarland & Company, Inc., Publishers
Box 611, Jefferson, North Carolina 28640

To all the actors who portrayed
Edgar Rice Burroughs' jungle hero Tarzan,
and especially to Johnny Weissmuller,
the greatest Tarzan of them all

ACKNOWLEDGMENTS

I gratefully acknowledge and thank from the heart all the following individuals and organizations who contributed their time and efforts to aiding my research for this Tarzan history and filmography.

My special appreciation goes to Maureen O'Sullivan, Bruce Bennett (Herman Brix), Denny Miller, Rudy Sigmund, Hank Brown, Ann McKee, Rhea Baldino, Mike Moody, Matt Wynans, David Hardy, Martin Williams, D. Peter Ogden, Martin Smiddy, Jodee Sunness, Frank Westwood and the Edgar Rice Burroughs Society, and George McWhorter.

I also warmly thank all my family members and friends for their unconditional support of this book and my other projects. A special remembrance goes to Dad, who used to watch the Tarzan movies with me when I was a kid and enjoyed them as much as I did.

In addition, I express my sincere gratitude to the Burroughs Bibliophiles and the Edgar Rice Burroughs Memorial Collection (University of Louisville Library), for the use of many of the photographs presented in this volume. Additional photographs were contributed by Rudy Sigmund, Martin Smiddy, and Frank Westwood; the remainder are from my own collection.

This book is in memory of my friend Chuck Connors, who was generous with his moral support of my projects and my biggest booster. Chuck Connors, The Rifleman, died on November 10, 1992.

CONTENTS

FOREWORD

I shall be ever grateful to Felix Feist, who directed the test that won me the role of Jane in the first of the MGM Tarzan series. I was 19 at the time, alone in Hollywood. I had exactly $250 in the bank and was a month behind in my rent at the Garden of Allah.

I was to be the new Janet Gaynor, a threat to the rebellious Janet who was biding her time in Honolulu while the studio threatened not to meet the demands she was making, financial or otherwise. The trouble was that her fans resented this new Janet, and when I was cast in a film that had been meant for her, they stayed away in droves. The studio became disgusted with me and dropped me as soon as my contract would allow, while Janet returned to the arms of her loving studio.

I was now adrift—almost broke, without a job and too proud to go home, a failure, to Ireland. So I gambled, got an agent, and spent my last money on some very un–Janetlike photographs. These photos led me to the test that I have just mentioned—which brings me to Felix Feist.

"Take One!" A year at Fox had only taught me my Janet Gaynor act. I was wistful, nauseatingly sweet. "Cut!" called Felix. "Stop that! Be strong and straight-forward!" he demanded. (Could I do that? I could and did.) "It's a wrap!"

said Felix, and I went home to wonder whether I had the part.

The next day my agent, a dear Irishman named Tom Conlon, called to tell me I had the role even though the director, Woody Van Dyke, had wanted someone else. After the usual wardrobe and makeup meetings, I was taken to the jungle set to meet Johnny Weissmuller, Edgar Rice Burroughs, and Woody Van Dyke.

Standing well behind the camera, I saw a Tarzan that the author could only have dreamed him to be. Golden makeup covered a body that was perfect. The setting sun lit his hair that was touched with gold. One foot was on a (sup-posedly) wounded lion. His arm was raised, and with the msot graceful gesture I have ever seen, he drove a spear into the animal's body. I watched in silence.

"Cut!" said Van Dyke, who seemed reconciled to the fact that I was to be Jane. "Come and meet Jane," he called to Johnny Weissmuller. "Hi Maggie!" said Johnny while extending that golden hand. (We had met once before, and he thought Maureen too dignified a name.) Edgar Rice Burroughs wanted a picture of us together. "My perfect Tarzan," he announced, "and my perfect Jane!" He sent me all his Tarzan books, and in the last book he wrote, "By now you should

The classic beauty of Maureen O'Sullivan with Johnny Weissmuller (circa 1940).

know everything there is to know about Tarzan."

I did get to know Johnny well, of course. It was difficult; he was a big, overgrown kid. I never saw him be less than happy. He had three wives who came and went during our jungle years. Johnny seemed the same happy-go-lucky person when they left as when they arrived. Of his love life he said, "Tarzan has a G-string, and women like to hang on." He never spoke of his Olympic triumphs or of the medals he had won. Nor did he speak of the countries that had honored him. I think he lived completely for the moment—happy with our make-believe life, with the crew, and with all the animals. Perhaps because he was a simple soul, they all adored him.

I had trouble with Cheetah, every Cheetah. Naturally, there was more than one during those nine years. The Cheetahs were jealous of me, and if I stood near Johnny, they tried to bite me.

When you see photographs of Johnny and me with Boy (John Sheffield) and Cheetah, you will always see the chimp next to Johnny and far from me. Often a wire was attached to the monkey's leg to keep her from me and still in the picture. Johnny liked practical jokes, such as giving me a birthday cake that blew up when I tried to cut it. Stage chemistry is an interesting thing. Johnny and I were very different, but on camera something must have been right.

Our lives and the lives of other Tarzans and Janes are documented in David Fury's lovely book. It is a knowledgeable book, and you will enjoy it as much as I do. I congratulate him and thank him for allowing me to be so much a part of our jungle magic.

Maureen O'Sullivan

Tarzan is the original superman, fighting for the rights of the under-dog. He's a terror to all villains, be they human or beast. He never enters into politics and rules his jungle domain with a minimum of words and a few pitched yells, hence he's understood by all. He represents pure escapist entertainment.

—Jock Mahoney, Tarzan #13

INTRODUCTION

Without a doubt one of the most fascinating characters in motion picture history is Edgar Rice Burroughs' courageous jungle demigod, Tarzan of the Apes. An untamed white man who was all-powerful within his viney domain and ruled over all the savage beasts of the deepest African jungles, Tarzan was indeed King of the Jungle.

Tarzan was born in the October 1912 issue of *The All-Story* magazine (cost: 15¢), in a tale called "Tarzan of the Apes (A Romance of the Jungle)." Certainly romance was an appropriately descriptive term, since fans of Tarzan have been carrying on a love affair with this jungle hero for the better part of a century. There seems to be no lessening of affection for the stories of Tarzan in film and pulp form.

Edgar Rice Burroughs' Tarzan character has inspired newspaper comic strips, radio programs, television series, comic books and children's toys and mesmerized millions of fans. Countless males and females of all ages have lived vicariously through the inspiring adventures of the heroic Tarzan, ruling the jungle and all its creatures, and swinging through the vines with the beautiful Jane by his side.

There have been over 40 authorized Tarzan feature films, and a multitude of actors have portrayed the sinewy ape-man on the silver screen, ever since Elmo Lincoln donned the loincloth in *Tarzan of the Apes* (1918). Tarzan movies are filled with thrilling adventure, jungle romance, tumultuous action, ferocious wild animals, and the comic antics and heroism of the faithful chimpanzees.

Undeniably the greatest Tarzan of all time was Johnny Weissmuller, the Olympic swimming champion who starred in 12 Tarzan films, beginning with the classic *Tarzan, the Ape Man* (1932). The vast majority of Tarzan fans will agree that Weissmuller was the definitive motion picture Tarzan—from his lean symmetrical physique, his dark brooding looks and snarling expressions of Tarzanian displeasure, to the blood-curdling Tarzan yell that Johnny made famous. With an almost innocent approach to his portrayal of the jungle man, Weissmuller has been the people's choice as their favorite movie Tarzan.

Maureen O'Sullivan is certainly the actress who will be most fondly cherished as Jane, Tarzan's better half. She seemed the perfect complement to Weissmuller's jungle man. Her unique beauty and shapely figure, along with the courage and loyalty she portrayed in the films, made her the ultimate mate for Tarzan. It's no coincidence that the film generally considered to be the greatest Tarzan

1

Edgar Rice Burroughs on the movie set of *Tarzan, the Ape Man* (1932) with Maureen O'Sullivan and Johnny Weissmuller.

picture of all time, *Tarzan and His Mate* (1934), is also the most memorable performance of O'Sullivan's distinguished acting career.

As a 1950s youth with a great imagination, I was enthralled by the weekend matinees of Tarzan, the apeman (the films of Johnny Weissmuller, with his spine-tingling war cry, shown on television and those of Gordon Scott, with his magnificent physique, at the movie theaters). I simply couldn't get enough of the thrilling adventures of the powerful jungle lord; Tarzan was just such a hero for a boy to dream about.

In my attic one day, I came upon a dusty early edition of *Tarzan of the Apes*, a novel by Edgar Rice Burroughs, that began a several-year odyssey in which I faithfully devoured the two dozen Tarzan novels, as well as other Burroughs classics, including the equally captivating John Carter of Mars series. Like millions of other Tarzan fans, I became a Burroughs aficionado, initially through the Tarzan films and then by reading the works of the legendary author.

From Burroughs' Tarzan stories came the dozens of exciting Tarzan motion pictures that are documented in this volume. Tarzan is idolized by millions of fans around the world to this day. The movies are simply another medium in which to enjoy the perilous and often-romantic adventures of Burroughs' extraordinary creation, Tarzan the ape-man.

This book covers all the Tarzan film adventures and all the actors who portrayed the ape-man. Undoubtedly there will be new Tarzan movies in the years to come. Regardless of what the future holds, the courageous jungle man will live in the hearts of all who cherish his brave deeds and romantic mystique.This book, a history and filmography of the Tarzan motion pictures, celebrates this fabled King of the Jungle.

With the fun of writing *Kings of the Jungle* now finished, I would like to add a few miscellaneous notes to clarify a few points. The sequence used in this book for the Tarzan actors has Elmo Lincoln as the first screen Tarzan (as a man). Actually, Gordon Griffith was the first actor to portray Tarzan on the screen (in *Tarzan of the Apes*) in 1918, but as a boy. For those who might be confused by the term "great apes" (in the synopses), as in "Tarzan's tribe of great apes," this is a fictional species larger and more powerful than chimpanzees, created by Edgar Rice Burroughs. Their mortal enemy was the gorilla. The spelling of the name of Tarzan's chimpanzee Cheeta was one of three used during the long run of the Tarzan films (along with Cheetah and Cheta). For the sake of uniformity, I chose to use Cheeta throughout the book (except for Maureen O'Sullivan's Foreword, which uses Cheetah).

David Fury

EDGAR RICE BURROUGHS DISCOVERS TARZAN

Tramping through the jungles of his mind, Edgar Rice Burroughs discovered perhaps the most famous fictional hero, Tarzan, the bronze-skinned jungle man. Burroughs' vivid imagination whirled over four decades as he authored 70 published adventure and science fiction tales that have delighted millions of readers worldwide, having been translated into 34 languages. His Tarzan novels were certainly his most famous works and were largely responsible for his international fame as an author. From these Tarzan stories came the Tarzan motion pictures.

The story of Tarzan is universally known: Englishman John Clayton and his wife Alice, Lord and Lady Greystoke, are put ashore in the wilds of Africa by the mutinous crew of the vessel *Fuwalda*. Some months after their abandonment, Alice Clayton gives birth to a son, the heir to the Greystoke name and legacy. Within a year of the boy's birth, Lady Greystoke succumbs to the mental duress of isolation in the savage African jungle. Almost mercifully in his grief, Lord Greystoke is killed by the great ape Kerchak, who storms their crude cabin in a fit of rage. Before Kerchak can kill the Clayton infant in his cradle, the child is swooped up in the arms of the she-ape Kala, whose own baby had died; Kala protects and nurtures the tiny creature as her own and names him Tarzan (meaning white skin). Raised by apes in the jungles of Africa, Tarzan, the young man, kills Kerchak in battle and becomes the ruler of the ape tribe and eventually master of all creatures in the jungle. He is Tarzan the ape-man, King of the Jungle.

This is the legend created by the master storyteller Burroughs, which in harmony with his other unique characters, earned ERB (as he is known to his worldwide legion of fans) the title Grandfather of American Science Fiction.

Born in Chicago on September 1, 1875, Edgar Rice Burroughs had a childhood that may be described as mostly average, with occasional spectacular exceptions. His parents and four brothers were a close family unit, and his father, George Tyler Burroughs, earned a respectable living as a businessman to provide an upper middle-class lifestyle. Ed Burroughs' most exciting chapter as a youth (in 1891, at age 15) was the several months he spent on his two older brothers' BAR-Y ranch in Idaho, learning to ride horses and to rope and herd cattle.

5

Edgar Rice Burroughs on the set of *Tarzan and the Golden Lion* (1927) with director J.P. McGowan.

In his unpublished autobiography Burroughs tells of breaking a fierce gelding named Whiskey Jack, who had killed a man and maimed several others. Thereafter he was the only one who could ride the cantankerous mount. In an interview with the *New York Sunday World* (October 27, 1929), Burroughs boasted that he had "ridden the ranges in the days of horse thieves, cattle rustlers, and pitched battles between sheep [herders] and cattlemen." The West was truly the Wild West during this period, and perhaps these months as a tenderfoot among hardened cowpokes helped mold the wet-behind-the-ears youngster into a man and later to inspire his highly imaginative writing. (In addition to his more famous Tarzan and Martian series, Burroughs authored four western adventure novels, undoubtedly influenced by his memorable sojourn as a teenager in the Idaho wilds.)

Although great success would come to Burroughs later in life, his early failings included dismissal from Phillips Academy in Andover, Massachusetts, in just his second semester (which subsequently landed him in Orchard Lake Military School to learn, as his father put it, "discipline"); failure to pass his examination after being appointed to West Point (1895); and, after enlisting in the regular army as a private in May 1896, a discharge in March 1897 because of a diagnosis of a heart murmur. His dreams of a service career were further dashed when his request for a commission in Teddy Roosevelt's Rough Riders was turned down in 1898.

During his brief career in the army, he was stationed at Fort Grant in the rugged Arizona Territory; his most memorable duty was being part of a cavalry troop assigned to hunt down a renegade Apache called the Apache Kid (although the renegade was never caught and apparently never even sighted). Almost a half century later, after having witnessed the Japanese attack on Pearl Harbor, a patriotic Burroughs acted as America's oldest war correspondent in World War II, finally getting a chance to serve his country at an age when the rocking chair beckoned most others.

Burroughs spent the initial half of his life often in disappointment and failure, seeking to find the proper vocation for his brilliant imagination—moving from job to job, staying with an occupation only long enough to know that that was not his life's work. The first 36 years of his life were basically an ordinary tale of a man searching, unsuccessfully, for his niche in the world.

Burroughs' list of occupations before he became a writer in 1911 is long and unimpressive, indeed, and includes being a railroad cop in Salt Lake City (rousting sleeping bums from vacant boxcars); working on a gold dredge on the Snake River in Oregon (and finding little gold); selling light bulbs to janitors, candy to drugstores, and Stoddard's Lectures from door to door; being an "expert" accountant (though he admitted he knew nothing about accounting); having a good job at Sears with excellent prospects that he quit to start his own business (which failed miserably); and being a collector for an ice company and a sales agent for lead-pencil sharpeners.

Often changing jobs and rarely making enough money to support his wife Emma (his childhood sweetheart) and their children (Joan, born January 12, 1908; Hulbert, born August 12, 1909; and John, born February 28, 1913). Burroughs admitted later in life that they lived perilously close to the poverty line in those early years. In truth, destitution was a state of anguish for Burroughs, who, at the nadir of their existence, had to sell his wife's jewelry just to buy food. Although he could have made a comfortable living working at his father's American Battery Company in Chicago (as he did for a period), this determined young man wanted to make it on his own without the crutch of working in a family-owned business.

Seeking both to find a release for his creative juices and to earn a respectable living, Burroughs finally stumbled onto his life's work in early 1911, with the penning of his first story, "Under the Moons of Mars." He had decided to try his hand at writing after poring over several all-fiction magazines, reasoning: "If people were paid for writing such rot as I read, I could write stories just as rotten. Although I had never written a story, I knew absolutely that I could write stories just as entertaining and probably more so than any I chanced to read in those magazines" (*Washington Post* interview, October 27, 1929).

It was surely a stroke of fortune that Burroughs submitted his initial literary effort to editor Thomas Metcalf, of *The All-Story* magazine. Metcalf was receptive to his visionary science fiction tale, a romantic Martian adventure complete with a dynamic hero, John Carter of Virginia, and, of course, a beautiful princess—and published it in six parts beginning with the February 1912 issue. Burroughs later admitted that without the encouragement of Metcalf, who saw great promise in Burroughs' imaginative style, he might have given up on writing before his marvelous career even began.

Curiously, and with a sarcastic sense of humor that often reared its head in his writing, Burroughs chose to use the pseudonym Normal Bean for "Under the Moons of Mars," which, of course, was his way of proclaiming his sanity to the world. Unfortunately, the humor was lost and replaced by irony when a proofreader corrected what he thought was a typo and changed "Normal" to "Norman." Thereafter, Burroughs abandoned his nom de plume, and used his given name, Edgar Rice Burroughs, for all his stories.

Having been paid $400 for his first published tale (a sum equal to several months' wages), Burroughs realized he was finally on the right track and followed his newfound career as a writer with remarkable dedication and zeal. It didn't take long for him to complete a second adventure, "The Outlaw of Torn," an historical romance about a 13th-century British prince. His latest effort didn't sell immediately, and Burroughs subsequently landed a job as a department manager for a business magazine called *System*. During his spare hours, Burroughs wrote "Tarzan of the Apes" on the backs of old letterheads and scraps of paper (with nary a penny in the family coffers to "waste" on writing paper).

Soon thereafter, a momentous literary era began with the publication of "Tarzan of the Apes," also in *The All-Story* (October 1912). Burroughs was paid the handsome sum of $700 for his first Tarzan story, and his career as an author was underway. Unfortunately, his joy over his newfound success was tempered by the death of his father on February 15, 1913; George Burroughs would not see the great heights his soon-to-be-famous son would eventually scale as an author.

When *Tarzan of the Apes* was published in book form in 1914 by A.C. McClurg (who, along with several other publishers, had originally turned it down), Burroughs was on his way to becoming one of the most prolific and well-known American authors of the 20th century. The McClurg edition of the book ultimately sold over 3 million copies, stamping Burroughs as an immediate triumph as an author after years of struggle and failure in business.

With the ever-increasing success of his Tarzan stories, Burroughs eventually became interested in bringing his jungle man to the silver screen. In late 1914 the author mailed a copy of *Tarzan of the Apes*, along with the unpublished "The Lad and the Lion," to Colonel William N. Selig, president of the Selig Polyscope Company in Chicago. Selig was a pioneer in the silent film era, producing many wild animal films from his studios in Los Angeles; Chicago; and Prescott, Arizona.

Interestingly enough, it was "The Lad and the Lion," rather than the original Tarzan story, that Selig chose to produce. Released in May 1917, the film was about the exciting adventures of a young man and a lion who are shipwrecked together in Africa and who become close companions. In the meantime Burroughs had pitched *Tarzan of the Apes* to the American Film Company in Chicago, but was rejected on the shortsighted premise that the story was "impractical for motion picture purposes."

Undaunted by rejection, Burroughs signed a contract with William Parsons, president of the National Film Corporation (an independent production company), in June 1916 to produce *Tarzan of the Apes*. The entrepreneurial Parsons had promised his new partner $5,000 in cash and $50,000 worth of stock in the film company, but it would be many months and several deadlines later when he finally fulfilled his contract. The first motion picture Tarzan was Elmo Lincoln, and with the opening of *Tarzan of the Apes* at the Broadway Theatre in New York, on January 27, 1918, the long history of the Tarzan film genre began.

In the decades that followed, and the dozens of Tarzan films that resulted, Burroughs wanted more involvement in the pictures than he was able to realize; *The New Adventures of Tarzan* (1935) and its sequel, *Tarzan and the Green Goddess* (1938) would be the only Burroughs-produced Tarzan films. The star of both, Herman Brix, was personally approved by Burroughs. Of particular disenchantment to the creator of Tarzan was the movies' depiction of his ape-man as an uneducated savage who could speak only in monosyllables; the hero of his novels was an intelligent man-beast (John Clayton, heir to the House of Greystoke) who combined a perfect command of several languages with the immense physical strength and instinctive cunning of a wild jungle creature.

Since Burroughs sold the film rights to the motion picture companies, however, the studios were able to characterize Tarzan as they thought the moviegoing public wanted him to be: a handsome, brawny jungle man with a limited English vocabulary. Burroughs had created a character that was vastly different from the movies' version of the ape-man, and this dichotomy was particularly agitating to him during his lifetime. Many years after his death, the first half of the 1984 film *Greystoke: The Legend of Tarzan* most closely adhered to the author's original concept of Tarzan.

Edgar Rice Burroughs continued to reap the financial rewards of negotiated film rights to produce the Tarzan films. To be closer to Hollywood, in 1919 he moved his family from their longtime home in Chicago to a sprawling 540-acre estate in California's San Fernando Valley that Burroughs christened Tarzana. Burroughs endured and persevered to create his thrilling adventure tales for almost 40 years and was planning a new series of stories on the planet Jupiter when he died of heart failure on March 19, 1950, at the age of 74.

The legacy of Edgar Rice Burroughs is the legendary characters he created and the universal appeal of his stories—flights of fantasy into savage and dangerous worlds of the unknown. His heroes, most notably Tarzan, are immortalized in the pages of books and the larger-than-life images of the silver screen.

I

The Silent Era Tarzans

Tarzan of the Apes

Release date: January 27, 1918; National Film Corporation of America/First National Pictures; eight reels. *Directed by* Scott Sidney; *produced by* William Parsons; *adapted by* Lois Weber and Fred Miller, *based on the novel* Tarzan of the Apes *by* Edgar Rice Burroughs; *director of photography,* Gilbert Warrenton; *cameraman,* Harry Vallejo; *wild animal photographer,* E.A. Martin; *editing,* Isadore Bernstein; *assistant director,* Charles Watt; *set designers,* M.J. Doner and Ted Bevis; *art director,* F.I. Wetherbee.

Tarzan	Elmo Lincoln
Jane Porter	Enid Markey
Tarzan as a boy	Gordon Griffith
Lord Greystoke	True Boardman
Lady Greystoke	Kathleen Kirkham
Binns	George B. French
Greystoke's nephew, Cecil	Colin Kenny
Professor Porter	Thomas Jefferson
Esmeralda, the maid	Bessie Toner
Innkeeper	Louis Morrison
Captain of the Fuwalda	Jack Wilson

Also featuring Fred Wilson, Eugene Pallette, and Rex Ingram.

John Clayton, Earl of Greystoke, is summoned by his government to investigate Arab slave trading in British Africa. En route to Africa on the sailing vessel *Fuwalda,* a mutiny takes place and the ship's captain is murdered. The crew wants to kill Lord and Lady Greystoke as well, but Binns, one of the sailors, with gun in hand, holds off the mutineers and orders that the Claytons be put ashore.

Binns and the two strangers he has saved from death are abandoned on the edge of an almost impenetrable jungle; Binns is captured by Arab slavers and

never sees the Claytons again. John builds a crude but sturdy log cabin for shelter from the hostile environment. Soon thereafter a baby's cry is heard — an heir is born to the noble House of Greystoke. Unfortunately, Lady Alice dies less than a year after her son's birth, and John writes in his journal, "Alice is dead and our baby is crying for nourishment. What shall I do?"

Clayton is mercifully relieved of his desolation, killed by Kerchak the great ape who storms the cabin in a rage. Kala, the she-ape whose own baby had died, claims the small human child, names

Advertising poster for *Tarzan of the Apes*, 1918.

him "Tarzan," and raises him among the apes as her own.

Years later, Tarzan discovers his parents' long-abandoned cabin and he begins to understand the printed word from a children's primer he finds. Armed with his father's hunting knife, he now has a weapon with which to dominate the other creatures. When one of his tribe of great apes is attacked by their mortal enemy, the gorilla, Tarzan kills the beast with his newfound blade and rejoices in his triumph.

Meanwhile, Binns finally escapes the Arab slavers. He reaches the Claytons' cabin, only to find their skeletons. Tarzan returns to the cabin and comes upon the sleeping Binns. They soon become friends, and the ex-sailor teaches the jungle lad to read and write. Binns eventually escapes Africa and reaches England, where the new countess has him locked away in a madhouse to keep him from telling his story of the Greystoke heir.

Back in the jungles, Tarzan's she-ape mother is killed by the arrow of a native. In his pain at the death of Kala, Tarzan tracks the murderer through the jungle and strangles him. He beats his chest and gives the victory cry of the bull ape.

Eventually, a search party makes its way to Africa, where Tarzan is now a full-grown man. Among the expedition are Professor Porter; his daughter, Jane; and Greystoke's nephew. When the searchers find Tarzan's cabin and the skeletons of the Claytons (including the tiny skull of Kala's ape baby), they falsely conclude that Binns' tale of a Greystoke heir is a concoction.

Tarzan watches Jane from a distance. He doesn't understand why, but he is in love with her. Tarzan bristles with jealousy when Greystoke's nephew makes a pass at Jane in the cabin. The ape-man reaches through a window and shakes the cad like a rag doll with one arm. Jane is impressed. When a lion tries to crawl through the cabin window to get to Jane, Tarzan springs to action to kill the beast. Later, Jane is carried off into the bushes by a renegade native, and the ape-man follows and fights the native to the death for the woman he loves.

Tarzan carries Jane through the jungles, while Jane's people are frantically searching for her. He and Jane run headlong into a tribe of angry natives, and the battle is on. Using his ingenuity, Tarzan starts their village on fire, and the natives race to their huts that go up in flames.

Jane is once again thrilled by the heroics of Tarzan, who brings her a gift of food. Tarzan aches to take Jane in his arms. He puffs his chest and woos her, but Jane politely rebuffs his advances. Tarzan's noble heart holds firm, and he guards Jane throughout the night as she sleeps.

The next morning Tarzan brings Jane through the jungle to her people and turns to leave, but Jane has made up her mind. She runs to Tarzan's arms, crying "Tarzan!"—the ape-man has found his mate.

•

Tarzan of the Apes, the motion picture version of Edgar Rice Burroughs' classic jungle tale, made its debut at the Broadway Theatre at 41st Street and Broadway in New York City on January 27, 1918. Starring in the First National eight-reel feature was 28-year-old Elmo Lincoln, who garnered a considerable amount of screen immortality as the motion picture's first adult Tarzan.

Born Otto Elmo Linkenhelter in 1889, the former railroad engineer was powerfully built, with a massive chest and huge thighs; he weighed over 200 pounds and stood around six feet tall. Square jawed, with a bullish neck and powerful arms, Lincoln indeed had the

Elmo Lincoln as Tarzan with Enid Markey as Jane and cast members (*Tarzan of the Apes*, 1918).

physical countenance to portray Burroughs' fictional ape-man.

Lincoln had broken into moving pictures in 1913, working in *The Battle of Elderbush Gulch* for legendary producer-director D.W. Griffith, who gave the burly actor his screen name. Elmo also appeared as a blacksmith in the Griffith masterpiece *Birth of a Nation* (1915) and as the mighty warrior in *Intolerance* (1916), as well as in other pictures, before landing his role as Tarzan.

The New York actor Winslow Wilson was originally signed by producer William Parsons to portray Tarzan in his production of *Tarzan of the Apes.* The filming was to take place in the backwoods of Louisiana. Director Scott Sidney settled on an area outside Morgan City. Winslow joined the company in Louisiana but soon thereafter enlisted in the army, leaving them without an actor to portray Tarzan.

It is reported that as many as 35 actors were screened in the search for the new ape-man before Lincoln was hired. In the role of Tarzan as a boy was 10-year-old Gordon Griffith, who, technically speaking, was the first actor to portray Tarzan. Griffith, a child actor in many early films, performed his initial scenes in the picture in the nude, until the young Tarzan "borrowed" a loincloth from a native who went swimming.

Enid Markey played the part of Jane Porter, and George B. French was the sailor, Binns. Listed in the credits was Rex Ingram, who eventually forged a long career as a character actor.

Ingram was cast as the native who abducts Jane and fights Tarzan when he comes to her rescue.

The film version of *Tarzan of the Apes* is true to Burroughs' novel, with minor exceptions; sailor Binns, who teaches young Tarzan to read and write in English, replaced French Lieutenant D'Arnot (in the book D'Arnot taught the lad his native tongue of French). In the novel Tarzan follows Jane Porter back to the United States to win her love; the filmed version ends in the jungle (until the sequel *The Romance of Tarzan* was released later in 1918). At least five different people contributed to the adaptation, including Fred Miller and Lois Weber. At times they actually worked without a script and improvised as they went.

Originally eight reels and approximately 95 minutes long, the version that is available on videocassette is five of the original reels equaling 61 minutes. (The omitted scenes are mostly of Binns' trip back to England.)

The Louisiana filming took place from late August to October 1917. Animal scenes were shot at the E & R Jungle film company in Los Angeles. Newspaper accounts of the shooting of the lion scenes included the instance of Elmo Lincoln actually killing an ancient lion that attacked him; the stuffed lion was later displayed at the Broadway Theatre when the picture was shown. Tarzan's tribe of apes were, of course, men in ape costumes—gymnasts hired from the New Orleans YMCA to don the goat-skin monkey suits and swing through the trees.

Actual jungle footage had been photographed previously in the wilds of Brazil and Peru and featured South American natives portraying their African counterparts. Native huts were built and then burned down for the final battle, and the blinding thunderstorm was also filmed in South America. The

New York Times reported that the filming headquarters was a place called Itejuca, 60 miles inland from the Amazon River. Back in Los Angeles in October, more wild animal scenes were shot in Griffith Park, where a replica of the Clayton cabin had been built in a wooded area. Aquatic scenes were photographed from a boat off the coast of San Pedro.

Filming was completed on January 15, 1918, with a reported cost of $300,000. (However, William Parsons had a wild imagination when it came to giving information to the press; for example, a press release published by the *New York Times* on February 3 included the following exaggerations: "Eleven hundred natives were used in the production.... Forty high-priced aerial acrobats were engaged and paid for an entire season's work [those were the YMCA gymnasts in ape costume].... Three hundred native huts were built in the Brazilian jungles [more like 30 for the fire scene]."

Parsons also hired Harry Reichenbach as publicity manager for the film. Reichenbach's stunts included dressing in an ape costume and attempting to register as a guest at the ritzy Knickerbocker Hotel in New York. Reichenbach also invited Edgar Rice Burroughs to the premiere by letter on January 16, but the author declined the invitation. On Sunday, January 27, the morning of the opening, an ad in the *New York Times* announced:

THE MOST STUPENDOUS, AMAZING, STARTLING FILM PRODUCTION IN THE WORLD'S HISTORY.... TARZAN OF THE APES ... SEE TARZAN'S STRUGGLE WITH THE LION—THE ELEPHANT RAID ON CANNIBAL VILLAGE—BATTLE BETWEEN AN APE AND GORILLA—ABDUCTION OF THE WHITE GIRL BY APES ... PRODUCED IN THE WILDEST JUNGLES OF BRAZIL AT A COST OF $300,000.

Tarzan of the Apes was indeed "stupendous," as the advertising described,

and grossed over $1 million worth of business; it was one of the first motion pictures to make seven figures in box office receipts. The monumental success of *Tarzan of the Apes* for National Film Corporation was largely responsible for making its distributor, First National Pictures, a major production force after 1915 and throughout the 1920s. First National had opened its doors for business in December 1917, and *Tarzan of the Apes* was its eighth general release.

For a film produced in the somewhat primitive filmmaking era of 1917, it was truly a remarkable achievement. Considering the efforts put forth in filming parts of the picture in the jungles of Brazil and on location in Louisiana, as well as the dangerous lions used (apparently at great risk to the actors), it was indeed cinematic history. Elmo Lincoln as Tarzan was certainly memorable, and young Gordon Griffith left a strong impression as the first screen Tarzan (as a boy). The critics were certainly impressed with the film, as the following reviews confirm:

New York Times (January 28, 1918): "*Tarzan of the Apes,* which excited considerable interest among the readers of the popular-priced fiction several years ago, was shown at the Broadway Theatre last night in film form. Being the story of a primeval man—or, rather, of a man brought up among apes and endowed with many of their abilities—it presents not a few difficulties to the movie maker. All of these have been overcome in the film at the Broadway, and apes swing realistically from bough to bough in the jungle, while lions and leopards seek their prey on the ground below. Intertwined with the jungle story is a domestic narrative which grows tedious at times, and the expedient of the cut-back is resorted to a trifle too freely. All of this is more than compensated for, however, by the stirring scenes of the jungle. A majority of these were photographed in Brazil, and several hundred natives appear before the camera. The picture as a whole, in addition to being interesting, also has a touch of educational value. An actor named Elmo Lincoln meets the difficult requirements of the hero satisfactorily."

Chicago Tribune (May 15, 1918): "Well folks, there's a brand new picture in town. And it's different from anything that's gone before it. It's *Tarzan of the Apes,* and is shown at the Colonial. Do you remember how you sat up most of the night to finish your first real adventure story? Well, it's better than that! And do you remember your first love story! Well, it's better than that! And all the wondering that's been done as to how they get animals to act in the movies—wait until you see the apes and lions and elephants "acting" in Tarzan.... Darwin's theory isn't particularly complimentary. Let's hope there was not one missing link but quite a chain of 'em. But anyway be sure to see *Tarzan.*"

Motion Picture Magazine (March 1918): "A thrilling, spectacular drama that contains a little of everything, including wild animals, African jungles, English lords and ladies, ships, yachts, dance-halls, fights, villains, heroes, high-brows and low-brows.... The photography is superb, and the acting, for the most part, fine."

Opposite: Elmo Lincoln with the ancient lion he actually killed (*Tarzan of the Apes,* 1918).

The Romance of Tarzan

Release date: September 1918; National Film Corporation of America/First National Pictures; seven reels. *Directed by* Wilfred Lucas; *produced by* William Parsons; *adapted by* Bess Meredyth, *based on the novel* Tarzan of the Apes *by* Edgar Rice Burroughs; *photographed by* Harry Vallejo; *production supervised by* Isadore Bernstein.

Tarzan	Elmo Lincoln
Jane Porter	Enid Markey
La Belle Odine	Cleo Madison
Cecil, Greystoke's nephew	Colin Kenny
Professor Porter	Thomas Jefferson
Tarzan as a boy	Gordon Griffith
Lord Greystoke	True Boardman
Lady Greystoke	Kathleen Kirkham
Binns	George B. French

Also featuring Bessie Toner, Monte Blue, Nigel de Brulier, Clyde Benson, Phil Dunham, and John Cook.

Lord and Lady Greystoke (John and Alice Clayton) are put ashore in West Africa by the mutinous crew of the ship *Fuwalda,* on the edge of a wild and savage jungle. Soon after giving birth to a son, Alice Clayton dies and husband John is killed by the great ape Kerchak. The tiny Clayton child is raised as her own by she-ape Kala, who lost her own ape baby.

The boy grows into the man Tarzan, and a search party comes from England in hopes of finding the truth: whether the son of Lord and Lady Greystoke is truly alive in the jungle, living as a primitive ape-man.

When the searchers (including Professor Porter and daughter Jane) are attacked by natives, they take refuge in the cabin built years before by John Clayton. Tarzan comes to their rescue by means of an emergency escape tunnel dug by his father and leads them to the shore where their boat lies waiting.

Tarzan holds off the enemy as Jane and company make for the boat, but Cecil, Greystoke's nephew, tells them that he has seen Tarzan die, so they depart (the scheming Cecil wants Jane, as well as the Greystoke fortune, for himself). Tarzan loves Jane with all his heart, and he jumps into the ocean to swim after them.

Tarzan's travels land him on an island, where he meets Father Raoul, a priest who furthers his education and teaches him the ways of civilized man. Eventually Tarzan stows away on a ship and lands on the coast of California, unaware that he is near his darling Jane.

Making his way to a dancing resort near the Mexican border, Tarzan hears a female cry for help. He is stunned to discover the voice is that of Jane, who has been kidnapped by thieves and brought to the resort. Tarzan breaks down a door and rescues his beloved, bringing her to her father.

Meanwhile, back at the resort, a beautiful "vamp" named La Belle Odine also has designs on the former jungle man, who is now dressed in a dashing tuxedo. The traitorous cousin Cecil arranges to have Tarzan killed, with the seductive La Belle as the bait in the trap. However, since she now loves

Tarzan herself, La Belle cannot go through with the treachery. Cecil also lies to Jane and tells her that Tarzan has fallen for La Belle. Jane naïvely believes this nonsense and chastises Tarzan for his infidelity.

Tarzan, by now fully confused with the ways of civilization, returns to his jungle home. Later La Belle admits to Jane that it was she who had plotted for Tarzan's love, not the other way around. Realizing how wrong she had been, Jane enlists her father to accompany her again to Africa to search for Tarzan.

•

Soon after the January 1918 release of *Tarzan of the Apes,* National Film president William Parsons signed Elmo Lincoln and Enid Markey to reprise their roles of Tarzan and Jane in a planned sequel, *The Romance of Tarzan.* However, author Edgar Rice Burroughs was not consulted about the production of the second film; he actually discovered the news in an article in the *Chicago Examiner* in May 1918, reporting a new Tarzan film in the works.

The main conflict between Burroughs and Parsons was that Parsons had obtained the rights to make a single Tarzan picture and, at least in the author's mind, this new venture was strictly unauthorized. From Parsons' standpoint, he owned the rights to the complete *Tarzan of the Apes* story and was now producing a "sequel" based on the second half of the book. Burroughs was understandably outraged, but his lawyer advised him that Parsons indeed had the right to produce a second picture, provided his scenario was based solely on *Tarzan of the Apes.* It's little wonder that Burroughs was once quoted, shaking his head, "The motion picture producer is the only man I care to have no further dealings with."

Despite the success of *Tarzan of the Apes,* Parsons selected a new director for the sequel, Wilfred Lucas, to replace Scott Sidney, who had done a marvelous job with the original film. Lucas was a well-known character actor in Hollywood for over three decades, often appearing in Laurel and Hardy comedies as a foil of Stan and Ollie (for example, as the warden in *Pardon Us,* 1931). He directed a number of films during the second decade of the century, then became strictly an actor around 1920. Filming took place at the National Film studio in Hollywood, with the location settings of Topanga Canyon and Griffith Park used once again.

The scenario for *Romance of Tarzan* was written by Bess Meredyth, who would forge a long career in Hollywood as a screenwriter (her many credits included the 1926 silent classic, *Ben-Hur*); in this instance, however, taking Tarzan out of the jungle proved to be a faux pas. Elmo Lincoln as Tarzan performing feats of derring-do in the jungle was more than believable, but Tarzan in a tuxedo mixing in high society was not the stuff that the Tarzan legend was built on. Even the title, which was chosen in hopes of luring film fans to see Tarzan in a "love affair," was misleading; Tarzan's romance was really more of a "runaround."

Cleo Madison portrayed the role of the femme fatale, La Belle Odine, the seductress who proves to be Tarzan's downfall in civilization. The pictorial prologue of *Romance of Tarzan* basically reviewed the events of *Tarzan of the Apes,* before the adventure moves to California, and reprising their roles were True Boardman and Kathleen Kirkham as Lord and Lady Greystoke; George B. French as Binns the sailor; Gordon Griffith again as Tarzan as a boy; and Colin Kenny as Cecil, the scheming Greystoke nephew. Sadly, this would be the final screen credit for True Boardman, who died of natural causes on September 28, 1918, at age 36.

Advertising poster, *The Romance of Tarzan*, 1918.

Elmo Lincoln would get one more opportunity to redeem himself as Tarzan in the 1921 serial, *The Adventures of Tarzan*, in which the ape-man was back in his domain—the African jungle. *The Romance of Tarzan* premiered in New York at the Strand Theatre on October 14, 1918, and ran for just seven days. For the most part, critics thought more of the highly regarded original *Tarzan of the Apes* than its sequel, as can be seen from these reviews:

***Motion Picture Magazine* (January 1919):** "The sequel to *Tarzan of the Apes* also has Elmo Lincoln and Enid Markey as the girl. Lincoln's chief action, when he reaches civilization from the jungle, seems to be to tear off first one coat and then another. As a matter of fact, he looks so uncomfortable in them we are glad when he goes back to the jungle and can remain coatless. This is not especially well done, but there is an adventurous spirit about it which is at least entertaining."

***New York Times* (October 14, 1918):** "To take Tarzan from his jungle and make him the hero of a trashy story of the popular novel is a literary crime. As the uncivilized Tarzan, Elmo is splendid, but as Tarzan in a dress suit—that is different."

The Revenge of Tarzan

Release date: May 1920; Numa Pictures Corporation/Goldwyn Pictures; seven reels. *Directed by* Harry Revier; *supervising producer,* George M. Merrick; *adapted by* Robert Saxmar, *based on the novel* The Return of Tarzan *by* Edgar Rice Burroughs; *prologue written by* John Wenger; *photographed by* John K. Holbrook and James C. Hutchinson; *technical directors,* Tom Tremaine and Frank Champrey.

Tarzan	Gene Pollar
Jane Porter	Karla Schramm
Countess de Coude	Estelle Taylor
Nicholas Rokoff	Armand Cortez
Ivan Paulovich	Walter Miller
Count de Coude	George Romain
Lieutenant Paul D'Arnot	Franklin Coates

Also featuring Betty Turner, Dorma Pepita Ramirez, Arthur Morrison, Jack Leonard, E.J. Sterne, and Phil Gostrock.

Tarzan is one of many passengers aboard a luxury ocean liner, bound for Paris from the United States, to seek his old friend and mentor, Paul D'Arnot. "Monsieur" Tarzan is dressed as an educated gentleman would dress, and his speech and mannerisms are impeccable.

Out of curiosity Tarzan enters the smoking room of the ship, where he finds a poker game in progress. He is just in time to find Count de Coude a victim of a card hustle. Tarzan notices one man slipping some cards into the count's pocket, and then with a pre-arranged signal to his confederate, the poker player (the Russian spy Rokoff)

leaps up and accuses the count of cheating. The former ape-man is quick to defend the count, who is grateful to Tarzan for saving his reputation. Rokoff vows to get even with this fool who has dared to interfere.

Once in Paris, Rokoff sets an ambush for Tarzan, who believes he is coming to the rescue of a woman in distress. Instead, Tarzan is cornered in a room by a dozen ruffians, who are intent on beating him to death. But Tarzan throws off the wraps of civilization and becomes a snarling beast and thrashes the cowards like they were a pack of cur dogs.

Later the count's wife befriends

Gene Pollar wrestles a lion (*The Revenge of Tarzan*, 1920).

Tarzan, and the unscrupulous Rokoff (who is the brother of the Countess de Coude) sets another trap for him. Rokoff manages to lure Tarzan to the countess' home at a late hour with a forged letter, and when the count arrives home on a mysterious tip (from Rokoff), he finds Tarzan and his wife together. They are innocent, of course, but the count demands a duel for his honor. Tarzan is wounded, but refuses to fire on his opponent. When the count discovers that Rokoff was behind the plot, he is grateful that his good friend Monsieur Tarzan has only a flesh wound.

Tarzan leaves France on a mission for the Foreign Office (a position arranged by his friend the count) and sets sail for Algiers. However, he is followed by Rokoff and his henchman Paulovich, who set upon him and overpower him in the desert. Tarzan is taken to an oasis, where he is bound to a tree and left to die.

Soon Tarzan hears the shattering roar of a man-eating lion and assumes he will soon meet his Maker. But to Tarzan's good fortune, a beautiful native girl happens along and sets him free. The ape-man makes short work of the

Gene Pollar as Tarzan (*The Revenge of Tarzan,* 1920).

battle to the death with the lion, choking the life from the snarling beast.

Eventually Tarzan is bound for Capetown aboard a ship, which also carries his mortal enemies Rokoff and Paulovich. As he leans over the ship's rail, they grab him by the heels and throw him into the sea. He is washed onto an island that is infested with the creatures of the jungles—apes, lions, leopards, and elephants. As fate would have it, a passing ship is wrecked and Jane, Tarzan's beloved, is washed onto the shore.

The incredulous Tarzan must save Jane from his enemies, who are quarreling over her, and once more he must strangle a lion that would take their fragile lives. Jane kisses Tarzan passionately, and thus the story ends.

•

When it came time to cast the important lead role of Tarzan for *The Return of Tarzan* (eventually changed to *The Revenge of Tarzan*), Elmo Lincoln, who had starred in the first two Tarzan features, was not considered. In fact, he was far from what author Edgar Rice Burroughs had envisioned his movie Tarzan would look like. In a letter to Pliny P. Craft of Monopol Pictures on January 28, 1919, ERB described his perfect screen Tarzan:

In the first place Tarzan must be young and handsome with an extremely masculine face and manner. Then he must be the epitome of grace. It may be difficult to get such a man but please do not try to get a giant or a man with over-developed muscles. It is true that in the stories I often speak of Tarzan as the "giant ape-man" but that is because I am rather prone to use superlatives. My conception of him is a man a little over six feet tall and built more like a panther than an elephant [Elmo Lincoln?]. I can give you some facial types that will give you an idea of about what I conceive Tarzan to look like though of course it is impossible to explain in detail. I should say that his face was more the type of Tom Meighan's or Tom Forman's but not like Wallace Reid. In other words, I conceive him of having a very strong masculine face and far from a pretty one.

It is doubtful that the actor chosen to be the next Tarzan, Gene Pollar, even remotely filled the bill as the demigod envisioned by Edgar Rice Burroughs; regardless, Pollar was indeed the movies' next jungle man. Pollar (real name Joseph C. Pohler) had never made a movie and was actually working in New York as a fireman when he was approached to play the role of Tarzan in early 1920 by Numa Pictures, owned by Louis Weiss and his brothers Max and Adolph. The Weiss brothers were looking for an actor about his size and weight (six feet two inches, 215 pounds), and Pollar had been recommended because of his solid physique and athletic skills. After passing a screen test, the new Tarzan gave up his job as a fireman and became the ape-man.

Pollar played Tarzan in an over-the-shoulder leopard skin that made him look more like a caveman than Tarzan. Once again the ape-man's travels brought him to civilization, where he donned a tuxedo and top hat and became John Clayton, Earl of Greystoke. The Weiss brothers made the mistake of putting Tarzan in clothes and running him around in civilization. The moviegoing public only wanted to see the King of the Jungle performing heroics in his natural domain.

Based on Burroughs' second published novel, *The Return of Tarzan*, the film adaptation by Robert Saxmar closely followed the book. Jane was played by Karla Schramm; the countess de Coude, by Estelle Taylor; the chief villains Rokoff and Paulovich, by Armand Cortez and Walter Miller, respectively; the count, by George Romain; and Tarzan's friend Paul D'Arnot, by Franklin Coates.

Photographed by John K. Holbrook and James C. Hutchinson, the film was shot in New York; Hollywood; and Lakewood, Florida. Wild animals were filmed at the Weiss brothers' zoo in Los Angeles. Critics of the film claim that the production values were poor and that the Weiss brothers cut financial corners at every opportunity; probably, the producers were only seeking to save money by casting an unknown as Tarzan instead of an established star who wouldn't come as cheaply.

Indeed, Pollar was duped with a salary of $100 per week to star in the picture, with more money promised if the feature was a success (it wasn't). Considering that he worked with live lions, Pollar's salary was paltry. Universal reportedly wanted Pollar to star in a jungle picture for them, but the Weiss brothers refused unless they were paid an exorbitant fee for his services. At the end of a year, Pollar's contract option with Numa Pictures expired, and his one-shot glimmer of fame as Tarzan the ape-man was over. It was the only picture he ever made. Pollar went back to his real name of Joseph C. Pohler and to his job as a New York City fireman. Edgar Rice Burroughs, speaking out on the movie Tarzans in the May 1934 issue of *Screen Play*, had the final word on Pollar as Tarzan: "As an actor, Gene was a great fireman. His selection is an outstanding example of the acumen of a certain type of motion picture producer."

The Return of Tarzan was produced

in the spring of 1920, and the Weiss brothers, seeking a quick profit, sold the world rights to Goldwyn Pictures on April 28 for a $100,000 advance plus a percentage of the profits. The film was previewed on May 30, 1920, at the Broadway Theatre in New York, with impresario Harry Reichenbach in charge of promotion. The original Numa Pictures nine-reel feature was subsequently cut to seven reels by Goldwyn, and on July 20, 1920, the picture was released under the revised title *The Revenge of Tarzan.* Apparently exhibitors were under the false impression that *The Return of Tarzan* was a rerelease of previous Tarzan pictures, and despite Burroughs' protests at the name switch, Goldwyn went ahead with the change. Film critics were divided on the merits of *The Revenge of Tarzan,* as noted in the following reviews:

***Moving Picture Herald* (Summer 1930):** "An exaggerated note of hectic melodrama is introduced in taking the hero out of the jungle and giving him a taste of civilization. The spirit of [*The Revenge of Tarzan*] is not conveyed until three or four reels have passed, when the onlooker is thankful that Tarzan is back with the birds and beasts. And even Gene Pollar's impersonation fails in its psychology. He appears to be as contented away from the jungle as in it.... Picture-goers who remember *Tarzan of the Apes* will probably reflect that the novelty is lost in the latest release."

***Stoll's Editorial News* (September 22, 1921) (England):** "Gene Pollar plays Tarzan with all the necessary vim and dash. Karla Schramm is excellent as Jane. Those who liked the preceding films will very much approve of the latest one. *The Return of Tarzan* [English title] is an excellent production."

***New York Times* (June 4, 1920):** "*The Return of Tarzan* is an improvement on the preceding Tarzan productions from at least one point of view—action. From start to finish Tarzan (Gene Pollar) is busy most of the time manhandling thugs or choking lions to death with his bare hands. His activities stamp him as a superman, for he tosses around human beings as easily as a grocery clerk handles pound packages of tea.... Mr. Pollar leaves nothing to be desired as Tarzan. Bearing in mind the superphysical attributes the story gives to Tarzan, which must dispel any tendency to carp at the seemingly impossible things he does, this is a good production and will undoubtedly please the majority of audiences. It certainly provides all the action the most exacting could demand."

The Son of Tarzan

Release date: December 1920; National Film Corporation of America; prologue plus 15 chapters. *Directed by* Harry Revier and Arthur J. Flaven; *adapted by* Roy Somerville, *based on the novel* The Son of Tarzan *by* Edgar Rice Burroughs; *photographed by* Lee Humiston and Walter Bell; *casting,* Jean Temple; *editing and titles by* Roy Somerville and Edgar Rice Burroughs.

Tarzan . . . . P. Dempsey Tabler
Korak, son of Tarzan . . . . Kamuela C. Searle

P. Dempsey Tabler as Tarzan with Karla Schramm as Jane (*The Son of Tarzan*, 1920).

Korak as a boy .... Gordon Griffith
Jane, Lady Greystoke .... Karla Schramm
Meriem (as a woman) .... Manilla Martan
Meriem (as a girl) .... Mae Giraci
Ivan Paulovich .... Eugene Burr

Also featuring Frank Merrill, Lucille Rubey,
De Sacia Saville, Kathleen May, Ray Thompson, and Frank Earle.

Chapters:

1. "The Call of the Jungle"
2. "Out of the Lion's Jaws"
3. "Girl of the Jungle"
4. "The Sheik's Revenge"
5. "The Pirate's Prey"
6. "The Killer's Mate"
7. "The Quest of the Killer"
8. "Coming of Tarzan"
9. "The Kiss of the Beast"
10. "Tarzan Takes the Trail"
11. "Ashes of Love"
12. "Meriem's Ride in the Night"
13. "Double Crossed"
14. "Blazing Hearts"
15. "An Amazing Denouement"

Kamuela Searle as Korak with Manilla Martan as Meriem (*The Son of Tarzan*, 1920).

It has been many years since Tarzan left the jungle to live in civilization with his wife, Jane, as Lord and Lady Greystoke. They both have fears that their son Jack has inherited the jungle instincts—indeed, his young heart is as savage as his brave father's. Meanwhile, stranded on the distant shores of Africa, Tarzan's bitter enemy, Ivan Paulovich, is saved by the crew of a sailing vessel. Paulovich heads for London and brings along one of Tarzan's ape friends, Akut, by trickery, to be exhibited in a theater as part of a vaudeville act.

Young Jack is instinctively drawn by his jungle instincts to the theater to see the ape. Akut, sensing that the boy is the son of Tarzan, goes berserk, and he and the boy cause a riot at the theater. Lord Greystoke (Tarzan) arrives and confronts his old enemy, Paulovich, and orders him to ship Akut back to Africa or face a severe thrashing. The cowardly Russian agrees, but tries to kill Jack when he comes to say good-bye to Akut. The loyal ape saves Jack from the deadly grip of Paulovich, and together the ape and the boy sail for Africa on a steamer, disguised as an elderly invalid (Akut) and her grandson.

In Africa, a series of events intertwine the paths of young Jack, the villain Paulovich, Tarzan and Jane, and many others. Fate brings them all together with the kidnapping of a small girl, Meriem, by an Arab sheik. Her father, Captain Jacot, offers a $100,000 reward for her return, which, in turn, brings Paulovich and his sinister cohort, the Swede, back to Africa. "I alone know where the girl is hidden!" boasts the Russian.

But young Jack, seeing the girl treated roughly from his perch high in the trees, rescues Meriem from the clutches of the Arabs. When he makes his first kill, he raises his mouth with a victory cry. He is now Korak the Killer, son of Tarzan! Korak and Meriem grow up together in the jungle, as Paulovich and the Swede beat the bushes in vain searching for them.

Eventually, Korak becomes King of the Apes by defeating the bull ape of the tribe in battle, a title he instead bestows on Akut. Korak has more important things in his life—he and Meriem have fallen in love. Tragically, Korak is injured by a spear and Meriem is once again captured by the Arab sheik. Meanwhile, Paulovich has lured Tarzan and Jane back to Africa with the news that their son is still alive, but it is vengeance alone that drives the evil Russian!

Jane is captured by the sheik, but Tarzan comes to her rescue. Reunited, they journey back to the Tarzan jungle ranch. Korak, wounded and weary, is wandering in the jungle in search of his beloved Meriem. Amid the chaos, the pieces of the puzzle are coming together. Paulovich is murdered in cold blood by the Swede, who is infatuated with young Meriem. A young suitor of Meriem's, Baynes, also dies, and she winds up in the hands of the sheik.

Soon, Korak and Tarzan are converging on the sheik's camp, following different paths. Korak arrives first and kills the sheik, but is captured himself and sentenced to burn at the stake. Only brave Tantor, the elephant, can save Korak. He rips the stake from the ground and carries Korak through the jungle to safety. Thinking Meriem is an enemy, Tantor is about to crush her when Tarzan arrives and shouts "Tantor!" calming his faithful old friend.

Korak is soon reunited with Tarzan and Jane, and Meriem is returned to her anxious father. It is truly a happy group that sets sail for England.

•

Although P. Dempsey Tabler played the part of Tarzan in *The Son of Tarzan*, the real star of the serial was muscular Hawaiian actor Kamuela Searle, who portrayed Korak, son of Tarzan. In the final chapter of the serial, "An Amazing Denouement," Korak is held captive by savages, tied to a stake in the Village of Death. Korak is unable to free his bonds and so gives the terrifying cry of the apes that he learned from Tarzan. Hearing his master's call, Tantor, the elephant, rushes to his rescue, ripping the stake from the ground and lifting Korak to safety in the same swift movement. Soon they are safely away.

As triumphantly as this heroic rescue of Korak worked on the screen, in real life it was tragic; after a long and dangerous chase scene, with the mighty beast carrying Searle on the pole at full speed through the jungle, the nervous elephant accidentally slammed the actor and the heavy pole to the ground after the scene was over. Kamuela Searle was grievously injured and died. A stand-in completed the final scenes. This grim tragedy was sensationalized in the newspapers, and with a certain morbid fascination, the moviegoing public flocked to the theaters for the final installments, in anticipation of seeing the scene in which Searle was fatally injured. In the final two scenes the stand-in for Kamuela Searle is shot only from the rear, his face out of view of the camera.

P. Dempsey Tabler (the *P* stood for Perce) was a professional singer and former athlete, as well as an actor in a number of director Thomas Ince's Triangle films of the period. Originally, cowboy actor "Lightning Jack" Hoxie had been announced as the new apeman, but instead the role went to the burly Tabler, who at age 40 (and showing his age) was probably miscast as the King of the Jungle. As a younger man Tabler had trained as a boxer and in track, as well as studied opera in Leipzig, Germany. In the supporting role of Korak's father, Tabler is undoubtedly

the least remembered of all the motion picture Tarzans, and indeed most of his scenes were in "civilized" attire, rather than in Tarzan's trademark loincloth. Tabler died on June 7, 1956.

Kamuela Searle, possessor of a classic physique and shoulder-length black hair, was physically perfect for the part of Korak, the son of Tarzan. The muscular Searle was also an athlete and performed most of his own stunts, including tree climbing, grappling with the villains, and riding elephants. The rest of the cast included Gordon Griffith (who played Tarzan as a boy in the original *Tarzan of the Apes*); as Korak as a boy he was superbly effective in this acrobatic role; Karla Schramm, again cast as Jane (as she had been in *The Revenge of Tarzan*); Manilla Martan and Mae Giraci as Meriem (the woman and the girl, respectively); and Eugene Burr, as the chief villain, Ivan Paulovich. Frank Merrill, who would be Tarzan number five in the serials *Tarzan the Mighty* and *Tarzan the Tiger*, had a small role in this film as an Arab sheik.

By the time production was ready to start on *The Son of Tarzan* in April 1920, Harry M. Rubey had ascended to the presidency of National Film Corporation, succeeding William Parsons, who died of kidney failure on September 28, 1919. The deal to produce the film with Edgar Rice Burroughs originally had the author writing the scenario for the serial; this never materialized, and Roy Somerville was hired to adapt the novel. Burroughs is listed in the credits as coeditor of the film, along with Somerville, and spent considerable time on the set during filming, which began in early June 1920 and concluded in January 1921.

Sharing the directing of the serial were Arthur J. Flaven and Harry Revier, the latter having directed the recently completed *The Revenge of Tarzan* for Numa Pictures. In charge of photography were Lee Humiston and Walter Bell. Filming took place at National's studios in Hollywood, as well as at Burroughs' Tarzana home in the San Fernando Valley.

An original song, "Tarzan, My Jungle King," with music by Norman Stuckey and words by Osborne Tedman, was written for *The Son of Tarzan*. The illustrated four-page sheet music contained the caption, "Written & Composed especially for SON ... the World's Wonder Jungle Serial."

One interesting note concerning Burroughs was a scene that was used before the serial. The scene was of the author (an accomplished horseman) charging hard at the cameras, riding a dark stallion that appeared to be bucking. (The film clip was inserted after screen promotion for the novel *Warlord of Mars*, which had recently been released in hard cover.) Burroughs later explained that the horse was really gentle and had

actually been running at an easy gallop, but that the cameras had been slowed when filming, so when the film was shown on the big screen at normal speed, he appeared to be riding a wildly gyrating bronco.

The initial chapters of *The Son of Tarzan* were released beginning in December 1920. The serial grossed $176,000 in three months, more than offsetting the $106,000 in production costs. In 1923, a feature film was edited from the serial and retitled, *Jungle Trail of the Son of Tarzan*. In 1992, this lost feature film was rediscovered and released on videocassette (with a running time of approximately 111 minutes). With its release, another precious missing link has been preserved in the film history of Tarzan. (The story's synopsis for this book was written from the 1992 videocassette; no complete copy of the serial is known to exist.)

The Adventures of Tarzan

Release date: December 1921; Weiss Brothers–Numa Pictures Corporation/Great Western Producing Company; prologue plus 15 chapters. *Directed by* Robert F. Hill; *adapted by* Robert F. Hill and Lillian Valentine, *based on the novel* The Return of Tarzan *by* Edgar Rice Burroughs; *film editor,* C.V. Henkel, Jr.; *titles by* Bert Ennis; *photography by* Joe Mayer and Jerry Ash; *editorial supervision by* George M. Merrick.

Tarzan	Elmo Lincoln
Jane Porter	Louise Lorraine
Nicholas Rokoff	Frank Whitson
Professor Porter	Charles Islee
La, Queen of Opar	Lillian Worth
Monsieur Gernot	George Monberg
William Clayton	Percy Pembrooke
Sheik Ben-Ali	Charles Gay
Arab guard	Frank Merrill
Waziri chief	Maceo Bruce Sheffield

Chapter Titles:

The adventure begins as the legend of Tarzan's origin is recounted once again. The orphaned babe of Lord and Lady Greystoke is raised by the she-ape Kala, and the lad grows up to become the mighty King of the Jungle. Tarzan meets the love of his life, Jane Porter, in the jungle, and their lives are forever after intertwined in romance and adventure.

Chapter 1 finds Jane, Nicholas Rokoff and William Clayton shipwrecked off the coast of Africa, with Jane's father apparently lost at sea in the storm. The scheming Clayton wants Jane for himself and tells her that he has seen Tarzan die. Rokoff also desires the young beauty and chases her into the jungle, where a mighty lion stalks his prey. Fortunately, Tarzan arrives in the nick of time and kills the beast, and the two lovers (the ape-man and Jane) are reunited—temporarily. From this point on, Tarzan would have to face many trials before he would be united once and for all with his beloved Jane.

Meanwhile, the Bolshevik villain Rokoff has stolen a secret formula for the development of a deadly nerve gas. As the story unfolds, the secret formula becomes secondary to a fortune in gold held by the lost primitives of Opar, that Rokoff and his cohort, Gernot, plan to steal. (The only map to Opar is tattooed on Jane's shoulder!)

Tarzan repeatedly foils Rokoff and Gernot, who kidnap Jane umpteen times, to be rescued each and every time by Tarzan. The ape-man also battles to the death the many lions that would have her for dinner, along with other snarling beasts, including a wild pig.

Besides Rokoff and Gernot, Tarzan must also save Jane from the Arab ivory bandits, who kidnap her; the treacherous beggar Hagar, who lusts after her; the fierce warriors of Opar, who would kill her; a burning cabin; a false stairway by which they are unceremoniously dumped into a dungeon; and even the beautiful Queen La of Opar, who also loves Tarzan and therefore plans to kill Jane, her rival.

In the conclusion, Tarzan traps Rokoff and Gernot in a cave and plans to turn them over to the French government to be imprisoned. He also makes his peace with Queen La, as they shake hands and part friends. Professor Porter has been found safe by this time, and the reunion is joyous as Tarzan and Jane kiss passionately and wander off together hand in hand.

•

The second Weiss Brothers/Numa Tarzan production, *The Adventures of Tarzan*, was loosely based on the concluding chapters of the novel *The Return of Tarzan*, and the weekly installments were a continuous run of thrilling escapades, with Tarzan saving Jane from one precarious predicament after another, both man and beast. Production was assigned to the Great Western Producing Company, owned by Oscar

Elmo Lincoln with Louise Lorraine (*The Adventures of Tarzan*, 1921).

and Louis Jacobs, along with Julius Stern, the nephew of Universal Pictures magnate, Carl Laemmle. Great Western had produced other Universal serials starring Elmo Lincoln, including *Elmo, the Mighty* (1919), and *Elmo, the Fearless* (1920). The 15-chapter serial was the final opportunity for Elmo Lincoln, who was the original and best of the early ape-men, to portray Tarzan.

Cast as Jane was 16-year-old Louise Lorraine, who would star in many serials during the 1920s. The teenager was obviously mature for her age and had large beautiful eyes, a pretty oval face, and a smile that literally lit up the screen. She was clearly superior to previous Janes and was a strong point in *The Adventures of Tarzan*. Miss Lorraine also starred in several more serials with Elmo Lincoln, including *Elmo, the*

Fearless (1920) and *The Flaming Disc* (1920).

Important cast members included Frank Whitson as the dastardly Russian, Nicholas Rokoff; George Monberg as Rokoff's equally vile partner, Gernot; Lillian Worth as the beautiful La, Queen of Opar; Charles Islee as the befuddled Professor Porter; and Frank Merrill (once again hoping to take over the role of Tarzan later), as an Arab guard. Also appearing was the famed orangutan, Joe Martin, as Ara the ape. However, Joe Martin performed in only a few scenes; in most of the scenes, Ara was portrayed by a man in an ape costume. Directing the production was Robert F. Hill, who would become a veteran of the serials in the 1920s and 1930s; he would also direct the serial *Tarzan the Fearless* (1933), which starred Buster Crabbe.

The film's strong points included a tremendous amount of action and convincing photography of the animal footage, including a great deal of exciting lion scenes. Probably the weakest aspect was the almost comedic nature of what was supposed to be a serious adventure. Elmo was draped in animal skins and looked like he was wearing a fur coat; the apes were most obviously men in ape costumes; the villains' facial expressions were often more ludicrous than menacing; and aside from Rokoff constantly kidnapping Jane in each chapter to build excitement, there was a distinct lack of a central plot menace in the meandering story line by Hill and Lillian Valentine.

Production was underway by late January 1921 and was completed on August 13; filming took place in Hollywood and in the Arizona deserts. Real lions were used most of the time, and a near-tragic accident occurred on July 15. During the filming of Chapter 12, three lionesses broke loose from the trainers and attacked and seriously mauled five actors, who were dressed like Arabs. Louise and Elmo were on the set at the time, but escaped injury; however, several cameras and the day's footage were destroyed, and two of the renegade lions had to be shot to be subdued. Another report had Elmo Lincoln being mauled by a lion during the filming of Chapter 2, with wounds serious enough for him to be laid up for several weeks.

The film was released to the public on December 1, 1921, and promotion was handled by the Weiss brothers' Adventures of Tarzan Serial Sales Corporation, which distributed tips to theater owners on how to generate the interest of patrons (including putting men in ape costumes in cages in the theater lobbies, as well as importing jungle foliage from local florists). A syndicated version that corresponded with each weekly chapter was featured in newspapers across the country, and Elmo himself went on a promotional tour in early 1922, wrestling with a young lion on stage after the weekly episode had been shown. This was the last new Tarzan picture or serial until 1927, when James Pierce would star in *Tarzan and the Golden Lion. The Adventures of Tarzan* was also reedited and released by Weiss Brothers Artclass as a 10-chapter serial in 1928, with added sound effects.

Elmo Lincoln would continue to work in films and adventure serials, including *King of the Jungle* (1927), but by the time the silent era ended in 1929, Elmo would be reduced to strictly bit roles. In later years Lincoln had a small part as a roustabout in *Tarzan's New York Adventure* (1942) and another cameo in Lex Barker's *Tarzan's Magic Fountain* (1949). Around 1929 Elmo wrote to Edgar Rice Burroughs hoping to obtain the rights to *Tarzan of the Apes* (1918); he planned to add sound effects and rerelease the film as *The Original Tarzan of the Apes*. This project never materialized, and his luck in finding work once "talking pictures" arrived amounted mostly to frustration. Elmo Lincoln died on June 27, 1952. His last role of importance was portraying himself in *The Hollywood Story* (1951).

Tarzan and the Golden Lion

Release date: May 1927; RC Pictures Corporation/FBO Gold Bond; six reels. *Directed by* J.P. McGowan; *executive producer,* Joseph P. Kennedy; *adapted by* William Wing, *based on the novel* Tarzan and the Golden Lion *by* Edgar Rice Burroughs; *photography by* Joseph Walker; *music compiled by* James C. Bradford.

Tarzan	James Pierce
Jane Porter	Dorothy Dunbar
Flora Hawkes	Edna Murphy
Esteban Miranda	Fred Peters
Waziri chief	Boris Karloff
Plantation overseer	Harold Goodwin
The old hermit	D'Arcy Corrigan

Also featuring Lui Yu-Ching.

At Tarzan's jungle estate in Africa, the ape-man awaits the arrival of Jane, her niece Flora Hawkes, and Flora's fiancé, who is also Tarzan's plantation overseer.

From out of the jungle comes Tarzan's friend, Weesimbo, who has narrowly escaped from the City of Diamonds—a strange land that no stranger has ever seen before and lived to tell of. Weesimbo reaches Tarzan's estate to tell his friend of his harrowing experiences. As the tale is being told, Jane, Flora, and her fiancé arrive.

While Tarzan is away from the estate on a mission in the jungle, the villain, Estaban Miranda, overhears Weesimbo's tale of the City of Diamonds and kidnaps him, as well as Flora and her fiancé. Miranda forces them to lead him to the city's fabled wealth of jewels.

When the ape-man returns from his jungle mission, Jane frantically tells Tarzan of her niece's abduction, along with Flora's fiancé and Weesimbo. Tarzan is enraged that anyone would invade the sanctity of his home and kidnap his friends and sets off in the direction of the City of Diamonds, accompanied by his faithful golden lion, Jad-bal-ja.

Meanwhile, at the mysterious City of Diamonds, Flora has been captured by the evil high priest and is to be offered as a sacrifice to the city's god and king (a real lion).

The ape-man manages to fight his way into the City of Diamonds and he and Jad-bal-ja rescue Flora from the clutches of the high priest and the lion-god. Victorious once again, Tarzan and the golden lion lead the party back to Tarzan's estate.

•

Tarzan and the Golden Lion, the last silent Tarzan feature film, starred a virtual unknown making his motion picture debut: James Hubert Pierce. The former All-American football player at Indiana University was employed as the football coach at Glendale High School outside Los Angeles, when he was discovered by Edgar Rice Burroughs at a party given for Burroughs' daughter Joan at the family's Tarzana ranch. At six feet four inches tall, with a trim physique and wavy golden hair, Pierce was indeed a handsome sight to behold.

It was the summer of 1926 when Burroughs contacted FBO Studios, requesting that Pierce be given a screen test for the part of Tarzan in the new film. The author was so enamored with his protégé that he commented (as noted in *The Man Who Created Tarzan* by Irwin Porges): "[Pierce] comes nearer approaching my visualization of Tarzan of the Apes than any man I have ever seen. If he can act, I believe that he is a distinct find...." The head of FBO Studios (Film Booking Offices, later RKO) at that time was financial genius Joseph P. Kennedy, patriarch of the Massachusetts Kennedys and father of future President John F. Kennedy.

Pierce, of course, passed the screen test and was chosen to be the new Tarzan; it was to be his only top-billed vehicle in a long career in Hollywood. However, Pierce became indelibly intertwined with the Burroughs family when he married Joan Burroughs, the daughter of the author, on August 8, 1928 (Pierce's birthday). As a wedding present, Burroughs promised Pierce the lead in a future Tarzan production. Although the film was produced (*Tarzan the Fearless*) in 1933 by Sol Lesser, Pierce did not get the role (which went to Olympic swimming champion Buster Crabbe). From 1932 to 1934, Pierce and wife Joan were the voices of Tarzan and Jane on the weekly Tarzan radio programs.

Production began in mid–October 1926 and wrapped up in mid–December, with most of the location shooting done at Sherwood Forest, a wooded "jungle" several miles west of Hollywood. The scenario was written by William Wing, whom Burroughs strongly disapproved of; regardless, FBO insisted on using Wing's script. Directing the film was J.P. McGowan, renowned for his suspenseful cliff-hanger serials and now planning the same brand of thrilling action for *Tarzan and the Golden Lion.*

Many years later, in his autobiography, *The Battle of Hollywood,* James Pierce related some of his personal traumas in making his screen debut:

> As soon as I arrived, [McGowan] rushed me to the camera set up and told me to lead a band of one hundred or more black extras dressed in native costumes. There was a war going on in the story between the good and bad tribes.
>
> I was dressed only in a leopard skin and barefooted when off we went through the rocks and brush. My feet were not tough enough for this, and after a few strides, I let out with the greatest Tarzan yell ever. The rocks and briars were killing me, and I stopped the scene and started limping back toward the cameras on my bruised and bleeding tootsies, walking like a frozen-toe rooster. McGowan the director yelled and screamed, "You really are some Tarzan!" I was terribly embarrassed of course, because here I was, the mighty Tarzan, "King of the Jungle," a real panty-waist! It seemed like a big joke to everyone but me.

The solution to this dilemma, suggested by Pierce, was to put him in sneakers, skin toned with body makeup. From that point on, "Tarzan" was able to jog through the underbrush without a problem.

Another time Pierce was attempting to cross a wide ravine at Santa Ana Canyon, on a rope covered with moss to make it look like a jungle vine. The ravine was some 60 feet deep, and 75 feet wide. As Pierce started to move across hand over hand, his hands started to lose their grip, and he was forced to throw his legs over the vine to keep from falling to his inevitable death. The ingenious solution here was metal hooks taped to his hands, which gave Tarzan a surefire grip to cross the ravine.

Pierce also had some interesting experiences with lions, again as noted in his autobiography, *The Battle of Hollywood:*

> The lion I was working with was not tame by any means, but with the

Top: James Pierce with Dorothy Dunbar (*Tarzan and the Golden Lion,* 1927). *Bottom:* James Pierce with the Golden Lion (*Tarzan and the Golden Lion,* 1927).

aid of trainer Charley Gay, of the famous Gay Lion Farm, who stood just out of camera range with a whip and a chair and a gun, we managed to get the scenes in good time. (In the story, the lion Numa was supposed to be my pet and everloving pal.) The day had been long and the lion was tired. The scene was to be the final wrap of the day.

I was standing on the porch of my jungle house with the golden lion beside me. I was to point into the jungle and Numa was to run off into the trees and brush. Each time the camera turned and the trainer cracked his whip (off camera) to make him run, the lion would yawn and turn to go back inside the house where his cage was located.

After several attempts, I became pretty disgusted. We had been trying to get the scene for a long time, the light was fading and it had been a hard day, so when he turned to go back into the house again, I just moved over in front of him and put my knees together and stopped him. No one had ever touched the animal in a scene before. The trainer went wild. He started yelling, shooting blanks, and running around like crazy to distract the lion before he decided to take a leg off. The crew ran for cover. Instead of going for me, he just sat down and looked at me quizzically.

In other scenes in which they needed to make a lion run fast through the jungle, the trainers would drip beef blood along the trail they wanted the lion to travel—with a juicy chunk of beef as the reward in his cage at the end of the run. Pierce recalled one scene in which he had to run through smoke and leap across a large ditch, followed hotly by a lion (hungrily smelling the trail of beef blood). "I traveled faster than the lion, believe me," said Jim, who kept his distance from the lions the rest of the film. Pierce was also involved in a serious head-on car crash (with a truck) during the shooting schedule and was laid up for several weeks with a collapsed lung. This caused the production

to fall considerably behind schedule and go well over budget.

The cast also featured Dorothy Dunbar as Jane; Edna Murphy as Flora Hawkes, the second lead heroine (Pierce and Miss Murphy had a serious love affair before he married Joan Burroughs and she married Mervyn LeRoy); and Harold Goodwin as Flora's fiancé. Boris Karloff played several roles, including the Waziri chief and a witch doctor (Karloff had been in silent films for almost a decade, but wouldn't become a star until the 1931 horror classic, *Frankenstein*); Lui Yu-Ching, an eight foot 300-pound giant who had once been a bodyguard to the emperor of China; and D'Arcy Corrigan who, in addition to stunt work in ape costume, played the old hermit.

As the star of the picture, the agentless Pierce was paid a measly $75 a week, with a promise of a $350 per week, five-year contract if the film did very well. Although *Tarzan and the Golden Lion* received limited bookings on the A-circuit, it was a pretty big hit on the B-circuit, proving that the adventure had its share of excitement and romance. The film was released in May 1927, and by August the worldwide receipts totaled $198,000. *Tarzan and the Golden Lion* played in Bloomington, home of Pierce's alma mater Indiana University, on May 12–13, 1927. Admission to the Indiana Theater for the double feature was 10 cents for children and 30 cents for adults.

Despite the moderate success of the film, there was no Hollywood contract waiting for James Pierce. He did go on to a career in films, often in westerns like producer Fred Thomson's *Jesse James* (1927) and *Kit Carson* (1928) and almost always as a heavy. His almost giantlike stature, six feet four inches tall, and a ballooning waistline, relegated him to lesser roles; indeed, his last opportunity to portray Tarzan in the 1933 production of *Tarzan the Fearless* was lost because he was seriously out of shape for the strenuous role.

It is not known whether any copies of this silent film have survived, but it seems unlikely. James Pierce himself spent many years in an unsuccessful search for a copy of it, hoping to preserve for film history his one and only starring role as Tarzan. He even went so far as to write to Joseph Kennedy, in hopes that there might be a copy of the film in the Kennedy family archives, but the elder Kennedy suffered a stroke and was unable to answer him. Pierce died in November 1983. His beloved wife Joan preceded him in death on New Year's Eve 1972. They are buried in the Pierce family plot in Shelbyville, Indiana.

Tarzan the Mighty

Release date: August 1928; Universal Pictures; 15 chapters. *Directed by* Jack Nelson; *adaptation and continuity by* Ian McClosky Heath, *based on the novel* Jungle Tales of Tarzan *by* Edgar Rice Burroughs; *supervised by* William Lord Wright.

Tarzan	Frank Merrill
Mary Trevor	Natalie Kingston
Bobby Trevor	Bobby Nelson
Black John	Al Ferguson
Lord Greystoke, Tarzan's uncle	Lorimer Johnston

Chapter Titles:

1. "The Terror of Tarzan"
2. "The Love Cry"
3. "The Call of the Jungle"
4. "The Lion's Leap"
5. "Flames of Hate"
6. "The Fiery Pit"
7. "The Leopard's Lair"
8. "The Jungle Traitor"
9. "Lost in the Jungle"
10. "Jaws of Death"
11. "A Thief in the Night"
12. "The Enemy of Tarzan"
13. "Perilous Paths"
14. "Facing Death"
15. "The Reckoning"

Mary Trevor and her little brother Bobby are the sole survivors of the ocean liner *Empress.* They are found by Black John, the beachcomber, who is the leader of a jungle colony descended from pirates. Black John hates Tarzan and is plotting to kill him at his first opportunity.

When Mary goes to bathe in the river, Tarzan happens to be in the trees above, and he greatly admires her beauty and lithe form. Tarzan's mighty jungle cry scares off Black John and his followers, and Tarzan befriends Mary and her brother. Later, Bobby goes into the jungle to warn Tarzan of a trap that Black John has set, a trap from which they both narrowly escape.

Back at the stockade, Black John demands that Mary be his bride that evening or she will never see Bobby again. Mary loathes Black John but she

Frank Merrill as Tarzan (*Tarzan the Mighty*, 1928).

is helpless to protest. At Tarzan's jungle hut, Bobby convinces Tarzan that Mary needs their help. Tarzan and his young friend speed through the trees, back to the stockade of Black John. Tarzan is just in time to stop the primitive marriage rites. He knocks Black John to the ground, and Tantor, the faithful elephant, arrives to rescue Tarzan and Mary from the angry natives.

At his camp, Tarzan shows Mary some papers that he does not understand. In fact, they are proof that he is the heir to the Greystoke title and fortune. Mary takes the papers for safekeeping, but once again winds up in the clutches of Black John, who, upon discovering the papers, plans to go to England to claim the title of Lord Greystoke.

This time, with Bobby by his side, Tarzan again rescues Mary and the patriarch of the natives asks Tarzan to be their king. In the confusion, Black John grabs Bobby and, in hopes of finding a ship to take them to England, heads for the shore. Unbelievable as it may seem, there is a ship, and a company is on shore already. It is the brother of Lord Greystoke with a search party hoping to find his long lost nephew!

Greystoke is unconvinced by Black John's tale that he is the lost relative. The villain says he will retrieve the family heirlooms from the jungle as further proof. Black John goes back to Tarzan's hut to steal the heirlooms. As luck will have it, he spots Tarzan in a tree nearby and fires his rifle at the ape-man, who falls to the ground unconscious.

Black John continues his evil doings by trapping Bobby and Greystoke in a cave and then assumes the clean clothes and trappings of Lord Greystoke. When Tarzan recovers from his fall, he and Mary find Bobby and Greystoke in the cave. Greystoke is now convinced that Tarzan is his nephew and the real Lord Greystoke.

Black John once again schemes treachery, this time with the help of Greystoke's unfaithful secretary, who stabs the elder Greystoke. Black John returns to finish the job and abduct Mary to be his wife when he escapes to England.

Tarzan and Bobby pick up the trail of Black John and reach the camp in time to save Greystoke. As Black John retreats into the jungle, he is torn to bits by leopards. Lord Greystoke wants Tarzan to return to England with him, but the ape-man knows he must stay in the jungle. Mary, too, knows where she belongs—at Tarzan's side.

•

The fifth Tarzan, Frank Merrill, was often referred to as the Hercules of the Screen, in tribute to his marvelous physique. Originally, another movie strongman, Joe Bonomo, was assigned the role. But Bonomo (known as Samson of the Circus), broke a leg on the third day of filming when a rope-vine snapped and the actor crashed to the ground suffering a compound fracture. Universal suddenly needed a new Tarzan.

Merrill was renowned as a weight lifter, and in his early years won 58 championships, mostly for rope climbing, Roman rings, and parallel bars. Born Arthur Poll in New Jersey on March 21, 1898, he later assumed the stage name Frank Merrill. With his marvelous athletic skills, Merrill got his start in motion pictures as a stuntman and a bit player; he previously appeared in *The Son of Tarzan* (1920) and *The Adventures of Tarzan* (1921), performing stunts and minor roles. By the mid–20s, he was starring in many films and serials, including *Perils of the Jungle* (1927), in which he played the hero, Rod Bedford, a young explorer in Africa.

Merrill certainly had the physique, the clean, handsome looks, and athleticism to fill the role of Tarzan. Because

Frank Merrill with Bobby Nelson (*Tarzan the Mighty*, 1928).

of his skill climbing ropes and on the gymnastics bars, he was able to swing through the trees, climb in and out of pits and traps, and generally perform the feats of Tarzan with realism; no stuntmen were needed with Merrill as the King of the Jungle. Merrill, like previous Tarzans, wore an over-the-shoulder leopard skin as his finery and a leopard headband that gave him a savage look. Tarzan also wore his father's hunting knife on a thong from his neck—another element that did not exist in Burroughs' Tarzan novels.

Costarring as Tarzan's love interest, Mary Trevor, was Natalie Kingston; there was no Jane in this serial (however, Natalie would be transformed into Jane in *Tarzan the Tiger*). The dastardly villain Black John was played with conviction by Al Ferguson, and he indeed looked the part; filthy animal skins for clothes, a pirate's headband, and a dirty black beard completed his vile appearance. Other major characters were Lorimer Johnston as Lord Greystoke and Bobby Nelson as Mary Trevor's brother. Directing was Jack Nelson (father of Bobby), from the imaginative scenario by Ian McCloskey Heath.

Tarzan the Mighty was originally to be called *Jungle Tales of Tarzan* and to be based on the novel by Edgar Rice Burroughs. After viewing the initial chapters of the film at Universal Studios on June 14, 1928, Burroughs was once again disappointed with what film producers were doing to his creation Tarzan. In a memorandum (noted in Irwin Porges' *The Man Who Created Tarzan*), an exasperated ERB wrote:

> There was only one character that appears in the original work, namely Tarzan, and no suggestion of any episode or action taken from the book. They have incorporated many characters, including a Lord Greystoke, some pirates, sailors and a castaway girl and her little brother, none of which appears in the original work. They have incorporated a love interest between Tarzan and the girl (Natalie Kingston), which does not exist in the book.

It was the "love interest" that particularly worried Burroughs, noting that Tarzan and Jane had been married in his second novel, *The Return of Tarzan*, so how could the ape-man possibly be interested romantically in Mary Trevor? The author thought that Frank Merrill would make a good Tarzan, but this was the only thing he liked about the new Tarzan serial.

Tarzan the Mighty began as a 12-chapter serial, with filming underway in late spring of 1928 and production wrapped up in October of the same year. Because of the popularity of the serial, the 12 original chapters were restructured to 15 chapters using footage previously discarded. It wouldn't be long before a sequel—*Tarzan the Tiger*—would be made, starring the same major actors—Frank Merrill, Natalie Kingston, and Al Ferguson.

Although Universal mogul Carl Laemmle had many of the silent masters in the Universal vault burned with the advent of sound pictures, it is believed that a copy of this serial still exists (and, it is hoped, will be on videocassette in the near future). Sadly, many great early Universal pictures and serials are lost forever because of this rash action by Laemmle.

Tarzan the Tiger

Release date: December 9, 1929; Universal Pictures; 15 chapters. *Directed by* Henry McRae; *supervision,* William Lord Wright; *continuity by* Ian McClosky Heath; *based on the novel* Tarzan and the Jewels of Opar *by* Edgar Rice Burroughs; *photography by* Wilfrid Cline; *art directors,* Charles D. Hall and David C. Garber; *film editor,* Malcolm Dewar; *titles by* Ford L. Beebe; *recording supervisor,* C. Roy Hunter; *synchronization and musical score,* Bert Fiske and David Broekman.

Tarzan	Frank Merrill
Lady Jane	Natalie Kingston
Albert Werper	Al Ferguson
La, Queen of Opar	Kithnou
Philip Annersley	Clive Morgan
Achmet Zek	Sheldon Lewis
Mohammed Bey	Paul Panzer

Chapter Titles:

1. "Call of the Jungle"
2. "The Road to Opar"
3. "The Altar of the Flaming God"
4. "The Vengeance of La"
5. "Condemned to Death"
6. "Tantor, the Terror"
7. "In Deadly Peril"
8. "The Loop of Death"
9. "Flight of Werper"
10. "Prisoner of the Apes"
11. "The Jaws of Death"
12. "The Jewels of Opar"
13. "A Human Sacrifice"
14. "Tarzan's Rage"
15. "Tarzan's Triumph"

Tarzan is planning a trip back to the city of Opar, to gather enough gold to pay off the debts that have mounted on the Greystoke estates in England. He discusses this plan with his "old friend" Werper, who is actually in a conspiracy with Tarzan's sworn enemy, Achmet Zek, the slave trader, and Tarzan's scheming nephew in England, Philip Annersley.

Werper follows Tarzan to Opar, while Achmet kidnaps Jane from their estate (he plans to sell her at the slave auction). Meanwhile, Tarzan enters the secret chamber at Opar and loads as much gold as he can carry (Werper is spying on this scene), but as he prepares to leave, a great storm hits Opar and Tarzan is knocked unconscious by falling rubble. Tragically, Tarzan loses his memory from the blow to his head. Before he leaves the temple, he fills a pouch with fabulous diamonds, thinking they are "pretty pebbles."

Using guile of her own, Jane manages to escape the clutches of Achmet Zek, but she is soon caught in the jungle by Taglat, the ape, who is an enemy of Tarzan. Fortunately, Tarzan is close by, hears her scream, and kills the ape in battle. However, Tarzan is unable to recall that Jane is his wife.

Entering the picture is Queen La of Opar, who is madly in love with Tarzan. In a wild skirmish, Jane is grabbed by Achmet, and Tarzan saves La and carries her back to Opar. Werper, who has stolen Tarzan's "pretty stones," has a falling out with Achmet and kills him. Soon, Tarzan reaches the Arab camp and rescues Jane, who has been sold at auction. Tarzan kills the man who bought her.

Tarzan and Jane return to the cabin

Frank Merrill with Natalie Kingston (*Tarzan the Tiger*, 1929).

of his birth, hoping to trigger his memory. Werper again tries to kill Tarzan but is foiled, and Tarzan once more reclaims his pouch of diamonds. Tarzan's memory is coming back in bits and pieces, and finally he remembers that Jane is his wife. They decide to return to Opar, the scene of Tarzan's loss of memory. Meanwhile, Tarzan's unscrupulous cousin Philip Annersley has joined Werper in Africa in the conspiracy against Tarzan; he hopes to claim the Greystoke title if Tarzan is proved dead.

At the city of Opar, Tarzan and Werper battle in the treasure chamber. Tarzan is knocked unconscious as Werper escapes with the jewels. When Tarzan wakes up, his memory is fully returned. Moments later, he hears Jane screaming from above, where La is

about to sacrifice Jane to eliminate her rival. Tarzan crashes the party to save Jane. Tarzan leads La and her people to the chamber of jewels and gold, and Tarzan and Jane are allowed to leave in peace.

As Tarzan and Jane head for home, they are confronted by Werper and Annersley. Tarzan is knocked out and tied to a tree, while Jane is dragged along toward Opar to help them find the treasure. Tantor, the elephant, answers Tarzan's yell for help and frees his bonds, and together they rush to Jane's rescue. As Tarzan arrives, Annersley is killed by a tiger and Werper dies in the jaws of a lion.

Tarzan and Jane are reunited and will use the pouch of jewels from Opar to save the Greystoke estates in England.

**Frank Merrill with Natalie Kingston (foreground) and Kithnou (center background)
(*Tarzan the Tiger,* 1929).**

•

Tarzan the Tiger was the final Tarzan silent production. It was released in both silent and sound versions, with the latter having a complete musical score, sound effects, and Tarzan's mighty victory cry the only recorded dialogue (Merrill's Tarzan yell was the first to be heard by movie fans; it sounded like a man's response to pounding his thumb with a hammer).

The film's title, *Tarzan the Tiger,* as well as the use of tigers in several scenes, was certainly misleading, since tigers are indigenous only to Asia (including India, the Malay Peninsula, and Siberia); there are no African tigers. (Edgar Rice Burroughs had made a similar mistake once in placing a tiger in

one of his novels; he later corrected the error and admitted his faux pas.)

Starring as Tarzan was Frank Merrill, who had been the ape-man in the previous serial, *Tarzan the Mighty.* Merrill once again made good use of his powerful arms and torso to perform his athletic stunts. He often scrambled up vines (ropes) using just his arms, shooting up to the heights like child's play. When an accident occurred during a vine-swinging scene (when Merrill reached for a vine 25 feet above the ground and did not connect), he was not injured despite the nasty drop, because the former tumbler rolled on hitting the ground and broke his own fall. One of Merrill's great stunts was an exciting ride through the jungle on an elephant in pursuit of a villain riding a camel—Tarzan leaps off his beast at top speed, grabs a vine in full flight, and knocks the rider right off the camel! In some lion scenes, Merrill was doubled by Melvine Koontz, grappling with Jackie, the lion.

Again, the female lead was the shapely, pretty, and dark-haired Natalie Kingston. This time Natalie played Lady Jane, wife of Lord Greystoke (Tarzan), whereas in the previous serial she was cast as Tarzan's love interest, Mary Trevor. Once again the chief villain was portrayed by Al Ferguson, this time minus his bushy beard from *Tarzan the Mighty*, but he naturally sports a pencil-thin moustache, twisted at the end. The exotic looking Kithnou played La, Queen of Opar, who often was dressed in skimpy harem outfits, as were the many Oparian dancers and the slave girls at the auction. Indeed, this was very much an "adult" serial; it included a scene in which Jane undresses to the buff, and runs through the jungle to a river to swim, only partially hidden from Tarzan's view by the jungle underbrush. Other villains included Sheldon Lewis as the lecherous slave trader, Achmet Zek; Paul Panzer, as another Arab of vile repute; and the scheming Greystoke nephew, Philip Annersley, this time played with gusto by Clive Morgan.

Directing *Tarzan the Tiger* was Universal's top serial director, Henry McRae, with a scenario by Ian McClosky Heath, based on Edgar Rice Burroughs' novel, *Tarzan and the Jewels of Opar*. All in all, it was an enjoyable adventure, and fortunately it has been preserved (unlike many "lost" silent films) for Tarzan film buffs to see Frank Merrill, the Hercules of the Screen.

After finishing production on *Tarzan the Tiger*, Merrill immediately hit the road for an extensive 18-month publicity tour for the serial, which had wrapped up filming in the winter of 1929-30. He would make few additional films, one of which was *The Wrestler*, in which he starred and directed. Frank Merrill went on to a public service job as a Los Angeles commissioner and died on February 12, 1966.

A fitting tribute to Frank Merrill came from Vern Coriell, the editor of the *Burroughs Bulletin* (Number 33, 1974) (fan publication), when he wrote of the Tarzan actor:

> Tarzan never dies. As long as there is someone who remembers the magic moments at the movies with *Tarzan the Mighty*, as long as someone passes on the remembrance to another, as long as histories of the movies are preserved in books and magazines and films—as long as the legend of Tarzan persists, so shall one of filmdom's greatest contributors to that legend also endure. "Tarzan the Mighty" . . . Frank Merrill!

II
The Johnny Weissmuller Era

JOHNNY WEISSMULLER, A BIOGRAPHY

Weissmuller not only had the physique but he had that kind of face—sensual, animalistic and good-looking—that gave the impression of jungle . . . outdoor life. Undoubtedly, Johnny was the greatest of all Tarzans.—Sol Lesser, producer of 16 Tarzan films (quoted in *The Big Swingers,* by Robert Fenton)

As difficult as it is to achieve fame and reach the pinnacle of success in a particular field, Johnny Weissmuller did it twice. He was the greatest swimmer of all time, and he then became eternally famous and internationally loved and remembered as Tarzan on the silver screen.

America had some truly legendary sports heroes during those exciting Roaring Twenties, including Babe Ruth in baseball; Jack Dempsey in boxing; Jim Thorpe in football; and the handsome, six-foot three-inch Adonis of swimming, Johnny Weissmuller. Johnny was the darling of the printed media in the 1920s, earning nicknames like Human Hydroplane, Prince of the Waves, Flying Fish, Aquatic Wonder, King of Swimmers, and America's Greatest Waterman.

Few athletes in the history of sports can claim that they retired undefeated, as was the case with Johnny, who never lost a race in his amateur swimming career. From his debut in competitive swimming in 1921, when he won his first AAU (American Athletic Union) cham-pionship in the 50-yard freestyle, Weissmuller was the winner in every race he ever entered through 1928, when he retired from competitive swimming to earn a living.

It was generally accepted as fact that Weissmuller was born in Pennsylvania on June 2, 1904, and thus was a citizen of the United States; however, research after his death revealed that Johnny was born in the town of Freidorf, in the Banat region of Romania (before boundary changes in 1918, this area had been a part of Hungary). Younger brother Peter was born in Windber, Pennsylvania, on September 3, 1905, which clearly reveals that Johnny spent only the first few months of his life in his birthplace. By the end of 1904, parents Peter and Elizabeth Weissmuller and their infant son had emigrated to the United States. When the issue of Weissmuller's citizenship came up before the 1924 Olympics, the baptismal documents for brothers Johnny and Peter were switched, thus allowing him to compete as a U.S. citizen.

The Weissmuller family started their new life in America in the coal town of Windber, Pennsylvania, where his father toiled as a miner in the murky and hazardous depths of the coal mines to eke out an existence for his family. Eventually, they moved to Chicago, where Mr. Weissmuller owned his own saloon for a time and Johnny's mother was head cook at Chicago's famed Turn-Verein restaurant. This son of poor immigrants would someday scale the heights of fame and fortune.

Johnny and brother Peter were avid swimmers, and later in life Johnny disclaimed the story that he was "sickly" as a youth: "That was something we put out to inspire the kids," Johnny admitted. "I was skinny, all right, but there was nothing sickly about me. I would have filled out even without swimming." But still, drawn to the power of swimming, young Johnny joined the Stanton Park pool, where he won all the junior swim meets, and at age 12 earned a spot on the YMCA swim team (he fibbed about his age because 14 was the minimum to be on the team).

Chicago's Oak Street Beach was his favorite summer hangout, and it was evident even in these early years that Johnny was a special human being when it came to aquatics. Throughout his life Weissmuller advocated that all children should learn to swim as a safety precaution. As a youth he witnessed a terrible boating accident, and he and brother Peter pulled 20 people out of the water, with only 11 surviving the tragic mishap. Johnny felt strongly that tragedies such as this could be averted if everyone learned to swim at an early age.

Family tragedy occurred in 1920 when Mr. Weissmuller died of tuberculosis, which he no doubt contracted during his employment as a coal miner. Years later, Johnny was philosophical about his childhood, as told in *Water, World & Weissmuller* by Narda Onyx:

I had to quit school after my father died. You know, your guts get so mad when you try to fight poverty and its constant inevitable companion—ignorance. I told myself, "I'm going to get out of this neighborhood, if only because he's got a quarter and I haven't." I fought my way out.... Maybe it is this drive to better oneself and one's surroundings that makes a champion out of the less-fortunate boy, instead of the one born with a silver spoon in his mouth, as the saying goes.

Young Johnny was indeed a fighter and a family man. When he quit school after his father died, he worked as a bellhop and as an elevator operator at the Plaza Hotel in Chicago to help support his family. Although that was the end of his formal education, Weissmuller would continue to learn and grow as a human being, with his newly gained responsibilities.

Johnny also gained a new father-figure around the time of his father's death in the burly 340-pound presence of "Big Bill" Bachrach, the red-mustachioed swim coach of the Illinois Athletic Club. Bachrach, famed as a trainer of Olympic champions, began training Johnny in October 1920, fully awakening the skills that would make Johnny a great champion. The fundamentals of Bachrach's approach were relaxation and form—one had to be relaxed with perfect form to achieve optimum speed. With Bachrach's guidance, Johnny developed his revolutionary high-riding front crawl, which allowed him to guide his sleek physique through the waves with a blazing speed no person had ever achieved.

Big Bill was also a con man in the P.T. Barnum mold, exploiting his young star's potential in exhibition matches at the Illinois Athletic Club (gathering donations from wealthy businessmen who lunched there), to provide Johnny with clothes, meals, and necessities. He

A young Johnny Weissmuller (circa 1931) with child actress Juanita Quigley.

was a strong motivating force, guiding both Johnny's swimming career and his life. They remained friends for years after his young protégé had moved out of the pool and into the jungle vines.

Seventeen-year-old Johnny Weissmuller made his amateur debut on August 6, 1921, winning his first AAU race (a 50-yard freestyle), and splashed his way to victory in every race he entered, from 50 to 500 yards, right up until the 1924 Olympics staged in Paris. At age 20, Weissmuller was the world record holder in the 100-meter race and seemed invincible. But the defending Olympic champion was 33-year-old Duke Kahanamoku of Hawaii, who had also won the gold medal in 1912 and 1920. Thus, the 1924 Olympics would certainly be a great challenge for the world's two top swimmers.

Also entered for the United States was Sam Kahanamoku, Duke's younger brother. With little thought to a rivalry among the Americans, Duke turned to Johnny before the race and said, "Johnny, good luck. The most important thing in this race is to get the American flag up there three times. Let's do it." And they did, Johnny winning the gold in 59 seconds flat, with Duke and Sam coming in second and third, respectively.

After his convincing victory, the appreciative throng of over 7,000 fans stood and called for Johnny to make an appearance, until it was announced that he would appear again later that afternoon. Johnny had won the 400-meter freestyle two days earlier, and then participated on the winning U.S. 800-meter relay team. At the Amsterdam games in 1928, Johnny carried the flag at the traditional opening ceremonies and then repeated his victories in the 100-meter freestyle and 800-meter relay.

During the 1920s, Johnny won 36 individual national AAU championships and 67 world championships. He was the first swimmer to break the one-minute mark in the 100 meters, and his world record of 57.4 seconds in the 100-meter freestyle set in 1924 would last for 10 years before being broken; among his record-setting performances were 51 world records and 94 American records (all individual). Weissmuller was chosen American Swimmer of the Year in 1922 (a nonrepeat award, for which if eligible, he undoubtedly would have also won in 1923, 1924, 1925, 1926, 1927, and 1928). Johnny also was Helms World Trophy Winner in 1923 (Athlete of the Year, North America) and was elected to the Helms Swimming Hall of Fame in 1949.

With his success in the 1928 Amsterdam Olympics under his belt, Johnny headed for Florida and performed in various water shows at posh hotels and resorts, receiving minimal compensation for travel and expenses. Under the advice of Bill Bachrach, Weissmuller decided to turn pro and signed a contract with B.V.D. to promote its swimwear. With his B.V.D. salary at a princely (for the times) $500 per week, Johnny actually had some folding money in his pocket for the first time in his life—and he liked it!

Johnny appeared in his first motion picture, *Glorifying the American Girl,* in 1929 (in a cameo role as himself), and the first of several Grantland Rice sport shorts, *Crystal Champions.* Weissmuller also coauthored (in collaboration with Clarence A. Bush) a full-length book in 1930, entitled *Swimming the American Crawl,* about his swimming techniques and career highlights. The book also spawned two articles for the *Saturday Evening Post,* "My Methods of Training" and "Diet and Breathing to Swim"; both the book and the articles were fascinating reading and included important techniques for serious swimming students.

On February 28, 1931, Johnny took

"the plunge" and married Bobbe Arnst, a Broadway actress who had appeared in several New York shows, including *Simple Simon* and *Rosalie*. According to an article in *Saga* magazine, they had met in Miami on Valentine's Day, where Bobbe was singing with Ted Lewis' band.

In 1931 MGM was casting for its new Tarzan film, *Tarzan, the Ape Man,* based on Edgar Rice Burroughs' heroic jungle character. Several actors were considered for the role but were rejected, and fate's sometimes fortuitous hand tapped Johnny Weissmuller on the shoulder to be the new ape-man. Screenwriter Cyril Hume, who was working on the screenplay for the new Tarzan picture, was impressed with Weissmuller's championship form in the pool at the hotel where both were staying. He immediately contacted MGM director W.S. (Woody) Van Dyke, who wanted a new actor for his Tarzan, "a man who is young, strong, well-built, reasonably attractive, but not necessarily handsome, and a competent actor."

Johnny certainly filled the bill: If God had ever created a man who was physically perfect for a particular movie role, it was Weissmuller for the part of Tarzan. The symmetry of his smoothly muscled physique had made him a champion as the world's greatest amateur swimmer, but he certainly wasn't muscle-bound. And his deep, brooding looks—that animal hunger in his eyes and his snarling expressions—would bring fear to any man or beast who aroused the displeasure of the ape-man.

After MGM worked a compromise with B.V.D., Weissmuller was signed on October 16, 1931, to the standard seven-year contract to be the new cinema Tarzan; his salary was to be $250 per week. With virtually no acting experience, the ex-swimmer fell into the role of Tarzan like he was made for it. His sleek, muscular yet symmetrical physique was like

that of a lion, and his noble face and black mane of hair indeed gave Tarzan a regal, King of the Jungle stature.

Johnny didn't need to be a great actor to portray Tarzan because he filled the role so naturally. He was able to capture the essence of invincibility that made his movie Tarzan legendary. The ape-man was ignorant only of the ways of the civilized world—call him naïve, uneducated, perhaps childlike in his puzzlement of things he did not understand. But in his world—his realm— Tarzan was cunning, junglewise, intelligent, and the absolute ruler of his kingdom. He ruled not only with his superior physical skills, but with a jungle savvy that clearly defined him as the Lord of the Jungle. Tarzan's "subjects" respected him, but, above all, they feared him—for he was indeed King of the Beasts.

Whereas Johnny Weissmuller was considered the archetypal actor for the role of Tarzan, the lovely 20-year-old Irish actress Maureen O'Sullivan was the perfect Jane. The curvy, sensual, and talented brunette played Jane in six Tarzan films with Johnny and made over 60 feature films in her lengthy career.

Released in March 1932, *Tarzan, the Ape Man* was a huge financial and critical success, and 27-year-old Johnny Weissmuller was a sensation as the screen's newest Tarzan. MGM had the hottest new star of the year, and seeing his obvious appeal to women, "requested" that Johnny end his marriage, so MGM could cash in on his sexuality. MGM reportedly paid Bobbe Arnst $10,000 to get a divorce, after which she returned to her singing career. While in New York that year promoting his hit film, Johnny met and swiftly fell in love with Latin actress Lupe Velez, whom he married in 1933.

Weissmuller's second Tarzan film, *Tarzan and His Mate* (1934), was as successful as the original, and there was no doubt now that this would be a series of films over many years. Johnny remained the number one movie Tarzan for 17 years—starring in a dozen Tarzan adventures, leaving the series then only with deep reservations.

Although at the triumphant beginning of Johnny's career in 1932, Clark Gable–like roles were predicted for the young star, none was offered. Johnny was pretty much stereotyped as Tarzan during his whole career. His only "straight" acting role came in the film *Swamp Fire* (1946), and Johnny joked when he said about his role, "I played a Navy lieutenant in that one—I took one look and went back to the jungle."

Johnny Weissmuller, the motion picture hero, was not called upon to serve his country as a soldier during World War II, but he did help to fight the war in his own way in the propaganda film *Tarzan Triumphs* (Tarzan fighting the Nazis who came to Africa to conquer the natives and steal their oil and wealth). Weissmuller also aided the war effort in other ways; he visited hospitals and military bases with other performers, washed dishes at the Hollywood Canteen near Sunset Boulevard, and for two years taught recruits how to swim out from under water covered with flaming petroleum. The U.S. War Finance Program honored Johnny with a citation for his patriotic efforts in 1945.

Johnny loved doing his Tarzan role over the years and thought that the part was "right up my alley," he recalled. "It was just like stealing. There was swimming in it, and I didn't have much to say." On another occasion Johnny noted: "The public forgives my acting because they know I was an athlete. They know I wasn't make-believe." Johnny would do his Tarzan yell for just about anyone who asked, warmly obliging his adoring public.

Immediately after retiring from his role of Tarzan, Johnny traded his loin-cloth for jungle fatigues and assumed the role of Jungle Jim, whom he portrayed in 16 films for Columbia Pictures between 1948 and 1955. The comic strip character Jungle Jim, created in 1934 by Alex Raymond, was an immensely popular Sunday newspaper strip for three decades. "Jungle Jim" became a television series for Columbia's TV arm, Screen Gems, for the 1955-56 season; the 26 episodes played over and over on network and syndicated TV for many years.

In 1950 Johnny Weissmuller's great swimming career was crowned when he was judged to be the Greatest Swimmer of the First Half-Century (1900–50) by the Associated Press. It's almost a shame that Weissmuller's greatness as a swimmer is partially overshadowed by his larger-than-life image as the movies' Tarzan.

After the "Jungle Jim" TV series ended in 1956, Johnny retired from films, making only an occasional cameo movie appearance. He did TV guest spots whenever he was asked, and on one episode of "You Bet Your Life" in the early 1950s, the inimitable Groucho Marx had Johnny do his Tarzan yell to impress his pretty, young female cocontestant. It was great fun for everyone, and the audience appreciated seeing the legendary Johnny Weissmuller in person.

In 1959 Johnny was participating in a celebrity golf tournament in Havana, while Castro's guerrilla soldiers were fighting Bautista's government troops. Rebel soldiers intercepted Johnny and his friends one afternoon as they were traveling to the golf course, pointing their guns dangerously at the unwelcome Americans. Rising to the occasion, Johnny beat on his chest and let out a blood-curdling Tarzan yell. Initially stunned, the rebels broke into smiles and happy cries of "Tarzan! Tarzan! Bienvenido! Ah, Juanito! Welcome to Cuba!" After Johnny shook hands and signed a few autographs, the guerrillas actually escorted him and his party to the golf course! Johnny was so well known and loved that he was universally respected, even by rebel soldiers fighting their own patriotic war.

In the late 1950s, Johnny returned to Chicago, started a swimming pool company, and lent his name to other business ventures. Johnny was never a great businessman, and fortunately the residuals from the "Jungle Jim" TV series kept him solvent for many years. His main fault as a businessman was that he was so honest (with an inherent naïveté) that he believed everything that people told him. The result was some bad business deals over the years that drained him of much of his earned wealth. In the mid-sixties he went to Florida to be curator of the Swimming Hall of Fame in Fort Lauderdale, and for a time in 1973 he was a greeter at the MGM Grand hotel in Las Vegas.

With his many championships and world records, Johnny Weissmuller was certainly the greatest swimmer of all time, and he unabashedly admitted as much in a 1972 interview after the Munich Olympics, where Mark Spitz won seven gold medals for swimming.

"I was better than Spitz is," said Johnny with frank honesty. "I never lost a race—never. The closest I ever came to losing was on the last lap of the 400 in 1924 when I got a snootful [of water]. But I knew enough not to cough. If you don't cough, you can swallow it."

In 1974 Johnny broke a hip and a leg; while in the hospital, he learned he had a serious heart condition. A number of disabling strokes over the next few years left him broken but not beaten, as literally thousands of cards and letters from his millions of fans (along with a daily swimming regimen), helped speed his partial recovery. His final public ap-

pearance was in 1976, when he was inducted into the Body Building Guild Hall of Fame.

Johnny loved life, and he loved the fair sex, but women didn't always bring him happiness. His wives included singer-actress Bobbe Arnst; Latin-born film star Lupe Velez; socialite Beryel Scott, the mother of his three children (Johnny Weissmulller, Jr., who has had occasional movie and television roles; Heidi, who died in a car crash in 1962 at age 19; and Wendy Ann); golfer Allene Gates; and German-born Maria Brock was his last wife. Maria married Johnny in 1963 and remained with him the rest of his life; they enjoyed a harmonious and loving relationship. (Camille Louier is listed in some sources as wife number one for Weissmuller. However, no such marriage was reported in the *New York Times,* and the union is not mentioned in Narda Onyx's authorized biography, *Water, World and Weissmuller.*)

For several weeks in 1979 Johnny was hospitalized at the Motion Picture and Television Country Home in Woodland Hills, California. Robbed of his good health by the strokes, Johnny and Maria moved to Acapulco later in the year and lived quietly until his death on January 20, 1984. Weissmuller was buried in Acapulco, per his request, the location of his last Tarzan film. At his funeral, a tape of Johnny's trademark Tarzan yell was played as his coffin was lowered into the ground.

Weissmuller always had a marvelous sense of humor, and the role of Tarzan was perfect for a man who never really grew up. One of his favorite lines was advice to new Tarzans who came to him after he gave up the role: with a twinkle in his eye, Johnny would say, "I tell them the main thing is don't let go of the vine when you're swinging through the jungle."

Maureen O'Sullivan,
a Biography

Just as Johnny Weissmuller will always be remembered as the movies' Tarzan, so Maureen O'Sullivan has been immortalized in screen history as Jane, the mate of the jungle hero. Her memories of the Tarzan motion pictures, all with costar Johnny Weissmuller, are shaded with warm recollections and personal pride.

In a 1991 letter to the author, O'Sullivan explained how Irving Thalberg, the MGM "boy wonder," had personally selected her for the choice role of Jane opposite Johnny Weissmuller. She recalled that, "Everything was very interesting—the Magic of the Jungle, the Romance, the animals, and of course—Johnny."

About her handsome, 27-year-old costar, she fondly remembered, "We were dear friends. He was simple, unpretentious, without conceit—a wonderful big kid." And of Johnny Sheffield, who portrayed Boy, she said, "Nice little boy, with a caring father—unspoiled."

O'Sullivan described the competent directors she worked with on the Tarzan pictures, including W.S. "Woody" Van Dyke, Cedric Gibbons, and Richard Thorpe: "Our directors were attractive men. All good-looking, strong. They could all have looked great on film."

She was born Maureen Paula O'Sullivan on May 17, 1911, in Boyle, County Roscommon, Ireland, and schooled at the Convent of the Sacred Heart at Roehampton, England (near London). One of her childhood classmates was Vivien Leigh, who also would pursue a life on the stage and in films. After advanced education in Paris, Maureen returned to her family in Ireland, with hardly a thought in her head toward an acting career.

But as fate would have it, O'Sullivan was spotted by sharp-eyed American director Frank Borzage, while both were attending a dinner-dance at the annual Dublin International Horse Show in 1929. Borzage was in Ireland filming location shots for *Song O' My Heart* and was attracted to Maureen's rare beauty and obvious talent. Borzage signed Maureen for 20th Century–Fox and brought the 18-year-old lass (along with her mother) to Hollywood, where she made her screen debut as Eileen in *Song O' My Heart.*

After doing a half-dozen films for Fox, including the female lead of Alisande in *A Connecticut Yankee* (1931), O'Sullivan left Fox and signed a long-term contract with MGM, which at the time was under the guidance of Louis

58

Weissmuller, O'Sullivan and Johnny Sheffield enjoy the Sunday Tarzan funnies.

B. Mayer and Irving Thalberg. (See Maureen O'Sullivan's Foreword to this book for more interesting notes on her signing with MGM and her role as Jane in the Tarzan motion pictures.)

The extremely busy O'Sullivan had nine films in release in 1932, including *Tarzan, the Ape Man.* While working in the MGM stable of stars in the 1930s, O'Sullivan was Mayer's favorite second leading lady in several classic films like *The Thin Man* (1934), *The Barretts of*

Wimpole Street (1934), *David Copperfield* (1934), *Anna Karenina* (1935), *A Day at the Races* (1937), *A Yank at Oxford* (1938), and *Pride and Prejudice* (1940), as well as the female lead in many of MGM's B-productions. Her six Tarzan films were A-pictures, and, of course, *Tarzan, the Ape Man* and *Tarzan and His Mate* are on a level of their own as legendary classic adventures.

After completing her sixth Tarzan picture, *Tarzan's New York Adventure,* in early 1942, O'Sullivan temporarily retired from films to raise a family with husband John Farrow, who had worked on the aborted version of *Tarzan Escapes* in 1935. She had been pregnant with her first child during the filming of *Tarzan Finds a Son!* in 1939, and she became pregnant with her second child in the spring of 1942. Around this time, John Farrow received a medical discharge from the navy after contracting typhus, and Maureen wanted to care for him herself. Producer Sol Lesser was desperate to get O'Sullivan to return to her role of Jane for the RKO Tarzan pictures, but eventually was forced to fill the part with Brenda Joyce.

By 1947, O'Sullivan was ready to return to acting on a limited basis, and she appeared in the thriller *The Big Clock.* Husband John Farrow directed the taut drama about a publishing magnate (Charles Laughton) who accidentally kills his mistress and then assigns one of his editors (Ray Milland) to solve the crime. O'Sullivan costarred with Robert Mitchum in another of her husband's pictures, *Where Danger Lives,* in 1950. John Farrow was a talented director who wrote many of his own scripts; he was also the author of historical books, such as a history of the papacy and a biography of Sir Thomas More, the English saint.

O'Sullivan appeared in only seven more films in the 1950s; her husband and children were obviously her most important career at this stage of her life. She did find time to serve as the congenial hostess of a syndicated television series, *Irish Heritage,* in 1954, and starred on dramatic television many times during the decade, including *Ford Theater, Lux Video Theater, Four Star Theater,* and *Playhouse 90.* O'Sullivan spent a great deal of her time taking care of her daughter Mia, who was stricken with polio in the mid-fifties. Further tragedy struck the family in 1958, when their oldest son Michael was killed in a plane crash while taking flying lessons.

In 1961, O'Sullivan's career moved to the legitimate stage when she appeared in the summer stock production of *Roomful of Roses,* which opened in Chicago. The following summer she appeared with Paul Ford in *Cradle Will Rock,* which moved to Broadway under the title *Never Too Late* and was a triumph when it opened in November 1962. O'Sullivan portrayed a well-to-do middle-aged housewife who becomes pregnant and must deal with the decisive change in her life.

Perhaps the most difficult period of O'Sullivan's life came two months after *Never Too Late* opened on Broadway, when her husband John Farrow died after suffering a heart attack. Struggling with an agonizing decision and wanting the best for her family, she decided to stay with the play and continue with her career. She and John had enjoyed an exceptional Hollywood marriage, raising seven children and staying happily married until John's death in 1963.

After the successful run of *Never Too Late,* O'Sullivan and Paul Ford starred in a screen version of the Broadway play for Warner Bros. in 1965. The following year she was back on the stage in *The Subject Was Roses,* a drama about a returning war veteran who finds the generation gap a barrier in trying to communicate with his parents. O'Sullivan did more summer stock in 1969, appearing in Neil Simon's *Barefoot in the Park*. Next was the role of Mrs. Grant in the Broadway play *The Front Page* in 1970. O'Sullivan stepped into the shoes of Amanda Wingfield in Tennessee Williams' *The Glass Menagerie* at Brandeis University in 1971 and starred in *Charley's Aunt* on Broadway.

She did a cameo appearance in the satirical *The Phynx* in 1970, with old friend and Tarzan costar Johnny Weissmuller, who did a cameo as well. Always dear friends in real life, Maureen O'Sullivan and Johnny Weissmuller shared the cover of the April 1970 issue of *Esquire*.

During the 1970s, O'Sullivan stayed busy on the stage with television appearances, including a segment with dancer Fred Astaire on *Alcoa Presents*. She also did an ABC television movie in 1972, *Crooked Hearts*, a charming comedy in which she and Rosalind Russell are members of a lonely hearts club, stalked by a murderer who kills wealthy widows. And it was back to the stage once more in *No Sex Please, We're British*, an English farce that toured the West Coast before reaching Broadway in early 1973. She appeared in another made-for-TV movie in 1976, *The Great Houdinis*, a well-produced drama about the life of the famed escape artist. Maureen also starred as Mrs. Higgins in *Pygmalion* on the Los Angeles stage in 1978–79 for an eight-month run and followed that with her Tony-nominated role as Esther Crampton in *Morning's at Seven* on Broadway in 1980.

The 1980s kept O'Sullivan active with television appearances and movie roles. One of the most marvelous films of her career was *Hanna and Her Sisters* (1986), an entertaining view of the neurotic lives of a New York family and their friends, in which she portrayed the family matriarch, with real-life daughter Mia Farrow as her screen daughter. Her final stage credit was *Barbarians* during a limited engagement at the Williamstown Theatre in Massachusetts in the summer of 1986. She also appeared in the Kathleen Turner "return to the '50s" escapade *Peggy Sue Got Married* (1986), and starred in a science-fiction drama entitled *Stranded* (1987) as a grandmother who is abducted by aliens. The Disney Channel production of *Good Old Boy* (1988) with Maureen as Aunt Sue was her most recent screen credit.

In March 1992, O'Sullivan appeared on the TNT special "MGM: As the Lion Roars," a history of the famed studio, and spoke fondly of the Tarzan pictures she had made with Johnny Weissmuller and her years with MGM. Today, Maureen O'Sullivan is married to James Cushing and still lives a full, active life with occasional movie roles and television appearances.

After more than 60 years in motion pictures and on the stage and television, Maureen O'Sullivan remains to most of us the forever-youthful Jane, mate of the legendary Tarzan the ape-man. Immortality is rarely gained from a single movie role, but both she and Johnny Weissmuller reached that lofty state for their memorable performances as Jane and Tarzan.

Tarzan, the Ape Man

Release date: March 1932; Metro-Goldwyn-Mayer; running time: 99 minutes. *Directed by* W.S. Van Dyke; *produced by* Bernard H. Hyman; *based on the characters created by* Edgar Rice Burroughs; *adapted by* Cyril Hume; *dialogue by* Ivor Novello; *photography by* Harold Rosson and Clyde de Vinna; *film editors,* Ben Lewis and Tom Held; *recording director,* Douglas Shearer; *art director,* Cedric Gibbons; *production manager,* Joseph J. Cohn; *animal supervision,* George Emerson, Bert Nelson, Louis Roth, and Louis Goebel; *photographic effects,* Warren Newcombe; *additional cinematography,* William Snyder; *opening theme, "Voodoo Dance" by* George Richelavie, *arranged by* Fritz Stahlberg and P.A. Marquardt; *composite effects by* Dunning Process Company and Williams Composite Laboratories.

Tarzan	Johnny Weissmuller
Jane Parker	Maureen O'Sullivan
Harry Holt	Neil Hamilton
James Parker	C. Aubrey Smith
Mrs. Cutten	Doris Lloyd
Beamish	Forrester Harvey
Riano	Ivory Williams

James Parker and his partner, Harry Holt, are adventurers who run a trading post in West Africa. The two men have decided to take a safari beyond the Mutia escarpment in search of the fabled elephant graveyard where a fortune in elephant ivory lies.

Jane Parker arrives to join her father, whom she hasn't seen in several years, and it's an emotional reunion for both. Jane wants to go along on the safari and enlists the support of Holt, who is already taken with the young beauty. Her father relents despite serious reservations.

The safari natives are superstitious of the Mutia, a sheer mountain of dizzying heights, and the narrow trail is perilous—one of the bearers falls to his tragic death. Meanwhile, a strange eerie cry from the jungle adds to the fears and tensions. "What do you make of that, Riano?" asks Holt. "Maybe hyena, bwana?" says the native. But Parker speaks the startling truth: "That was a human cry!"

A treacherous river crossing becomes deadly when they are attacked first by a herd of hippopotami and then by crocodiles, who make a grisly meal of two of the unfortunate safari natives. The hippos are called off by the strange cry that comes from the jungle once again, and this time they get a glimpse

Advertising poster for *Tarzan, the Ape Man*, 1932.

Tarzan hunts for his dinner (*Tarzan, the Ape Man,* 1932).

of a savage white man who leaps through the trees—Tarzan the ape-man!

Jane is the first white woman Tarzan has ever seen, and following a primitive instinct, he abducts her and carries her through the trees to his lofty lair. At first Jane is frightened of Tarzan, who can only mimic her English, but soon falls in love with the jungle man, who is brave and noble and fearless.

Parker and Holt discover Jane in the treetops while Tarzan is away hunting and kill one of the great apes guarding the girl. Tarzan is enraged and takes his revenge on the safari, picking them off one by one until the ape-man is himself wounded in the head by a bullet from the rifle of Holt, who is jealous and covets Jane for himself. Saved by one of his apes, Tarzan is carried to safety by Timba, the elephant. The

great apes lead Jane through the jungle, and she nurses Tarzan back to health.

When Tarzan recovers, he and Jane discover romance in their viney "garden of Eden." Their playful fun turns into serious passion for both. Tarzan's feelings are hurt when Jane rejoins her father, who has been desperately searching the jungles for her. As the ape-man walks dejectedly into the jungle, Jane pleads with him, "Tarzan! Tarzan, please come back!" But the Lord of the Jungle rejoins his world, and Jane reluctantly rejoins hers.

When the safari is captured by a tribe of savage dwarfs, Cheeta races to warn Tarzan of Jane's precarious plight. With his thundering war cry, Tarzan incites his elephant allies to action, and together they charge the dwarf village. The diminutive hostiles begin throwing their captives into a pit containing a giant ape, who crushes his victims like toys. When Jane is thrown into the pit, both Holt and her father jump in to save her. They all seem doomed until Tarzan arrives in the nick of time to battle and kill the savage brute.

Tarzan's mighty elephants arrive and destroy the village and trample the dwarfs, while Jane, her father, Holt, and the ape-man escape on the backs of two elephants. One of their huge mounts is wounded. Dying, the noble beast leads them through a waterfall to the secret entrance of the sought-after elephant graveyard. "It's worth millions!" cries Holt, but their jubilance is short-lived when Parker dies of his wounds. Jane is heartbroken at her father's death. "He found what he was looking for. I know that somewhere, wherever the great hunters go, he's happy." Jane sends Holt back to civilization by himself and remains with Tarzan in the African jungles to share a new life with him.

•

A classic motion picture like *Tarzan, the Ape Man,* which introduced Johnny Weissmuller as Tarzan to the moviegoing public, is a collaborative effort of many skilled and creative individuals. Starting with the extraordinary concept of Tarzan, developed into a screen story with strength and character, produced and directed with extreme competence, and using the perfect actors for the characterization, the result in this case was a heart-pounding, romantic adventure that stands the ultimate test—time. *Tarzan, the Ape Man* was the first "talking" feature in this long-running series, but it will be remembered for many more reasons than that. The initial premise of the film (and all its African photography) got its start a few years earlier.

In 1929, MGM studio chief Irving Thalberg assigned W.S. (Woody) Van Dyke to direct a jungle picture called *Trader Horn* (based on the journals of Alfred Aloysius Horn and edited by Ethelreda Lewis), which was to be filmed on location in Africa to achieve an unparalleled authenticity and realism. The jungle and wild animal footage was shot in Tanganyika, Uganda, Kenya, the Sudan, and the Belgian Congo. To ensure against attack by beast or man, the camera crews were escorted and protected by a team of professional white hunters.

The story of *Trader Horn* was a twist on Edgar Rice Burroughs' Tarzan theme, with a veteran trader and his young partner (Harry Carey as Horn and Duncan Renaldo as Peru) discovering a beautiful white woman, Nina (Edwina Booth), who is the leader of a tribe of savage natives. Nina falls in love with the handsome Peru, and the small band narrowly escape the jungle hazards of wild beasts, starvation, and bloodthirsty tribes to return to civilization. Portraying the role of Renchero, Horn's faithful gun bearer, was a genuine African chief, Mutia Omoolu, who was brought back to the United States to complete his scenes in the picture.

There were plenty of problems for the crew of *Trader Horn,* including the dangerous wild animals that abounded in their jungle settings, as well as tribes of hostile natives who were not exactly enamored to have their country invaded by an American film company. The truck carrying the sound equipment veered off a trail and landed in a river. Lead actress Edwina Booth contracted an exotic disease while in Africa and later sued the studio. Halfway through the African filming, MGM decided that *Trader Horn* must be a "talkie," which resulted in numerous additional headaches and technical problems for the already-beleaguered Van Dyke.

Disastrous would seem to describe

Tarzan battles the giant ape (with O'Sullivan and C. Aubrey Smith at Weissmuller's feet) (*Tarzan, the Ape Man,* 1932).

the entire expedition, and it would be many years before motion picture companies dared venture back to Africa to film on location. Further magnifying their trials and tribulations, the jungle and wild animal footage shot by cinematographer Clyde de Vinna was simply not enough to make the motion picture they envisioned, and the entire company returned to Hollywood and the MGM sets to continue filming.

At this point, with production costs skyrocketing toward an eventual $1.3 million, Thalberg was reported to be ready to fire director Van Dyke and to scrap the entire project. Fortunately, Van Dyke got off the hot seat and was allowed to complete his exciting jungle adventure that would bring in hordes of appreciative audiences around the world. The film was even nominated by

the Motion Picture Academy for Best Picture of 1930-31 (the winner was *Cimarron*).

Searching for a follow-up to *Trader Horn* (1931), Irving Thalberg negotiated with Edgar Rice Burroughs to produce an MGM picture based on his jungle legend, Tarzan. The deal was inked in April 1931 and sealed with a check for $20,000 (there was also an option for two additional sequels). With plenty of leftover footage from the *Trader Horn* expedition available (and no desire to return to Africa to go back on location), producer Bernard Hyman assembled basically the same crew who worked on *Trader Horn,* including director W.S. Van Dyke, scriptwriter Cyril Hume, photographer Clyde de Vinna, editor Ben Lewis, and recording technician Douglas Shearer.

The deal MGM struck with Burroughs was that the new motion picture would use his characters, including Tarzan, but would not be based on his works. Burroughs was also paid $1,000 per week for five weeks to read the scripts, pointing out any material that conflicted with or infringed on his original stories. There were certainly similarities between Burroughs' Tarzan novels and the plot of the new film, but ERB let them pass without complaint. Unable to use the author's fictional ape language for the MGM movie, the scriptwriter invented new words for Tarzan, including the classic "Umgawa" (which meant "up," "down," "halt" or "go," and in later pictures just about any actions needing a command!).

The original draft of *Tarzan, the Ape Man* had Trader Horn leading an expedition (which included a lovely lady scientist) in search of a lost primitive tribe in the bowels of the Dark Continent. From the lofty treetops drops Tarzan, and infatuated with the female of the species, kidnaps her. Later, Tarzan must save the expedition from the clutches of the lost tribe, moon worshippers who make human sacrifices to a sacred, but deadly, gorilla. Tarzan and his ever-faithful elephants arrive at the lost city to rescue the woman, who falls in love with the brave and noble hero. Trader Horn and safari return to civilization, while the lady remains to live with Tarzan.

Eventually, scriptwriter Cyril Hume replaced Trader Horn in his story with James Parker, an adventurer who runs a trading post; the lady scientist became Jane Parker, a beautiful young English lass, who comes to Africa to visit her father. This change cut the cords for using *Trader Horn* as a precursor to *Tarzan, the Ape Man,* and the rest of the story was modified into its final form: a search for the fabled elephant graveyard, rather than a scientific expedition.

Dozens of actors were considered for the role of Tarzan, including Herman Brix, but the former Olympic shot-putter knocked himself out of the running by breaking a shoulder during the filming of *Touchdown* (1931). Director W.S. Van Dyke couldn't find the actor he wanted for Tarzan within the MGM stable of stars and envisioned his ape-man to be rugged looking, as well as physically capable. "I want someone like Jack Dempsey, only younger," said Van Dyke. This turned out to be Olympic swimming champion Johnny Weissmuller, who had no acting experience but definitely filled the bill.

When MGM signed Johnny Weissmuller as Tarzan and Maureen O'Sullivan as Jane, the studio's brilliant bit of casting produced an unbeatable team as the jungle man and his mate. Weissmuller and O'Sullivan had a special chemistry that worked remarkably well, giving a warmth and genuineness to their roles as Tarzan and Jane.

Johnny was a little rough on Maureen at times during filming, but necessarily so. In one scene Tarzan literally knocks Jane off her feet with a playful chop to the legs, and she lands on her derrière with a loud plunk (this obviously stung the actress quite a bit). Moments later, the playfulness turns to passion in their eyes; Tarzan lifts Jane in his arms and carries his woman, now submissive, to an obvious treetop romantic interlude. Although only implied as the scene fades, the sensuality of this cinematic romance was extremely effective.

O'Sullivan appeared on the TNT special "MGM: As the Lion Roars" in March 1992, and recalled the instinctive relationship formed between Tarzan and this woman he had found in the jungle:

> He was a man who had never seen a woman before, so it was a fairy tale—and yet it was two real people.

He didn't know what to do with a woman—I guess he found out pretty quick. But he didn't know what it was, when he found her—was it a monkey? She was able to teach him many things that he was unaware of. It was a lovely, innocent concept, and yet very sexy.

Years after the filming of *Tarzan, the Ape Man,* O'Sullivan fondly recalled another playful incident between her and her costar.

I was deathly afraid of height. And one day, Johnny Weissmuller and I had to cower in the high branches of a tree for one of our scenes. Johnny was a practical joker. He knew I was afraid of height. So he began to shake our branch and I screamed. As I shrieked, Johnny smiled.

The story goes that moments later, Johnny responded with a sarcastic wit becoming his lighthearted personality, "Me—Tarzan! You—Jane!" Of course, this famous comic variation of the dialogue that was actually spoken in the film, "Tarzan—Jane" (with the ape-man poking first his own chest and then Jane's), broke up cast and crew members alike.

The superb cast also included Neil Hamilton as Harry Holt, a jealous guy (in love with Jane) who misguidedly tries to murder his rival (Tarzan); C. Aubrey Smith (of the noble aristocratic profile), who portrayed Jane's father, James Parker (Smith had a similar role in *Trader Horn* in which he played a trader friend of Horn's); and Forrester Harvey, who supplied comic relief as Beamish, a clumsy Londoner who is a friend of the Parkers. Of course, the real comedian in the Tarzan films was Cheeta, the chimp, in this film portrayed by Emma (the first of many chimps to fill the role). Johnny Weissmuller was always close to the chimps who played Cheeta, and they, in turn, were fond of him.

The fictional scenario for the MGM Tarzan pictures was beyond a rugged, mountainous barrier, almost a sheer cliff, called the Mutia escarpment (named after Mutia Omoolu, the African chief who portrayed Trader Horn's loyal gun bearer). The Mutia was often represented by one of the many matte paintings used by movie studios in those days; most were realistic enough and blended smoothly with sets (especially with the use of black-and-white photography, which hid more flaws than did color film).

The MGM jungle, complete with its own river, was the Toluca Lake region of North Hollywood. The area west of Hollywood, known as Sherwood Forest (named after the legendary forest in Douglas Fairbanks' classic production of *Robin Hood,* 1922), was also used. The safari river crossing and the realistic hippo attack were shot at Lake Sherwood. An African landscape was created in Hollywood by bringing in truckloads of tropical fruit trees, plants, and other lush vegetation, all planted especially for the jungle production.

Despite the somewhat primitive cinematic techniques of 1931, the film succeeded on both a technical and an artistic basis. Rear projections for the wild animal shots, with the actors moving in the foreground, were realistic enough to be believable and were used over and over in the MGM Tarzan pictures. Yet they were somewhat less effective in some early scenes in which Jane is supposedly standing close to some beautifully plumed native tribespeople, who have come to trade with Parker and Holt.

The incredibly conditioned and athletic Weissmuller did many of his own stunts in the Tarzan films, such as riding elephants, climbing trees, swimming and diving, and battling his enemies (both human and animal). One stunt that required especially great strength was Tarzan being pulled by one arm from the giant ape's pit by an elephant, while he was lifting Jane and Holt (O'Sullivan and Hamilton) out of the pit with his free arm.

Of course, the most dangerous stunts were pulled off using stunt doubles. Alfredo Codona, a renowned aerialist and one-third of the Flying Codonas, did all the shots of the ape-man swinging through the trees on specially constructed trapezes. Skilled "lion man" Bert Nelson, animal trainer for the A.G. Barnes circus, did the scenes with Tarzan in a death struggle with a ferocious lion (a lion Nelson was familiar with). Many of the wild animals used in the film were leased by George Emerson, MGM's full-time studio trainer. Four additional lions were supplied by the Goebel Lion Farm in Thousand Oaks, with trainers Louis Goebel and Louis Roth working on the set to see that the beasts didn't get out of control. Again, these stock shots were reused many times over the next decade in the MGM Tarzan films. Future Tarzan Buster Crabbe reportedly worked on the picture as well, as an extra and stuntman.

Indian elephants were easier to work with than the African species, so the Indian pachyderms were fitted with false ears (covering their own small ears) and extended tusks. The climactic elephant stampede of the dwarf village took five days to orchestrate and was dramatically thrilling as the giant beasts, summoned by Tarzan with his reverberating jungle cry, pummeled the village and its inhabitants to smithereens.

Johnny Weissmuller originated the famous yell that became the standard used in most of the Tarzan pictures, including the films made after he retired from the role. Starting with Johnny's own cry, MGM sound technician Douglas Shearer mixed in a strange variety of unrelated sounds, timed a split-second apart, including: a hyena's yowl played

backwards, a camel's bleat, the pluck of a violin string, and a soprano's high-C. In its review of the film, the *New York Times* said of the Tarzan yell, "a peculiar cry, a noise like blowing on a comb covered with paper."

Years later in a television interview, Weissmuller recalled the origin of his Tarzan yell:

> When I was a kid I used to read all the Tarzan books, and they had kind of a shrill yell for Tarzan. And I never thought I'd ever make Tarzan [movies], but when I finally got it [the role of Tarzan], they were trying to do yells like that. And I remembered when I was a kid I used to yodel at the picnics on Sundays, and I said, "I know a yell!"

At this point the former Tarzan broke into his famous jungle cry, "Aaahhhh-eeeeeeeee-aaaahhhh-eeeeeee-aaaahhhh-eeeeeee-aaaahhhhhhhh!"

Actual filming of the jungle classic began on October 31, 1931, and concluded just eight weeks later in late December. The modest budget for the film was $652,675, almost exactly half the cost of filming *Trader Horn. Tarzan, the Ape Man* eventually paid for itself many times over, and indeed was one of the top 15 money-makers of 1932. Previewed in February 1932, the film was released to an appreciative public in late March.

The opening musical theme, "Voodoo Dance," composed by George Richelavie and arranged by Fritz Stahlberg and P.A. Marquardt, was haunting, primeval, even savage—it actually raised the hairs on one's neck! The music was also used as the opening theme for the sequel, *Tarzan and His Mate* (1934).

From the opening credits right down to the final moments when Jane decides to stay with the man she loves (appropriately enough, a clip of Tchaikovsky's "Overture to Romeo and Juliet" played over the final scene), *Tarzan, the*

Ape Man succeeded unconditionally as both an electrifying adventure and a satisfying romance of the heart. Fans around the world loved the picture and the dynamic duo of Weissmuller and O'Sullivan and stampeded to the box offices, shelling out their hard-earned quarters for admittance to the classic jungle picture. The critics applauded the film as well, as attested to by the many testimonial reviews, as follows:

Literary Digest **(April 16, 1932):** "Fame as a champion swimmer may help Mr. Weissmuller to the eminence he seems bound to achieve, but his acting qualities will also help. A subtle touch of the animal nature in *Tarzan* is indicated in his frequent turning of the head, in his alertness in the presence of danger. It was something shown by Nijinsky in his impersonation of the *Fawn.* Athletically, he competes with exalted predecessors."

New York Evening Post **(excerpted from** *Literary Digest,* **April 16, 1932)** (Thornton Delehanty): "Whereas *Trader Horn* made a grim effort to impress you with its fidelity, this *Tarzan* is a frank and exuberant frolic in the imaginative literature of the screen.... It even has a way now and then of making fun of itself, a ruse so disarming that you are tempted to enjoy the picture most when you are believing it least.... However credible or interesting Tarzan may be on the printed page, I doubt very much if he emerges in such splendor as he does in the person of Johnny Weissmuller, the swimming champion.... As Tarzan, Mr. Weissmuller makes his bow to the moviegoing public, and as Tarzan he will probably remain bowing through a whole series of these pictures, even tho the public may clamor to see him in Clark Gable roles.... There is no doubt that he possesses all the attributes, both physical and mental, for the complete realization of his son-of-the-jungle role. With his flowing hair, his magnificently proportioned body, his catlike walk, and his virtuosity in the water, you could hardly ask anything more in the way of perfection. And for the portrayal of Tarzan, nothing short of perfection would be permissible.

"As the English girl who has gone to Africa with her father in search of treasure, Maureen O'Sullivan gives one of her most charming performances. One can understand why Tarzan swings her around that way in the trees, and why he calls out his elephant friends to save her when she is about to be devoured by a horrible gorilla. She helps to make this infatuation of Tarzan's the most plausible thing in the picture."

Photoplay Magazine **(June 1932)** (Katherine Albert): "The most vital statistic of all is the fact that a lad who had never been in a picture before, who had been interested in nothing but swimming all his life, and who frankly admits he can't act, is the top-notch heart-flutterer of the year."

New York Sun **(excerpted from** *Literary Digest,* **April 16, 1932)** (John S. Cohen, Jr.): "Johnny Weissmuller is the ideal choice, representing as he does, the movie maiden's prayer for a cave man, ape man, and big fig-leaf-and-bough man. Tall, built like a Greek statue.... *Tarzan* is a first-rate show."

New York Times **(March 28, 1932)** (Mordaunt Hall): "Johnny Weissmuller, Crack Swimmer Makes His Film Debut as a Wild Man of the Jungle.... Youngsters home from school yesterday found the Capitol a lively place, with all sorts of thrills in the picture *Tarzan, the Ape Man,* and Johnny Weissmuller as the hero, a so-called ape man.... Mr. Weissmuller does good work as Tarzan and Miss O'Sullivan is alert as Jane."

•

Even author Edgar Rice Burroughs was delighted with the film, which was not the case with the majority of the Tarzan films made previously. After the preview in February 1932, Burroughs sent director Woody Van Dyke a letter thanking him for the marvelous finished product, as quoted in Irwin Porges' *The Man Who Created Tarzan:* "This is a real Tarzan picture. It breathes the grim mystery of the jungle; the endless, relentless strife for survival; the virility, the cruelty, and the grandeur of Nature in the raw."

Burroughs continued by describing Johnny Weissmuller as a "great Tarzan with youth, a marvelous physique, and a magnetic personality." And of Maureen O'Sullivan, who he thought was "perfect" as Jane, Burroughs said, "I am afraid that I shall never be satisfied with any other heroine for my future pictures...." Burroughs concluded his letter with a final salute to Van Dyke and company: "Mr. Hamilton and Mr. Smith have added a lustre of superb character delineation to the production that has helped make it the greatest Tarzan picture of them all.... Again let me thank you for the ability, the genius, and the hard work you have put into *Tarzan, the Ape Man...."*

High praise indeed from the creator of the legend of Tarzan, who wrote to producer Bernard Hyman on May 31, suggesting that Tarzan movies should be released as seasonal events, each spring, so that people would look forward to the occasion, much as they did to the circus, "to which the Tarzan picture is analogous." With the accolades pouring in from the critics and the dollars pouring in from the moviegoing public, it was now time to plan a sequel to the original — *Tarzan and His Mate.*

Tarzan and His Mate

Release date: April 1934; Metro-Goldwyn-Mayer; running time: 116 minutes at preview, 95 minutes in general release (104 minutes in 1991 videocassette release). *Directed by* Cedric Gibbons (*uncredited direction by* Jack Conway); *produced by* Bernard H. Hyman; *based on the characters created by* Edgar Rice Burroughs; *screenplay by* James Kevin McGuinness; *adapted by* Howard Emmett Rogers and Leon Gordon; *photographed by* Charles G. Clarke and Clyde de Vinna; *film editor,* Tom Held; *recording director,* Douglas Shearer; *art director,* Arnold Gillespie; *production manager,* Joseph J. Cohn; *second unit directors,* James McKay, Erroll Taggart, and Nick Grinde; *animal supervision,* George Emerson, Bert Nelson, Louis Roth, and Louis Goebel; *special effects director,* James Basevi; *art effects,* Warren Newcombe; *photographic effects,* Irving Ries; *sound effects,* T.B. Hoffman, James Graham, and Mike Steinore; *opening theme,* "Voodoo Dance," by George Richelavie, *arranged by* Fritz Stahlberg and P.A. Marquardt; *closing theme,* "My Tender One," by Dr. William Axt; *song,* "Soldier on the Shelf" by Sherman Myers and Erele Reaves; *additional composite effects by* Dunning Process Company and Williams Composite Laboratories.

Tarzan	Johnny Weissmuller
Jane	Maureen O'Sullivan
Harry Holt	Neil Hamilton
Martin Arlington	Paul Cavanagh
Beamish	Forrester Harvey

Weissmuller and O'Sullivan with Paul Cavanagh (left) and Neil Hamilton (*Tarzan and His Mate,* 1934).

Saidi	Nathan Curry
Tom Pierce	William Stack
Henry Van Ness	Desmond Roberts
Monsieur Perron	Paul Porcasi
Native bearer	Everett Brown

Almost a year after leaving Jane Parker with Tarzan in the African jungles, Harry Holt is planning another safari to the elephant graveyard. Holt is joined in the quest for ivory by old friend Martin Arlington; their plans are temporarily sabotaged by the unscrupulous Tom Pierce and Henry Van Ness, who steal Holt's map and all the safari natives.

Catching up with Pierce and Van Ness near the taboo Mutia escarpment, they are found dead, tortured by Gibonis, a fierce native tribe. Holt and Ar-

lington barely escape the savages, only to be attacked by ferocious apes. This time they are saved by the familiar cry of Tarzan, who calls off his worthy subjects.

Harry is in love with Jane, and the roguish Martin lusts for the enchanting jungle woman. The two men concoct a plan to lure Jane back to England (each for his own selfish reason), but she loves only Tarzan and declines to leave. "I wouldn't want to live without Tarzan, and where would he be without me?"

Advertising poster for *Tarzan and His Mate* (1934).

Tarzan leads the charge of his mighty elephant army (*Tarzan and His Mate,* 1934).

The ape-man sees through the facade of Holt and Arlington and refuses to lead the ivory hunters to their destination. "Tarzan's the only law here in the jungle, and mine—won't you let us guide you back?" Jane asks. Undaunted, Arlington shoots an elephant, and the poor wounded beast follows his instincts to his place of dying—the elephant graveyard with its fortune in ivory. Tarzan halts the ivory caravan with a herd of elephants as a blockade, but the corrupt Arlington has a plan. He lies to the ape-man when he says he'll return the ivory to the graveyard the next day, after the men in the caravan have rested.

Meanwhile, Jane gives her mate a trinket of her father's. "I want you to wear it always, Tarzan," she says. When Tarzan goes to fish by the waterfall, Ar-

lington wounds him with a bullet to the skull. He then lies to Jane and tells her he has seen the jungle man die in a grim fight with a crocodile. Jane is convinced Tarzan is dead only when she finds the "always" bracelet in the river. "Nothing matters anymore," she says in despair.

Unknown to Jane, Tarzan's faithful jungle creatures have saved his life, and the apes are nursing him back to health. Later, Cheeta manages to convince Jane that her mate is not dead. "Tarzan's alive!" rejoices a rejuvenated Jane.

Suddenly, amid the drone of ju-ju drums, the entire safari is surrounded by fierce natives. Somehow, Jane, Holt, Arlington, and Saidi barely escape to a rocky cave, and Cheeta runs to warn Tarzan of Jane's perilous plight. When the hostiles loose an entire pride of lions, Saidi and then Holt die in acts of bravery. Arlington is the last to die, leaving Jane to face the lions alone.

With only the fire she has started between herself and a certain grisly death, Jane bravely holds off the hungry beasts until Tarzan arrives in the nick of time to save her. Tarzan's elephants and ape friends kill off the rest of the lions and savages, as the ape-man gathers his mate in his arms with great relief. Jane tells her beloved Tarzan that "always is just beginning for us," as they ride Timba, the elephant, toward their jungle home.

•

Tarzan and His Mate, the sequel to *Tarzan, the Ape Man*, is considered by a vast majority of film buffs to be the greatest Tarzan picture ever made. It is charged from stem to stern with action and adventure and, as in all the MGM Tarzan pictures, with the romantic mystique of the Weissmuller/O'Sullivan relationship. Beautifully photographed by Charles G. Clarke and Clyde de Vinna and cleverly crafted from the story by Kevin McGuinness, adapted by Howard Emmett Rogers and Leon Gordon, it is virtually cinematic poetry in motion.

The film starred Johnny Weissmuller, whose dark hair, masculine good looks, and a perfect physique combined to form the definitive Tarzan. It also starred Maureen O'Sullivan, who has reaped accolades for her sensuous beauty and convincing portrayals; she also received a certain amount of fame and notoriety simply from the skimpiness of the costume she was asked to wear as Jane.

In her March 1992 appearance on the TNT special "MGM: When the Lion Roars," Maureen O'Sullivan gave her thoughts on the obvious appeal of the sexuality of *Tarzan and His Mate:*

> They tried different things to make Jane look pretty sexy. And first off

they had the idea of having Jane wearing no bra—no brassiere at all—and she would always be covered with a branch, and they tried that and it didn't work. So then, they made a costume and it wasn't that bad at all. There was a little leather bra and a thing (loincloth) with thongs on the side. But it started such a furor, that the letters just came in. So it added up to thousands of women who were objecting to my costume. And I think that was one of the things that started the Legion of Decency.

> Now in those days, they took those things very seriously, the public did. Do you know I was offered land in San Francisco, I was offered all kinds of places where I could go in my shame—to hide from the cruel public who were ready to throw stones at me. It's funny you know—we were unreal people and yet we were real.

Indeed, Johnny and Maureen breathed life into Edgar Rice Burroughs' fictional characters, capturing the essence of a primeval man and his mate. The playfulness between Tarzan and Jane was often endearing, and also provocative. In the scene where Jane puts on a dress, stockings, and French perfume (gifts from Holt and Arlington to try to persuade her to return to England), the ape-man approves; he scoops her up and carries her away to their lofty love nest, with hardly a protest from Jane.

Some years after the picture was released, producer Sol Lesser offered his view of O'Sullivan as Jane in Robert Fenton's book, *The Big Swingers:*

> Maureen O'Sullivan was an ideal Jane with a figure that is greatly revealed in the second Metro picture— but done so beautifully that it couldn't be criticized (but of course, it was). As I recall the situation she is standing on a tree limb with Tarzan. He tugs at her garment, dives in the water and she dives in after him. Then she comes up from the swimming scene with her breast exposed. It was done in such good taste—I think

that a kind of snobbishness developed afterwards with Miss O'Sullivan from her role as Jane. Maybe the public kidded her too much—or maybe she thought it wasn't good acting, I don't know. But I do know the movie audiences worshipped her.

The beautifully choreographed underwater swimming sequence that followed O'Sullivan being tossed into the drink by Tarzan was actually performed by Weissmuller and Josephine McKim, a petite Olympic swimming champion who doubled for Maureen. (Josephine McKim won a gold medal in the 1932 Olympics as a member of the women's 4×100-meter freestyle relay. She knew Weissmuller from the 1928 Olympics in Amsterdam, where she won a bronze medal in the 400-meter freestyle.) This underwater "ballet" is memorable for its graceful beauty and again the playful love between Tarzan and Jane; the ape-man kisses his beloved mate underwater in a classic moment.

Weissmuller wears his loincloth during the scene, but Jane (McKim) is nude, which, of course, raised a furor with the Production Code Office that previewed the picture. Metro bent over backwards to appease the censors by reshooting the scene with Jane clothed (apparently, three versions were released to different areas of the country, depending on local codes and restrictions). When Ted Turner released the first three MGM Tarzan pictures on videocassette in 1991, the nude swimming sequence was included in all its splendor; fortunately for film fans, the scene had not been lost.

Although the winning tandem of Johnny and Maureen wasn't tampered with for *Tarzan and His Mate,* a major change was made in the director's chair. Woody Van Dyke was busy on another project, and was unavailable to direct the picture. Taking the helm was Cedric Gibbons, who worked as art director on

most of the MGM Tarzan adventures. Although the film is considered a classic, it had its share of problems, including a change in director in the early stages of the production schedule.

Filming began on the MGM back lots on August 2, 1933, under the direction of Gibbons; the secondary cast included: Rod LaRocque as Martin Arlington, Murray Kinnell as Tom Pierce, Frank Reicher as Henry Van Ness, and Neil Hamilton as Harry Holt. Near the end of August, an unexplained happenstance occurred. Longtime MGM director Jack Conway supplanted Gibbons as director of the first unit, and Rod LaRocque was replaced by Paul Cavanagh in the second lead role of Arlington. Other cast changes included William Stack and Desmond Roberts stepping, respectively, into the characters of Pierce and Van Ness, in place of Kinnell and Reicher.

Cedric Gibbons is given full director's credit, but it was to be his first and only shot at directing a picture at Metro; afterward, he resumed his job as art director, working on hundreds of MGM pictures from 1924 through the 1950s. (Gibbons won several Oscars for art direction and is credited with designing the Oscar statuette.) Gibbons was given one additional honor for the picture; the fierce native tribe that chase the safari to the base of the Mutia escarpment, the "Gibonis," were named after him, tongue in cheek, of course.

When filming resumed in early September, Conway directed the dialogue segments of the film, and James McKay, Errol Taggart, and Nick Grinde worked with the second units. Once again Sherwood Forest and Lake Sherwood were the basic shooting scenarios, in addition to the swamplands of Woodland Park and Big Tujunga and China Flats. Some of the realistic scenes filmed for the picture included Tarzan's underwater river battle with a giant crocodile, a classic scene that was to be used several times in future MGM Tarzans. It was even used in the 1959 MGM remake of *Tarzan, the Ape Man.*

When Tarzan swims frantically to save Jane from a monster-sized crocodile, he barely manages to vanquish the savage beast after a savage battle. Working in approximately 18 feet of water in a tank on Lot 1, Weissmuller grappled with the huge mechanical reptile, finally stabbing it to "death"; dye sacks in the neck of the creature were cut open by Johnny's knife, and "blood" gushed out from the fatal wound. Josephine McKim doubled as Jane, with the crocodile thrashing in the water and trying to flatten her with its wildly spinning tail.

During production, Mary, the rhinoceros, made her "acting" debut, again a classic scene with Tarzan riding on the back of the beast and finally killing it with his knife. MGM animal trainer George Emerson imported the beast from Germany (reportedly paying $10,000) and rode Mary in the most dangerous scenes shot in the rhino corral on Lot 2. However, accounts of the filming relate that Weissmuller also rode Mary during part of the scene, despite the pleadings of his wife, Lupe Velez, not to do so; Johnny also filmed part of the scene on a dummy rhino. Johnny was never afraid to try dangerous stunts, if it was possible and within the realms of reason to do so. Mary was indeed a dangerous beast and at one point charged a frantic camera crew, who were shaken up but saved from certain tragedy only by the heavy metal cage that enclosed the men and the cameras.

Weissmuller looked every bit the part of a magnificent jungle king, riding the lead elephant of the herd called by Tarzan to surround the elephant graveyard, while by his side the savagely beautiful Jane (Maureen, this time doing her own stunt) was riding on the head and trunk of a smaller animal. There is

something primitive and majestic in Tarzan and his mate riding to the rescue on the mighty beasts, especially when you realize the real risks the actors took in working with dangerous and often skittish wild creatures.

At one point in the story, after Arlington (Paul Cavanagh) shoots one of the elephants to give them a trail to follow to the elephant graveyard, Tarzan (Johnny) picks up the other man and lifts him over his head like he was merely a rag doll. No trick photography was involved here, just the brute strength of Weissmuller.

Tarzan and His Mate again featured the thundering war cry of Tarzan and something new. Jane unveiled her own female version of the ape-man's yodel, which she used mainly to enlighten Tarzan that she was in a threatening predicament and needed his help pronto.

Alfredo Codona once again doubled for Weissmuller in the treetops, and the Flying Codonas aerial act performed the entire scene in which Tarzan, Jane, and Big Cheeta (a man in an ape costume) do their own jungle "trapeze" act. An adagio (balancing act) team executed the stunt of Jane diving from a high branch into Tarzan's waiting arms below; actually Maureen and Johnny also did the stunt themselves, but Maureen's leap was from a much lower platform (the effect being that it looked like they had done the trick themselves).

As in the previous film, "big cat" man Bert Nelson doubled for Weissmuller in battles with first a lion and then a lioness, as well as for Paul Cavanagh in the scene in which Arlington meets his death in the jaws of a lioness (Johnny did grapple with a real lion in the climactic scene, before Nelson took over the balance of the sequence). Betty Roth, wife of lion trainer Louis Roth, doubled for O'Sullivan in scenes in which two snarling lions have her trapped on a narrow ledge.

The heart-pounding finale, with Tarzan backing slowly through dozens of the killer beasts (Weissmuller on a sound stage in front of the rear projection of the lions), emitting his thunderous plea for help to his always faithful elephant friends, is a cinematic masterpiece. The sequence was so ingeniously conceived and edited that it impresses you even though you know they are using "trick" photography.

The mysterious "Voodoo Dance" was again used over the opening credits, and in a moment of déjà vu, the picture opens with the exact scene as in *Tarzan, the Ape Man:* native bearers carrying ivory along a path. This was about the only expense that was spared; the rest of the picture is a veritable panorama of drama and expensive adventure. The final tab was $1.3 million, an enormous sum for the Depression era and almost double the cost of filming *Tarzan, the Ape Man.*

On the set in August 1933 as a guest of MGM was Edgar Rice Burroughs, who wrote to his son Hulbert, as quoted in Irwin Porges' *The Man Who Created Tarzan,* that "the underwater shot of Weissmuller fighting the croc" was going to be "very thrilling." A later note to Hulbert from ERB reported that Metro was sparing no cost in the production: "I am fearful that they are going to spend too much. They are very anxious to make it outshine Lesser's picture to such a degree that there will be no comparison...." MGM had paid Burroughs $45,000 for the rights to produce *Tarzan and His Mate,* and his appearance on the set indicated that his interest was more than simply financial.

The elaborate production of *Tarzan and His Mate* took approximately eight months to film, but if it had taken eight years to produce, it still would have been worth the wait: The second Weissmuller-O'Sullivan collaboration is simply the definition of a classic motion picture. In the United States and abroad, the film was a resounding success, playing to massive audiences (especially in foreign markets, punctuating the international appeal of Tarzan). When the picture opened in New York in mid–April 1934, it was received with thunderous applause by fans and critics alike, as these reviews indicate:

***New York Times* (April 21, 1934)** (Mordaunt Hall): "Having apparently dwelt in the jungle since they met in *Tarzan, the Ape Man,* Johnny Weissmuller, the swimming ace, and the comely Irish colleen, Maureen O'Sullivan, are now to be seen at the Capitol in a sequel to their first adventure. The current offering, which is hailed as *Tarzan and His Mate,* is, if anything, even more fantastic than its predecessor.... Aside from the wild tale, this film is a marvel from a photographic standpoint. Tarzan has his hand-to-hand encounters with leopards, hippopotamuses, and other beasts, and Jane has anything but a merry time with several lions.... Needless to say that Miss O'Sullivan and Mr. Weissmuller acquit themselves in the same favorable fashion they did in their former hectic experiences."

***Newsweek* (April 28, 1934):** "*Tarzan and His Mate* is the mild name Metro-Goldwyn-Mayer have chosen for the most exciting movie of the season. So exciting is it that even in the most ludicrously impossible scenes, the audience sits on the edge of the seats, cheering lustily and praying for the safety of the agile ape-man.... The most daring feat of all is the hero's dangerous act on the back of a bona fide rhinoceros. George Emerson, former big animal man of Ringling Brothers, declared that he had never heard of anyone, trainer or actor, who had ridden on the back of this fierce animal.... Johnny Weissmuller, as well as Tarzan, must have been born under a lucky star."

***The Nation* (May, 16, 1934)**
(William Troy): "*Tarzan and His Mate*, happens, it is true, to be much the best directed and best photographed film in the entire Tarzan cycle. With an admirable sense of delicacy, the producers have refrained from intruding for too long at a stretch on the tropical intimacies of Tarzan and his noble English-born mate.... In brief, this addition to the Tarzan saga achieves all the charm and interest of so-called documentary pictures like *Chang* and *Africa Speaks*, without any of the disturbing strain on our credulity which such pictures usually involve."

Tarzan Escapes

Release date: November 1936; Metro-Goldwyn-Mayer; running time: 95 minutes. *Directed by* Richard Thorpe; *associate producer,* Sam Zimbalist; *screenplay by* Cyril Hume, *based on the characters created by* Edgar Rice Burroughs; *recording director,* Douglas Shearer; *art director,* Elmer Sheeley; *photographed by* Leonard Smith; *film editor,* W. Donn Hayes; *set decorations,* Edwin B. Willis; *special effects director,* A. Arnold Gillespie; *photographic effects,* Thomas Tutwiler; *art effects,* Warren Newcombe; *opening theme,* "Cannibal Carnival," *by* Sol Levy; *closing theme,* "My Tender One," *by* Dr. William Axt.

Tarzan	Johnny Weissmuller
Jane	Maureen O'Sullivan
Captain Fry	John Buckler
Rita Parker	Benita Hume
Eric Parker	William Henry
Herbert Henry Rawlins	Herbert Mundin
Masters	E.E. Clive
Bomba	Darby Jones
Riverboat captain	Monte Montague

Eric and Rita Parker arrive in Africa in search of their cousin Jane, who has made a life in the jungle with her mate, Tarzan. They must find Jane to tell her of a large inheritance that she must return to her homeland to claim.

The naïve Londoners hire an unscrupulous safari guide, Captain Fry, to lead them to the Mutia escarpment, Tarzan's home grounds. Fry schemes to capture Tarzan and bring him back to civilization to exhibit like some sort of "wild man from Borneo." Fry brings along a metal cage to hold his prize trophy. A funny little man named Rawlins is Fry's "man Friday"—he jumps when Fry commands.

The safari is attacked by the savage Gibonis, who scurry back to their village when they hear Tarzan's war cry. As they approach the Mutia, the safari natives are afraid of the ju-ju (the taboo region guarded by the escarpment) and refuse to go any farther. "All right, let them stay if they want. See how they like the Gibonis," barks Fry. The reluctant bearers quickly fall into line as the safari departs.

Eventually, Eric and Rita are reunited with their cousin Jane, who is

Tarzan and Jane, treed by lions (*Tarzan Escapes*, 1936).

Tarzan calls for his mighty elephants! (*Tarzan Escapes*, 1936)

overjoyed to see old friends from home. Jane is sympathetic to their cause, but doesn't want to leave Tarzan for any reason (especially money). However, when Jane finds out that Eric and Rita have invested all their money in the safari to locate her, she reluctantly agrees to go temporarily to London with them.

The suggestion to bring Tarzan back to London is rejected by Jane: "Out here Tarzan is a king. How do I know what he'd be back there?" Tarzan is dejected when he discovers Jane is going to leave him, even for a short while. The two lovers spend a final afternoon together in their secluded "Garden of Eden."

When the safari breaks camp, Fry doubles back to capture Tarzan. Rawlins, whom the ape-man has befriended, attempts to warn Tarzan, but the brave little man receives a bullet in the back from Fry as his reward. The treacherous Fry tricks Tarzan into entering his cage, lying to him that Jane has left him forever.

Jane and the safari are surrounded by the fierce Hymandi tribe, who also seize the caged ape-man. Desperate to help Jane, Tarzan escapes with the help of his elephant friends, who rip open the bars of his cage. Tarzan rescues Jane, and the remaining safari narrowly escapes, traversing a swamplike cave filled with strange man-eating creatures. Barely making their way through the swamp safely, Tarzan orders the murderer Fry back the way they came, where he slips into the ooze and dies a horrible death.

Eric and Rita confess to Jane that they lied and that only her signature is necessary to gain the inheritance. "We wanted to take you back to where we thought you belonged—civilization, I think they call it," said Rita. "But I couldn't ever forget the look in Tarzan's eyes when he thought he was going to lose you." Jane forgives them because she realizes their intentions were honest and sends them on their way with her blessings. Tarzan rejoices to find that his mate Jane is staying with him in their jungle home.

•

After the immense critical and box-office success of the first two MGM Tarzan pictures and the international adulation of stars Johnny Weissmuller and Maureen O'Sullivan, it was obvious that this would be a long-running series of films for many years to come. Next in line would be *Tarzan Escapes,* a troubled production that took 14 months to complete and underwent almost a complete metamorphosis before it was finally released in November 1936. Actually two films were made; the initial version was shelved, rewritten, and rephotographed with a new director, producer, scriptwriter, a drastically altered story line, a revised cast, and a substantially altered crew.

Credited with directing the finished product was Richard Thorpe, the efficient and prolific director who worked exclusively for MGM from 1935 through 1965. Thorpe had already directed over 100 films for several studios before he joined MGM in 1935. Screenwriting credit went to Cyril Hume, who wrote the dialogue for *Trader Horn* and the adaptation for *Tarzan, the Ape Man;* and the associate producer for the film was Sam Zimbalist, under Bernard Hyman.

The original production staff had included James McKay as director (McKay had worked as a second unit director on *Tarzan and His Mate,* directing animal sequences); Philip Goldstone as producer; and Karl Brown authoring

a treatment tentatively titled *Tarzan Returns.* Contributing to the screenplay were Louis Mosher and John Farrow, as well as Wyndham Gittens and Otis Garrett.

The story line of the ill-fated *Tarzan Returns* had Rita and Eric Parker (Benita Hume and William Henry) seeking their cousin Jane in Africa, their safari guided by the shady Captain Fry (John Buckler). Rita was portrayed as a shallow vamp, who not only hopes to find Jane dead so she can inherit her fortune but makes seductive overtures to Tarzan. Fry's callous intentions are to cage Tarzan and exhibit him like a sideshow freak; both Rita and Fry die justified deaths in the jungle, while Eric returns to England. Also filmed was a terrifying scene with vampire bats and pygmies in the smoky bogs; working titles at various times included *Tarzan and the Vampires* and *Capture of Tarzan.*

Filming got underway in July 1935 and concluded in October after 95 days. After the screening, the MGM decision makers decreed that the picture in its present form was unacceptable for various reasons, including the lack of a central plot menace. By early 1936, the hard facts had been laid out: The picture must be rewritten, restructured, and rephotographed.

Major changes included Richard Thorpe stepping into the director's shoes, with Sam Zimbalist in charge as associate producer. The new script was written by Cyril Hume (with input from MGM story editor Edwin Knopf), W. Donn Hayes bumped Basil Wrangell as film editor, and Elmer Sheeley stepped up from associate to art director. Darby Jones replaced Everett Brown as Bomba, and the character of Herbert Henry Rawlins was added, portrayed comically by Herbert Mundin.

The character of Rawlins was an interesting one, especially from the viewpoint that he was the first white man whom Tarzan truly liked and called "friend." Rawlins provided comic relief for the most part. At first he was terrified of the ape-man when Tarzan dropped from the trees and abducted Rita, but he developed a strong affinity for Tarzan after he got to know him. "Mr. Tarzan is the finest gentleman I've ever known," says Rawlins to Jane. Later on, Rawlins suspects that Captain Fry (John Buckler) is planning to lure Tarzan into his cage and doubles back to warn his friend. Fry catches up with Rawlins in the jungle, and shoots the little man in the back in cold blood.

After their escape through the cave filled with smoke and slimy creatures, Tarzan's eyes fall on Fry and his henchman, Bomba. The native falls to his knees, and Tarzan mercifully waves him to go with the others; but he orders Fry back into the bog, knowing he will die. In the jungle Tarzan is the judge and jury, and in this case the sentence was death for murdering Rawlins. Fry reenters the cave; moments later, he trips into the ooze and is sucked down as man-eating reptiles eagerly attack their prey. Fry's hat floating on the scummy water is his only grave marker.

Tarzan Escapes went back into production in July 1936 and concluded in September; the final cost was just over $1 million. Several scenes photographed for earlier films were reused, including the memorable crocodile fight and Jane's leap from the treetops into Tarzan's arms, both reprised from *Tarzan and His Mate;* Tarzan wrestling and killing a wildebeest for dinner from *Tarzan, the Ape Man;* a charging lion killed by rifle shot from *Trader Horn;* and salvaged footage from the earlier aborted version. The vampire bat scene (reportedly an exciting one) was unfortunately lost on the cutting room floor; the scene may have been too horrifying for the juvenile audiences who were expected to view the film.

Tarzan Escapes featured life-style changes for Tarzan and Jane, including an elaborate six-room treehouse constructed by Tarzan that had running water, overhead fans (powered by Cheeta), and an elevator operated by an elephant. The treehouse was built on location in the Santa Monica Mountains, in an area known as Brent's Mountain Crags (Crater Camp). A bit of tongue-in-cheek humor was calling the fierce interior tribe who capture Tarzan and the safari, "Hymandis," named for producer Bernard Hyman.

In response to the restraints of the Production Code of 1934, Jane's revealing outfit from *Tarzan and His Mate* was replaced with a ragged jungle shift, covering her midriff and mid-thigh in length. An underwater swimming "ballet," similar to the one used in the previous film, featured Jane in her redesigned dress along with Tarzan (taking no chances with the censors this time, MGM kept Jane's clothes on). After their playful swim, Jane looks up to see a more serious look on Tarzan's face: Jane's expression melts into submissive sensuality, and she drops the orchid in her hand into the slow river current. The scene fades at this point, but the obvious implication is that Tarzan and his mate consummate their love as a final good-bye.

Given the limited vocabulary that Tarzan was allowed to use in the MGM Tarzan films, Johnny Weissmuller did an excellent job of portraying remorse and desolation at the thought of Jane leaving him to return to England. Again the love scenes of Weissmuller and O'Sullivan were tender and touching, giving the story a clearly memorable romantic theme, as well as being a thrilling jungle escapade.

Replacing "Voodoo Dance" as the opening theme was "Cannibal Carnival," by Sol Levy, which had been used previously in *Trader Horn* over the opening credits. Though there was no musical sound track, as such, there were the realistic sounds of the jungle, the wild animals roaring and grunting, the tropical birds and their peculiar cries, and the authentic jungle drums and native chants (recorded during the 1929 foray into the African wilds on the *Trader Horn* filming expedition). This symphony of jungle instruments was indeed a musical sound track all its own.

Although not a classic in the sense of the first two films of the series, *Tarzan Escapes* succeeded as a first-rate adventure that thrilled audiences worldwide once again. By the time the fourth film in the series—*Tarzan Finds a Son!*—was released in 1939, the Tarzan family would include a progeny.

Tarzan Finds a Son!

Release date: June 1939; Metro-Goldwyn-Mayer; running time: 95 minutes. *Directed by* Richard Thorpe; *produced by* Sam Zimbalist; *screenplay by* Cyril Hume, *based on the characters created by* Edgar Rice Burroughs; *recording director,* Douglas Shearer; *art director,* Cedric Gibbons; *associate,* Urie McCleary; *photographed by* Leonard Smith; *film editors,* Frank Sullivan and Gene Ruggiero; *special effects,* A. Arnold Gillespie, Warren Newcombe, and Max Fabian; *animal trainer,* George Emerson; *assistant director,* Dolph Zimmer; *musical director,* David Snell; *music by* Sol Levy and Dr. William Axt.

Tarzan	Johnny Weissmuller
Jane	Maureen O'Sullivan
Boy	Johnny Sheffield
Sir Thomas Lancing	Henry Stephenson
Austin Lancing	Ian Hunter
Mrs. Austin Lancing	Frieda Inescort
Mr. Sande	Henry Wilcoxon
Mrs. Richard Lancing	Laraine Day
Richard Lancing	Morton Lowry
Pilot	Gavin Muir
Mooloo	Uriah Banks

Richard Lancing, nephew of Lord Greystoke, is en route to Cape Town, along with his wife and infant son. Suddenly losing power, their small plane crashes on the Mutia escarpment, near the jungle home of Tarzan and Jane. All the passengers except the baby, who is next in line to inherit the fortunes of the earl of Greystoke, are killed.

Tarzan finds the baby in the jungle and brings him to Jane, whose maternal instincts immediately take over. The jungle couple adopt the orphaned child and name him Boy. Tarzan is at first a reluctant father, but he soon loves Boy as his own. As Jane endearingly puts it, "the King has a son!"

Several years later, a safari makes its way to the escarpment in search of the lost plane and passengers. The search party includes Sir Thomas Lancing; Mr. and Mrs. Austin Lancing; and

Weissmuller, O'Sullivan and Johnny Sheffield (*Tarzan Finds a Son!*, 1939).

their guide, Mr. Sande. Sir Thomas truly hopes to find his nephew and family alive, while the unprincipled Lancings hope to find them dead, so they can collect the late Lord Greystoke's fortune. Eventually, the searchers come face to face with the ape-man and his mate in the jungle.

Jane and Tarzan both hide the fact that Boy is indeed the missing child from the plane, but Sir Thomas is able to see through their deception. Naturally, Jane is dead-set against letting her beloved son go to England. However, the shady Mrs. Lancing convinces her that it's the best thing for the boy to grow up in London, rather than the dangerous African jungles. (With Boy in London, the greedy Lancings would control his inheritance.)

Knowing her mate won't go along with the plan to take Boy away, Jane traps Tarzan in a deep grotto by cutting his vine, so he can't follow when they leave. "Tarzan, I know you'll never forgive me—but I'll be back for you. And if you want to send me away, I'll go," says Jane in a soliloquy meant for Tarzan. Indeed, the ape-man takes Jane's deception very hard, and he is totally despondent.

As the safari departs, Sir Thomas reveals to Jane the Lancings' plan to steal the boy's fortune. Bravely trying to slip back to set Tarzan free, Sir Thomas is shot in the back by the corrupt Austin Lancing. The ill-fated safari is soon captured by the savage Zambeli tribe, who have a fate worse than death planned for the party. Sir Thomas's death is avenged with the murder of Austin Lancing.

Boy manages to slip out through a break in the village barricade; Jane is wounded by a spear as she creates a

Weissmuller and Johnny Sheffield ... swimming lessons (*Tarzan Finds a Son!*, 1939).

diversion for her brave little son. "Did you see him? Clean away, just like Tarzan," whispers Jane proudly. The jungle lad narrowly averts the ferocious wild creatures in his path home and frees Tarzan from his cavernous trap. Tarzan and his elephant friends ride to Jane's rescue. The ape-man battles a dozen Zambelis by himself, and the elephants destroy the village.

Tarzan is angry with Jane for deceiving him but when he sees his mate is wounded, he is panicky. "Jane not die! Jane not die! Jane all right?" begs Tarzan. "Yes darling, everything's all right," says Jane. The family of Tarzan, Jane, and Boy are reunited and return to their home on the back of Timba, the elephant.

•

The Metro-Goldwyn-Mayer production of *Tarzan Finds a Son!* introduced a major addition to the winning team of Johnny Weissmuller and Maureen O'Sullivan as Tarzan and Jane: a son, portrayed by seven-year-old Johnny Sheffield. The hunt for the son of Tarzan began with an MGM ad in the *Hollywood Reporter,* posing the question, "Do you have a *Tarzan, Jr.* in your backyard?" In excess of 300 young boys were screened for the enviable role; the search was for a lad who not only looked the part of a boy raised in the jungle, but who had the physical stamina to handle the difficult stunts involved.

Johnny Sheffield was raised in an acting family (his father was English-born actor Reginald Sheffield) and had just finished working in the Broadway play *On Borrowed Time,* which starred

Dudley Digges (Sheffield portrayed the grandson). Weighing only four pounds at birth, Sheffield had been a frail and underweight child. But a program of vigorous exercise and healthy food administered by his father had the future son of Tarzan the picture of perfect health by age five. After his parents responded to the ad, Sheffield was interviewed by the MGM brass and by Johnny Weissmuller.

Weissmuller personally gave the final okay to the selection of Sheffield as Boy and gave his movie son swimming lessons before and during the production of their first film. Big John developed a strong affection for Little John (as he would be called), and they were close during the decade in which they filmed their eight Tarzan pictures together. The fine cast also included Ian Hunter as the immoral Austin Lancing; Henry Wilcoxon as the shady safari guide; Laraine Day in a small role as Boy's natural mother; and Henry Stephenson as Sir Thomas Lancing. The veteran actor Stephenson lent a modicum of class to every picture he appeared in, and as the most honest person in *Tarzan Finds a Son!* he was superb.

With the important selection of Sheffield as Boy completed, MGM began spinning the wheels to turn Cyril Hume's imaginative Tarzan script into the newest jungle adventure. A 1938 agreement with Edgar Rice Burroughs had given MGM the rights to produce three new Tarzan pictures, with options for two additional films. (Burroughs was extremely discouraged by the two pictures, *The New Adventures of Tarzan* and *The Green Goddess,* that his company had produced. From this time on, agreements with MGM and close friend Sol Lesser to produce all future Tarzans would end his personal involvement with the production of Tarzan pictures.)

This would be Cyril Hume's third and final MGM Tarzan script, and the author had to find a way around the Hays Code (censorship) to give Tarzan and Jane a son. They had never been formally married, so the character of Jane would not be allowed to have a baby. The solution to this dilemma was simply to have Tarzan find a baby in the jungle (the sole survivor of a small plane crash) and to have the child adopted by Tarzan and Jane.

There is mention early in the film that the child is the grandnephew of a certain Lord Greystoke. This is the only reference in the MGM Tarzan pictures to the famous heritage of Edgar Rice Burroughs' fictional Tarzan. There is no mention in the MGM pictures either of where Tarzan came from (other than that he was raised by apes) or of the House of Greystoke in his lineage.

Reliable Richard Thorpe had settled into the position of director for the balance of the MGM Tarzan films, and many of the same crew who had worked so effectively in the three previous films were on hand, including Leonard Smith handling the photography; Cedric Gibbons in charge of the art department; perennial recording director Douglas Shearer; and the special effects men who had worked their magic on the previous jungle films—A. Arnold (Buddy) Gillespie, Warren Newcombe, and Max Fabian (who was in charge of miniatures: for this picture, the small plane and subsequent crash). Bumped up to top producer was Sam Zimbalist. Music director David Snell rerecorded "Cannibal Carnival" and "My Tender One" and used them once again over the opening credits and final scene.

Filming began on January 9, 1939, with a potentially traumatic experience to all movie fans written into the script: Maureen O'Sullivan's character of Jane was to die at the end of the film, the victim of a Zambeli spear. O'Sullivan was pregnant during the production of

Tarzan Finds a Son! and she had asked to be written out of the series so she could concentrate on raising a family with husband John Farrow (they would eventually have seven children). However, an alternate ending was also filmed about a month after the close of production in which Jane did indeed survive her spear wound. The MGM brass had fortunately realized after previewing the picture that audience reaction would have been so negative to the death of Jane that it might have doomed the series. (In the latter stages of her pregnancy, Maureen was photographed from the waist up or partially hidden behind tables and other props, to camouflage her condition.)

Some of the finest underwater swimming scenes of any Tarzan picture were photographed for *Tarzan Finds a Son!* at Silver Springs, Florida, near the end of the shooting schedule. The crystal-clear water of Silver Springs was the perfect playground for Big John and Little John, who frolicked and splashed underwater for approximately four minutes—at first swimming with a baby elephant named Baby Bea, then playing below-surface hide-and-seek, and then "hitching" a ride behind a huge sea turtle who pulled the ape-man and son along as if he barely knew they were there.

The playful cavorting, swimming, and diving were so genuine that it was obvious there was a real affection between the screen father and son, and the extended underwater sequence was absorbing and enchanting. The final three minutes of the seven-minute scene had Boy lounging on a giant lily pad, then floating downstream in the swift current toward the waterfalls; a thrilling moment ensued when Weissmuller showed his best Olympic champion swimming form in speeding to rescue Boy. The MGM river back in Hollywood was the scenario for Boy's near-tragic mishap,

with a "dump tank" on Lot 1 creating the waterfall effect.

As in previous Tarzan films, a fascinating collection of wild animal footage (mostly reclaimed from *Trader Horn*) was skillfully edited in, including great flocks of birds; crocodiles hungrily gulping their dinners; roaring lions; a herd of elephants; and hippos yawning, exposing cavernous mouths. There were also a vicious battle royal between a leopard and several baboons and a wild free-for-all involving a black panther, a spotted leopard, and a pack of hyenas.

Stock shots included the Giboni attack at the base of the Mutia escarpment, as well as Tarzan riding and killing the rhinoceros (borrowed from *Tarzan and His Mate*—this time Boy was the near-victim). The jungle king swinging from vine to vine (actually stuntman-aerialist Alfredo Codona) had its origin in *Tarzan, the Ape Man.*

Audiences were also treated to a new process that produced an effective aqua hue to the film print, derived from a sepia tone and a platinum tint—not exactly color, but it did give a more lifelike quality to the film texture. Thanks to the extensive use of the stock footage, the cost of producing *Tarzan Finds a Son!* was $880,000.

Johnny Weissmuller again showed his great physical strength, twice lifting Zambeli warriors over his head like they were lightweight toys, rather than 160-pound men. (The Zambeli name was another tongue-in-cheek salute to a crew member, this time producer Sam Zimbalist.) With the limited vocabulary that his Tarzan character was allowed to use, Weissmuller was confined as an actor and had little latitude for artistic expression; but he was always able to show strong emotion that welled up from the soul, and as Tarzan, he continued to be a natural.

Johnny Sheffield as Boy was an athletic, miniature version of Tarzan. The lad did most of his own stunt work and portrayed his role to the highest expectations. The Tarzan family tradition was handed down in many ways, including the Tarzan yell. Boy developed his own version of the mighty cry that was used whenever he was in trouble—which was often! The doubling and stunt work for Sheffield was performed by a 32-year-old midget named Harry Monty, known professionally as the "Midget Strong Man with the most muscular perfect physique of any small person in the world."

Maureen O'Sullivan portrayed her role of Jane with the same depth of character and sensitivity she had used so well before, and the scenes in which she struggles with her own conscience and must decide what's best for her son—and what's best for Tarzan—are heart-rending. O'Sullivan really was a marvelous actress, and made Jane, the mate of Tarzan, a woman who was believable and courageous, as well as simply beautiful. Her near-fatal confrontation with a Zambeli spear produced the touching, emotion-evoking reunion of Tarzan and Jane near the picture's conclusion. The ape-man's tears weren't crocodile tears, and there wasn't a dry eye in the house when Tarzan gathered his love in his arms with grateful joy and Jane opened her eyes, saying, "Darling, everything's all right."

Various working titles had been bandied about by the MGM executives during production, including *Tarzan in Exile* and *Son of Tarzan*, but the final title was perhaps the most appropriate: *Tarzan Finds a Son!* When the film was released in June 1939, the moviegoing public had waited almost three years for the genuine article of a Weissmuller-O'Sullivan Tarzan picture. Movie fans certainly weren't disappointed, since the new adventure was one of the best of the long-running series. With the world on the verge of a world war, it would be more than two years until the next foray into Tarzan's jungle world: *Tarzan's Secret Treasure*.

Tarzan's Secret Treasure

Release date: December 1941; Metro-Goldwyn-Mayer; running time: 81 minutes. *Directed by* Richard Thorpe; *produced by* B.P. Fineman; *screenplay by* Myles Connolly and Paul Gangelin, *based on the characters created by* Edgar Rice Burroughs; *director of photography,* Clyde de Vinna; *recording director,* Douglas Shearer; *art director,* Cedric Gibbons; *associate,* Howard Campbell; *set decorations,* Edwin B. Willis; *film editor,* Gene Ruggiero; *special effects,* Warren Newcombe; *assistant director,* Gilbert Kurland; *musical score by* David Snell; *music by* Sol Levy and Dr. William Axt.

Tarzan	Johnny Weissmuller
Jane	Maureen O'Sullivan
Boy	Johnny Sheffield
Professor Elliot	Reginald Owen
O'Doul	Barry Fitzgerald
Medford	Tom Conway
Vandermeer	Philip Dorn
Tumbo	Cordell Hickman

Cheetah's leap for life into Tarzan's arms (*Tarzan's Secret Treasure*, 1941).

Joconi chief .... Everett Brown
Headman .... Martin Wilkins

The Mutia escarpment is a sheer cliff that, legend says, "rises from the plains to support the stars." Beyond the escarpment are the jungles that Tarzan, Jane, and Boy call home.

When Boy finds pure gold nuggets at the bottom of their swimming pool, Tarzan tells a story of a vast vein of gold up the river. Boy is further intrigued by Jane's tales of civilization and the power of gold in civilized lands. "Now darling, just you forget about civilization. Our world here is far more lovely and exciting than the outside world, I promise you," warns Jane. But Boy's curiosity is aroused.

One night, Boy leaves a note for his parents: "Gone to see civilization, be back tomorrow." During his travels, Boy saves a young native boy, Tumbo, from a charging rhino, and they soon become friends. Tumbo's village is infested with the plague, and the boy's mother dies of the fever. The medicine man blames the "ju-ju" on Boy and plans to burn him at the stake. In the nick of time, Boy is saved by men on a safari, and Tarzan arrives on their heels to save them from the attacking natives.

Tarzan offers to lead the men to the lost city they seek as a reward for saving Boy and takes along Tumbo, the or-phaned native boy. The ape-man makes friends with Professor Elliot and O'Doul, an Irishman with a strong pen-chant for Irish whiskey. Meanwhile, Boy is naïvely impressed by Medford and Vandermeer and lets a secret slip. "Tar-zan knows where there's a whole moun-tain of gold," he says, as a greedy fire lights in the eyes of the two men.

The white men have gold fever, but O'Doul and Boy catch the deadly plague. Fortunately, Tarzan's jungle medicine is strong, and they both re-cover. Medford and Vandermeer plot against the professor and prevent him from taking Tarzan's medicine and thus his death is murder.

The mutineers kidnap Jane and Boy and force Tarzan into a trade—the gold for his family. Tarzan keeps his word and brings Medford to the mountain of gold, but the black-hearted Medford shoots the ape-man's vine, and Tarzan plummets to the bottom of a ravine. Only Tumbo has seen Tarzan fall to the earth, unconscious.

When the escaping gold thieves foolishly try a shortcut through Joconi country, savage natives capture and tor-ture the trespassers. O'Doul pretends to be killed, and together with Tumbo they brave the dangerous jungles to find Tar-zan and warn him of Jane's imminent danger.

The Joconis are transporting their prisoners upriver to their village, where they will be killed. Tarzan, with help from his elephants, overturns the canoes and saves Jane and Boy from their cap-tors. Medford and Vandermeer are not so lucky, meeting a grisly demise in the hungry jaws of the river's crocodiles.

The Tarzan clan send their new friend O'Doul on his way home on the back of Timba, the elephant, with a basket of gold as his reward for his faithfulness. "If there were more folk like you in the world, it would be a sweet and smiling place," says O'Doul as he waves good-bye to his new friends, Tarzan, Jane, and Boy.

•

When *Tarzan's Secret Treasure* was released to moviegoing audiences in De-cember 1941, the United States was at war with Japan and Johnny Weissmuller had been portraying Tarzan for almost 10 years. At age 36, Weissmuller had lost the lean swimmer's physique of his youth, but he was still powerfully built and cut a commanding figure as Tarzan. O'Sullivan, at age 30, probably was at her peak in all the feminine ways: Mau-reen as Jane was still the ultimate match for the King of the Jungle.

Directing once again was Richard Thorpe, who had the reputation as a "one take" director; certainly efficiency was one of his virtues, but he was also able to get the most out of the material he was given to work with. Shooting began on June 14, 1941, and Thorpe had no problem completing the picture on schedule, wrapping up production on August 18. Behind the cameras was

Weissmuller, O'Sullivan, Sheffield and Cordell Hickman (*Tarzan's Secret Treasure*, 1941).

Clyde de Vinna, who had photographed the first two classic Tarzan pictures (*Tarzan, the Ape Man* and *Tarzan and His Mate*) a decade earlier, and the venerable Cedric Gibbons was again in charge of the art department.

After Jane had been "killed" and her death was reprieved in *Tarzan Finds a Son!*, MGM screenwriter Cyril Hume again wanted to kill off the character of Jane, making the ape-man a bachelor open to new romantic situations. Hume's early outlines included a beautiful "glamour girl" hunting big game in Africa, where she encounters the handsome (and now available) Tarzan, and the natural mating instincts take over.

This plot line was rejected by the MGM brass, who refused to write Maureen O'Sullivan out of the Tarzan pictures. At this point Hume asked to

be relieved, and responsibility for the script was turned over to Myles Connolly and Paul Gangelin, whose story ideas were not entirely new to the Tarzan pictures. Film number five in the MGM Tarzan series was, in fact, strictly formula: Greedy white men invade Tarzan's jungle (this time gold is the booty, the "secret treasure" of the title), and there's plenty of excitement and adventure as the ape-man drives the interlopers from his jungle. One pint-sized addition to the standard plot formula was the small native boy, Tumbo (portrayed effectively by Cordell Hickman), who becomes friends with Boy; the two take turns saving each other, and the innocence of their friendship is touching.

The decent cast also included veteran British character actor Reginald Owen as Professor Elliot; Tom Conway as the number one villain, Medford (brother of actor George Sanders, Conway was famed as the Falcon during the 1940s); and Barry Fitzgerald, who provided comic relief as the alcoholic Irishman who develops a strong affection for and loyalty to Tarzan. Fitzgerald was his usual screen self (a warmhearted bumbler), who starred in many classic films during his career, including his Academy Award–winning role in *Going My Way* (1944).

In one of the warmest scenes in any Tarzan picture, the jungle couple discuss their son Boy and how easily he is impressed by the outsiders from civilization—and what fools Tarzan feels these people are:

> "None of them have what we have," says Jane warmly.
> "Tarzan have Jane," replies the ape-man with conviction.
> "Has it seemed a long time, Tarzan?" asks Jane romantically.
> "Sun make one safari for Jane and Tarzan," answers Tarzan poetically.
> "Oh Tarzan, a poet couldn't have said that more beautifully," coos Jane.

This was a lovely romantic scene that was the hallmark of the MGM Tarzan movies: a true romantic relationship between Tarzan and Jane that often wasn't present in later Tarzan pictures (these scenes were always played very well by Weissmuller and O'Sullivan, their best opportunities for any real acting in the pictures). After a swim together, there's more romantic love talk as Tarzan and Jane lie together on the riverbank and then kiss sensually.

The Tarzan family treehouse received further "modernizations," including a "refrigerator" and a hot spring used to boil eggs. Their diet included fresh African caviar (which was quite a change from the days when the ape-man was an uncivilized bachelor and fresh raw meat was his dietary staple!). And Cheeta, the chimp, began playing a

larger role in each story and getting into more and more mischief; this time the chimp takes a liking to O'Doul's Irish whiskey and gets drunk (as only an ape can!).

As was now standard, scenes filmed for earlier Tarzan pictures were reprieved once again, the most notable being the crocodile fight (Tarzan saves Boy this time), the rampaging rhinoceros (Boy saves Tumbo) from *Tarzan and His Mate*, and the wild animal footage shot years before on the *Trader Horn* expedition to Africa. New and effective action scenes that were shot included Tarzan crossing a cavernous gorge on a vine and the dandy final battle royal in the river, with scores of hungry crocodiles and Tarzan's always faithful elephants coming to the rescue. A young man named Gouley Green did some doubling for Johnny Sheffield.

Underwater filming in Florida had worked well for *Tarzan Finds a Son!* and an excursion to Wakulla Springs produced a new scene (although similar and mixed with footage from the previous film). Tarzan, Jane, and Boy frolic and cavort underwater with Baby Bea, the elephant, and the giant sea turtle. Weissmuller even catches a large fish with his bare hands for the jungle family's dinner. Photography for the Florida sequences was supervised by Lloyd Knechtel, whose cameramen worked from a specially designed camera bell attached to a barge. The bell was actually a large, weighted metal drum set several feet below the surface, with an optical glass window for the camera port. Also photographed in Florida were the underwater portions of Tarzan's rescue of Boy and Jane in the film's grand finale.

The Tarzan series at MGM was beginning to wear thin after a full decade, and the formula plots, the stock footage used over and over again, and MGM's waning interest in Tarzan pictures signaled the coming end. The pictures were also getting shorter, relegating them to the lower half of twin bills at the theaters; *Tarzan's Secret Treasure* was only 81 minutes, whereas the first four MGM Tarzan films had averaged over 95 minutes each. Production costs for this jungle feature were just under $1 million. The familiar opening and closing themes of "Cannibal Carnival" and "My Tender One" (rerecorded by music director David Snell) were used once again per custom.

Johnny would still have several good years to come as Tarzan, but the ape-man's peak years were now behind him. In fact, to give the series a jolt of life, the scenario for the next (and last) MGM Weissmuller Tarzan picture would be moved to New York City, a drastic change that left all those overworked jungle scenes far behind. The crocodile fight, Tarzan riding the rhinoceros, the vines swinging, and underwater swimming were all classic scenes in their day; but audiences were not so naïve that MGM could continue using them forever. Next up for Johnny Weissmuller and Maureen O'Sullivan (her final role as Jane) was a foray into the strange and unfriendly world of civilization in *Tarzan's New York Adventure.*

Tarzan's New York Adventure

Release date: August 1942; Metro-Goldwyn-Mayer; running time: 71 minutes. *Directed by* Richard Thorpe; *produced by* Frederick Stephani; *screenplay by* William R. Lipman and Myles Connolly, *story by* Myles Connolly, *based on the characters created by* Edgar Rice Burroughs; *director of photography,* Sidney Wagner; *recording director,* Douglas Shearer; *art director,* Cedric Gibbons; *associate,* Howard Campbell; *set decorations,* Edwin B. Willis; *gowns by* Howard Shoup; *film editor,* Gene Ruggiero; *special effects,* Arnold Gillespie and Warren Newcombe; *opening theme,* "Cannibal Carnival," *by* Sol Levy; *musical score by* David Snell.

Tarzan	Johnny Weissmuller
Jane	Maureen O'Sullivan
Boy	John Sheffield
Connie Beach	Virginia Grey
Buck Rand	Charles Bickford
Jimmy Shields	Paul Kelly
Manchester Mountford	Chill Wills
Colonel Ralph Sargent	Cy Kendall
Judge Abbotson	Russell Hicks
Blake Norton	Howard Hickman
Gould Beaton	Charles Lane
Roustabout	Elmo Lincoln

Also featuring Miles Mander, Milton Kibbee, Mantan Moreland, Anne Jeffreys, Hobart Cavanaugh, Matthew Boulton, Willie Fung, William Forrest, William Tannen, Dick Wessel, Joe Offerman, Jr., Eddie Kane, Harry Tenbrook, Harry Semels, George Magrill,

The Tarzan family take a cab ride (*Tarzan's New York Adventure*, 1942).

Wade Boteler, Eddy Chandler, Frank S. Hagney, Frank O'Connor, Emmett Vogan, Ken Christy, Jack Perrin, Harry Strang, John Dilson.

Tarzan sees a small plane in the skies above his jungle and knows that white men will bring trouble with their arrival. The airborne safari is led by Buck Rand, who has come to Africa to trap lions for the circus. Because he likes the pilot Jimmy Shields, Tarzan gives them one day to complete their mission and leave the escarpment.

Boy is intrigued by the airplane and visits the site where the trappers are readying to depart. Boy has his trio of young elephants do tricks for the men, and Rand contemplates kidnapping the jungle lad for the circus. Jimmy Shields nixes the idea and orders Boy to go home.

The warlike Joconi tribe attacks the hunters, and Tarzan and Jane come to rescue Boy, but they plummet through the trees into tall grasses when their vine is cut, and the grasses are set on fire. The men escape by plane, taking Boy along, wrongly assuming that the jungle man and his mate have been killed. Cheeta saves Tarzan and Jane from the burning grasses and then warns them that Boy has been taken away in the "iron bird."

Tarzan and Jane travel cross-country to civilization, and using gold nuggets for money, charter a plane to New York where Boy has been taken. Jane convinces her husband that he must follow her guidance while in civilization. "I'll be the only guide you have. Will you follow me? Will you do as I say? I'll try not to fail you," says Jane.

Tarzan in the shower (*Tarzan's New York Adventure*, 1942).

The ape-man responds from the heart, "Jane lead way. Tarzan follow always!" Jane tells Tarzan he must also wear clothes, and he is fitted with a custom-made suit.

Upon arriving in New York, Tarzan and Jane track Boy to a circus run by Rand and Colonel Sargent, who has legal custody of the jungle lad. The two men are conspiring to sell Boy to another circus for $100,000. When Tarzan arrives at the circus (ready for action), he is convinced by Jimmy Shields to go to court to regain Boy's custody.

Their day in court fails to get Boy returned to Tarzan and Jane, so the ape-man takes the law into his own hands. Tarzan evades the police by diving 200 feet from the Brooklyn Bridge into New York harbor, while Jane and Shields travel by car to the circus.

When Tarzan arrives, Rand and Sargent are trying to retreat with Boy as their hostage. Tarzan, overpowered and caged by Rand's men, calls the circus elephants to his aid, and the elephants bend the bars and free him. Leaping into the speeding car, Tarzan saves Boy as Rand and Sargent are killed in a spectacular car crash.

Back in court, the judge is compassionate and returns Boy to Tarzan and Jane. "Law good—judge good," says Tarzan and calls the judge his friend. Tarzan and his family travel back to their home in the African wilds, away from the civilized "jungle."

•

In the original Tarzan story by Edgar Rice Burroughs, *Tarzan of the Apes* (1912), the ape-man follows the woman he loves, Jane, back to America to capture her heart. But it took a full decade to get Johnny Weissmuller out of the jungle and into a suit, in *Tarzan's New York Adventure*. Weissmuller cut a striking figure in a 1940s double-breasted suit, his broad shoulders highlighted by the well-tailored cut of the garment. Maureen O'Sullivan also looked sharp in the latest female fashions of the civilized world.

This plot line was decidedly different from the previous MGM Tarzan pictures, and for the most part, a refreshing change of pace. It still contained plenty of action and adventure, and the first half of the story takes place in Tarzan's Africa, thus not stretching credibility too far. The imaginative story was the brainchild of Myles Connolly (who had co-written the script for *Tarzan's Secret Treasure*), and the script was co-authored by William Lipman and Connolly. The final opportunity to direct a Tarzan film went to Richard Thorpe (his fourth consecutive ape-man picture), who ground out pictures at MGM at a frenetic pace; this time only six weeks were required from the start to the end of production. *Tarzan's New York Adventure* was filmed from December 1941 to February 1942, under the working title *Tarzan Against the World*.

Featured players included Charles Bickford as the lion trapper without a conscience; Paul Kelly as the pilot who helps Tarzan find his son; Virginia Grey as the torch singer and girlfriend of Jimmy Shields (Kelly); and Chill Wills as the good guy who befriends Boy and gets murdered for his efforts (this plot device, of course, allowed for the villains Buck Rand and Colonel Sargent to die at the end of the picture, thus receiving just retribution for their vile deeds). One other cast member worth noting was the original silent Tarzan, Elmo Lincoln (*Tarzan of the Apes*, 1918), in a bit part as a roustabout (circus laborer). Lincoln had bounced around Hollywood for years finding small roles and working as

an extra—certainly a comedown from his days as the King of the Jungle.

MGM borrowed perhaps the most classic moment from any Tarzan picture, the "me Tarzan, you Jane" scene from *Tarzan, the Ape Man* (1932) and reworked it slightly for *Tarzan's New York Adventure*. This time, on the veranda of their treehouse, Tarzan and Jane are discussing the dangers of the jungle that Boy must face every day:

> "I know there's never any need to worry as long as you're with me," says Jane. "At first I used to have many little fears—for myself—for Boy. One by one you chased them all away. Wouldn't it be strange if someday I became as brave as you are?" Tarzan responds, "Jane no need to be brave—Jane beautiful." Jane answers to her husband, "You're my goodness, darling—my strength." Now comes the reenactment of the classic scene, as Tarzan taps Jane's bosom and then his own, and says, "Jane—Tarzan. Tarzan—Jane."

Of course, the ape-man is steamed up by now and has romance in mind. He kisses Jane passionately and then scoops her up and carries her away, as the scene fades and the audience is left to imagine the rest of the scene.

As was standard operating procedure, scenes photographed for earlier Tarzan films were reused in *Tarzan's New York Adventure*, including the killing of the lion and miscellaneous wild animal footage from the *Trader Horn* expedition of 1929; the vine swinging from *Tarzan and His Mate*, used for the last time; and the underwater swimming segments with Tarzan, Jane, and Boy left over from *Tarzan's Secret Treasure*, used at both the opening and close of the picture.

New animal material that was filmed included three highly trained young elephants that Boy commands, with Johnny Sheffield actually putting the talented beasts through a series of circus tricks and balancing stunts. Johnny Weissmuller also did a number of stunts in the picture, such as the exciting scenes of Tarzan climbing on the exterior of the New York skyscraper (filmed on sets, of course). Tarzan's classic dive off the Brooklyn Bridge into the murky waters 200 feet below was actually a weighted dummy captured on film by Jack Smith, perched at the top of the scenic tower on the MGM backlots. Only a few establishing shots were actually photographed on location in New York City.

Besides the plentitude of action, there was a wealth of humor, which was provided mainly by Cheeta, the cutup, who gets into all kinds of mischief. The chimp puts on Jane's makeup, drinks her perfume (and gets tipsy), makes a prank telephone call, scares the wits out of two pretty hatcheck girls, and just generally makes a monkey nuisance of herself. A funny scene has Tarzan taking a shower with his clothes on and giving his mighty war cry to Jane's utter disbelief. Then the ape-man shows that his savvy goes beyond the jungles and has the gallery in stitches, when he makes a monkey out of the opposing lawyer (Charles Lane) in the courtroom battle over Boy's custody.

"Cannibal Carnival" was used over the opening credits for the last time. The torch ballad, "I Must Have You or No One," was written by Marty Melnick and Jay Livingston, and additional music was composed by Earl Brent, Daniele Amfitheatrof, and Herbert Stothart.

At 71 minutes long, *Tarzan's New York Adventure* was the shortest adventure yet for Johnny Weissmuller as Tarzan. With Sol Lesser having purchased the rights to produce future Tarzan pictures (to be distributed by RKO), MGM didn't go beyond what was necessary to hold the budget in line; the final cost was approximately $700,000. Weissmuller was crossing over to RKO with producer Sol Lesser, along with Johnny Sheffield, to continue their roles as Tarzan and his son; their first feature without longtime mate Maureen O'Sullivan would be the war propaganda picture, *Tarzan Triumphs*. With the United States already into the rapidly escalating war, there was a plea to all Americans below the words, "THE END":
"America needs your money. Buy Defense Bonds and Stamps Every Pay Day."

Tarzan Triumphs

Release date: February 1943; Sol Lesser/RKO; running time: 78 minutes. *Directed by* William Thiele; *produced by* Sol Lesser; *screenplay by* Roy Chanslor and Carroll Young; *story by* Carroll Young, *based on the characters created by* Edgar Rice Burroughs; *director of photography,* Harry Wild; *art director,* Hans Peters; *film editor,* Hal Kern; *production design,* Harry Horner; *assistant director,* Clem Beauchamp; *wardrobe,* Elmer Ellsworth; *sound technician,* John C. Grubb; *music director,* Constantine Bakaleinikoff; *music by* Paul Sawtell.

Tarzan	Johnny Weissmuller
Boy	Johnny Sheffield
Zandra	Frances Gifford
Colonel von Reichart	Stanley Ridges

Sergeant	Sig Rumann
Patriarch	Pedro de Cordoba
Bausch	Philip Van Zandt
Achmet	Stanley Brown
Schmidt	Rex Williams
German soldier	Otto Reichow
German soldier	Sven Hugo Borg

Against Tarzan's orders, Boy visits the hidden city of Palandria, whose people are peaceful, gentle folks. When Boy slips and falls to a treacherous ledge, he is saved by the beautiful Zandra; then both are saved by Tarzan, who arrives just in time.

Jane has gone to London to be with her sick mother, and a letter to Tarzan and Boy tells of a world war and her longing to return to them. As Tarzan and Boy prepare for bed that evening, Tarzan looks at Jane's letter and repeats the words his beloved has written: "All my love—always—Jane." Tarzan rolls over to sleep, missing her very much.

When a German war plane crashes in Tarzan's jungle, the radioman Schmidt is the only survivor. Tarzan brings the soldier to his jungle tree-house, where the young man is delirious with fever. When he recovers, Schmidt tries to radio Berlin the coordinates for landing an invasion force in the jungle, which would be a strategic stronghold for the Germans. The radioman is foiled by Cheeta, who steals his antenna. The Nazi soldier tries to kill the ape, but justly falls to his death from a cliff.

Meanwhile, a Nazi safari arrives in Palandria, where the soldiers are greeted with hospitality by Zandra and her family. The despicable Colonel von Reichart repays the family's kindness by conquering the city and enslaving its people. When Zandra's brother Achmet is killed by the Nazis, Zandra flees through the jungle to seek help from Tarzan.

Zandra asks Tarzan to save her people from the Nazis, but he wants no more trouble from the Germans, as long as they leave him alone. However, when Boy is kidnapped by the soldiers in their quest for the radio, Tarzan declares: "Now, Tarzan make war!"

Under cover of nightfall, Tarzan infiltrates the Nazi compound, but both the jungle man and Zandra (who has followed Tarzan) are captured. Cheeta returns the missing radio antenna to the Germans and sneaks Tarzan his knife. The ape-man frees himself and recruits an army of Palandrians, who take up the fight against the Nazis. Bravely, Boy does his part by shooting a soldier who took dead aim at Tarzan.

As the battle rages, Colonel von Reichart escapes into the jungle with the radio, still hoping to signal Berlin. But von Reichart is in the jungle man's domain now, and he is tricked by Tarzan into falling into a lion pit—already occupied by a lion. With irony in his voice, Tarzan speaks von Reichart's epitaph: "In jungle, strong always survive."

Zandra and her people are saved, and justice is served, as Tarzan triumphs once again.

•

In 1938 a three-way deal between MGM, Sol Lesser, and Edgar Rice Burroughs was struck whereby MGM purchased three of the five Tarzan stories that Lesser owned at the time; these rights were turned into *Tarzan Finds a Son!, Tarzan's Secret Treasure,* and *Tarzan's New York Adventure,* the final three Tarzan pictures at MGM. Thus, when MGM withdrew from the Tarzan market in 1942, Lesser also acquired Johnny Weissmuller's contract from

"Now, Tarzan make war!" Weissmuller with Frances Gifford in *Tarzan Triumphs,* 1943.

MGM for "unspecified considerations." Also included in the bargain were Johnny Sheffield, who played Boy, and Maureen O'Sullivan (should she decide to be available for any further Tarzan pictures). Edgar Rice Burroughs, Inc., also benefited immensely through the new deal with Lesser, being paid both an advance and a percentage of the profits.

With Weissmuller set as Tarzan and Johnny Sheffield returning as Boy, Sol Lesser needed an actress for Jane; his first choice was Maureen O'Sullivan, who was pregnant for the second time and declined the role. To find the female lead for his coming production of *Tarzan Triumphs*, Lesser conducted extensive screen tests and an exhaustive search before deciding on 21-year-old Frances Gifford, whom he had spotted in the 1941 Republic serial *Jungle Girl* (based on another Edgar Rice Burroughs story).

Gifford, who was under contract to Paramount at the time, was vehemently against doing the film because she hoped to move on to more challenging acting roles. Paramount, however, would not relent and lent her to Lesser, despite her protestations. After Lesser presented her with an orchid on the first morning of shooting, all potential problems were smoothed over. Gifford as Zandra, the Palandrian, was a stunning beauty; although she wasn't a romantic replacement for Jane (the ape-man remained lonely), she definitely complemented any scenes she appeared in.

The cast also included veteran German character actor Sig Rumann, the rough sergeant who dies by Tarzan's knife, and British actor Stanley Ridges, who effectively portrayed the vile Colonel von Reichart. A classic scene has Tarzan toying with von Reichart in the jungle in a game of cat and mouse, with the German going in circles. Tarzan keeps repeating the name, "Nazi—

Nazi—Nazi—Nazi," until his opponent's bullets are gone. He then tricks von Reichart into falling into a pit filled with a hungry lion.

Chosen to direct *Tarzan Triumphs* was William Thiele, who had come to Hollywood in the 1930s, in exile from his homeland of Germany (an interesting choice given that this was an American propaganda film targeted at Hitler's Nazi regime). The German soldiers were all portrayed as either evil or ignorant; of course, Adolph Hitler was a hated figure throughout the world by this time (even by many people in Germany). In this picture, the Nazis were the bad guys (usually represented by greedy white men on safari), invading Tarzan's jungle to pilfer its treasures. The clever screenplay by Roy Chanslor and Carroll Young, from a story by Young, managed to stay on course despite the heavy propaganda message.

With independent producer Sol Lesser now in charge of producing the Tarzan pictures, a new jungle had to be found to replace the MGM jungle. The area chosen was the Los Angeles State and County Arboretum in Arcadia, California, about 15 miles northeast of downtown Los Angeles. The Arboretum was complete with a lagoon and natural lush vegetation, making it the perfect backdrop for all the studio Tarzan films produced by Lesser for RKO distribution. Other exterior location settings included Lake Sherwood, with city scenes photographed at the RKO Encino Ranch; interiors were shot at RKO studios.

Wild animal and jungle footage that Lesser borrowed included a savage battle between a spotted leopard and a warthog. A new treehouse was designed and built for the ape-man, but the same mischievous Cheeta appeared—for half the picture, the chimp had the Nazis chasing him for the critical radio antenna. The final scene with the Germans

Tarzan disposes of von Reichart (*Tarzan Triumphs*, 1943).

in Berlin speaking to Cheeta, who is playing with the radio, is hilarious and the ultimate insult to Hitler; the voice on the other end of the radio says, "Idiot—this is not von Reichart! This is der Fuhrer!"

Johnny Weissmuller had added a few pounds, but his great physical strength pulled him through the role just fine; he still looked strong enough at age 38 to fight a whole army by himself. Indeed, the action is almost nonstop as Tarzan takes on the German army and wins. The ape-man's hair was also longer and shaggier than in previous Tarzan pictures, and a new (slightly modified) Tarzan yell was recorded for the RKO series.

With Jane back in England and out of the picture, Tarzan is a lonely fellow; Zandra uses her feminine wiles on him (with Boy's permission) to get him to change his mind about helping her

people against the Nazis, but he sees through the plan. After Tarzan is wounded by the soldiers, Zandra revives him and relates that the Nazis took Boy away. "Took away? Boy?" says Tarzan with grief in his voice. Then in a classic, unforgettable scene, Tarzan grabs his knife and gritting his teeth, pronounces with fierce emotion, "Now! Tarzan make war!" Patriotic American audiences actually got to their feet and cheered after Weissmuller growled this immortal line.

Johnny didn't get to say much in the RKO Tarzan films, and years later Sol Lesser explained his philosophy for the minimal dialogue in *The Big Swingers* by Robert Fenton. "Tarzan is an international character and about 75 per cent of the film grosses came from foreign countries during the period I was producing the films. Their demands were for action, not words. Too much dialogue would only serve to slow up a Tarzan picture and weaken its strongest appeal to the foreign theatergoer—the universal understanding of action and pantomime."

One major change for a Tarzan movie was an actual musical score, with music by RKO contract composer Paul Sawtell (conducted by Russian-born Constantine Bakaleinikoff, who was with RKO from 1941 through 1952). Released in February 1943, *Tarzan Triumphs* was Lesser's biggest money-maker of all his Tarzan films. By the end of 1943, Johnny Weissmuller would be riding a wild stallion and once again battling the forces of evil in *Tarzan's Desert Mystery.*

Tarzan's Desert Mystery

Release date: December 1943; Sol Lesser/RKO; running time: 70 minutes. *Directed by* William Thiele; *produced by* Sol Lesser; *screenplay by* Edward T. Lowe; *story by* Carroll Young, *based on the characters created by* Edgar Rice Burroughs; *associate producer,* Kurt Neumann; *photography by* Harry Wild and Russ Harlan; *art directors,* Hans Peters and Ralph Berger; *interiors by* Victor Gangelin and Stanley Murphy; *film editor,* Ray Lockert; *assistant director,* Derwin Abrahams; *wardrobe by* Elmer Ellsworth; *sound technicians,* Jean L. Speak and Bailey Fesler; *musical director,* Constantine Bakaleinikoff; *musical score by* Paul Sawtell.

Tarzan	Johnny Weissmuller
Boy	Johnny Sheffield
Connie Bryce	Nancy Kelly
Paul Hendrix	Otto Kruger
Karl	Joe Sawyer
Prince Selim	Robert Lowery
Sheik	Lloyd Corrigan

Also featuring Frank Puglia, Phil Van Zandt, Nestor Paiva, and Frank Faylen.

An airplane flies over the escarpment and drops a package for Tarzan and Boy—a letter from Jane, who is nursing wounded troops in a British hospital during the war. Jane sends her love and an urgent request that Tarzan send her a supply of his fever medicine to save soldiers who contracted jungle fever in Burma. Tarzan listens intently as Boy finishes reading Jane's letter: "Take good care of yourselves, my darlings—you are always in my thoughts and prayers. With all my love, Jane."

It is a great distance across a mighty desert to reach the jungle with the fever medicine vines. Boy talks Tarzan into taking him along. Near their destination is the city of Bir-Herari, ruled by the sheik and his son, Prince Selim. The sheik has naïvely allowed a heartless profiteer, Paul Hendrix, to oppress his people and has put Hendrix in charge of the city's industries. Tarzan releases a beautiful wild stallion captured by Hendrix's men, who swear vengeance against the jungle man.

Weissmuller, Johnny Sheffield, and Nancy Kelly (*Tarzan's Desert Mystery*, 1943).

Meanwhile, Sheik Emir of Alakibra has enlisted the aid of Connie Bryce, an American magician, to deliver an urgent secret communication hidden in a bracelet to Prince Selim. The message exposes Hendrix as a spy who plans to take over the whole region.

Tarzan, Boy, and the desert stallion find Connie stranded at an oasis and escort her to Bir-Herari, where the apeman is immediately imprisoned by Hendrix's henchmen. Connie gains the confidence of Selim and delivers her message, but the prince is murdered by Hendrix, who tightens his evil grip on the people of Bir-Herari.

Connie is framed for the prince's murder and is sentenced to die by hanging. Tarzan escapes his lofty prison and riding the stallion, Jana, frees Connie with not a moment to spare. Together

with Boy and Cheeta, the fugitives take flight into the desert. Remembering his mission, Tarzan goes into the jungle to gather the fever medicine vines for the serum he must send to Jane.

Hendrix pursues Boy and Connie into the desert and chases them through the jungle into a mysterious cave. When Boy is caught in the web of a man-eating spider, Cheeta races to warn Tarzan. Escaping a deadly trap himself, Tarzan saves Boy from the spider, who instead settles for the bitter taste of Paul Hendrix for his dinner.

Connie is honored by the sheik for her bravery in delivering the vital message, and she bids her new friends, Tarzan and Boy, farewell. "Well, Tarzan old scout, what else can I do for you in London besides bringing Jane the fever medicine?" she asks. Tarzan speaks for

Tarzan in action (*Tarzan's Desert Mystery*, 1943).

both Boy and himself when he replies, "Tell Jane, Tarzan very lonesome—send much love."

•

Tarzan's Desert Mystery, released in December 1943, was another Tarzan movie without a Jane, leaving the ape-man and Boy sans the female touch around the treehouse. Producer Sol Lesser hadn't quite given up on getting Maureen O'Sullivan to return to the series, so in this story Jane is still in London, nursing wounded soldiers in a British hospital, as her letter to Tarzan and Boy details.

For the female lead, Lesser chose Nancy Kelly, an RKO contract player who received her best roles on the Broadway stage (except for an Academy

Award nomination for *The Bad Seed* [1956], in which she re-created her stage role). In *Tarzan's Desert Mystery*, Kelly played Connie Bryce, a lady magician who somehow becomes the secret emissary to Sheik Emir; she runs into Tarzan and Boy in the desert and forms an alliance with the jungle man and his son. The balance of the ordinary cast included Otto Kruger as the villainous Paul Hendrix, Joe Sawyer as Karl (the second villain in command), suave Robert Lowery as Prince Selim, and the usually comical Lloyd Corrigan as the sheik.

Bluntly put, *Tarzan's Desert Mystery* (shooting title, *Tarzan Against the Sahara*) was easily the poorest of the 12 Johnny Weissmuller Tarzan pictures; unfortunately, it was long on desert and desperately short on mystery. Basically a standard programmer (only 70 minutes long), it was more of a light melodrama with slices of humor or even a desert "western" (with all the horses in it) than it was a Tarzan picture.

Poor Johnny Weissmuller must have felt forgotten; his dialogue consisted of about 40 words for the whole picture, and he spent much of his time locked in a prison (off-screen). The most dangerous creature Tarzan had to fight was a man-eating plant; he even needed his elephant friends to get him out of the trap. Admittedly, Johnny had let himself get out of shape for this picture; at age 39, the years and a few too many pounds were starting to show. (By the time *Tarzan and the Amazons* was filmed, the jungle man was back in trim. Weissmuller had too much pride to let himself go indefinitely).

Meanwhile, Kelly carried the lead, cavorting with Boy and Cheeta and matching wits with the despicable Otto Kruger as Herr Heinrich (who calls himself Hendrix to conceal his nationality). Although this was a milder propaganda film than *Tarzan Triumphs,* the bad guys were once again Germans.

William Thiele directed his second RKO Tarzan feature, from a story by Carroll Young; these two men had successfully collaborated on the previous picture, but this entry turned out to be weak. The best action scene in the film is when Tarzan hops on the wild stallion, Jana, frees dozens of other wild horses, and escapes into the desert with Boy, Connie, and Cheeta. The expansive desert and blowing sands recalled the 1939 desert classic *Beau Geste,* but the similarities between the two abruptly ended there. The desert action was photographed at the Olancha sand dunes near Lone Pine, California, while the jungle scenes were shot at the Arboretum and the city scenes were filmed at the RKO Encino Ranch.

Tarzan's Desert Mystery simply failed as an action-adventure picture, and with Jane missing from the story, there was no romance to rescue it. By the time the next Tarzan picture was released in April 1945, World War II was nearing its end, and Jane would be back in the ape-man's arms. A new Jane (Brenda Joyce) would be joining Weissmuller and Sheffield in the next adventure, *Tarzan and the Amazons.*

Tarzan and the Amazons

Release date: April 1945; Sol Lesser/RKO; *running time:* 76 minutes. *Director and associate producer,* Kurt Neumann; *producer,* Sol Lesser; *screenplay by* John Jacoby and Marjorie L. Pfaelzer, *based on the characters created by* Edgar Rice Burroughs; *photography by* Archie Stout; *production design,* Phil Paradise; *art director,* Walter Koessler; *interiors by* James E. Altweis; *film editor,* Robert O. Crandall; *assistant director,* Scott R. Beal; *wardrobe by* Earl Moser; *makeup artist,* Norbert Miles; *sound technician,* Jean L. Speak; *musical score by* Paul Sawtell.

Tarzan	Johnny Weissmuller
Boy	Johnny Sheffield
Jane	Brenda Joyce
Sir Guy Henderson	Henry Stephenson

Weissmuller with Brenda Joyce and Johnny Sheffield (*Tarzan and the Amazons,* 1945).

Amazon queen	Maria Ouspenskaya
Ballister	Barton MacLane
Athena	Shirley O'Hara
Andres	Don Douglas
Splivers	J.M. Kerrigan
Brenner	Steven Geray

After living in England for many months during the war, Jane is returning to her African home to be with Tarzan and Boy, who are happily anticipating her return. "I guess it'll take Jane months to tell us all about the wonderful things she's seen," beams Boy.

The trip to Randini to meet Jane proves eventful when Tarzan saves a beautiful young woman, Athena, from the jaws of a panther. Tarzan carries Athena back to her people, an ancient race of Amazon women. No one is allowed to enter or leave Palmeria, but Tarzan is an exception—he is welcomed by the queen. "You need not plead for Tarzan," rules the queen. "He is our friend. May the great sun god protect you on your way, Tarzan."

Tarzan and Boy meet the riverboat in Randini, and the reunion with Jane is indeed a joyous occasion. Also arriving are a party of archaeologists led by Sir Guy Henderson, who is fascinated by the idea of a lost culture of Amazon women. But Tarzan respects the women's laws and refuses to show the archaeologists the way to Palmeria. "Not good for man to look directly into sun," is Tarzan's wise reasoning.

Athena begs the queen for Tarzan's life (*Tarzan and the Amazons*, 1945).

Undaunted, the archaeologists equip a scientific expedition guided by Ballister, a fortune hunter whose sole motive is greed. Jane and Boy are miffed with Tarzan for not helping their friends. Thinking he is doing the right thing, Boy leads the archaeologists to the hidden city of Palmeria, where they are indeed unwelcome. The queen suspends the mandatory death sentence and instead orders them to work in the quarries for the rest of their lives.

Searching the jungle for Boy, Jane is pinned by a fallen tree and threatened by an angry lion. Fortunately Tarzan is nearby to save her. Meanwhile, the loyal Athena tries to lead Boy and the party of men safely out of Palmeria. Her reward is a knife in the back from Ballister. Sir Guy tries to stop the others from pilfering the priceless treasures, but he is ruthlessly murdered as well.

Ballister narrowly escapes Palmeria with two priceless golden sacraments and plans to return for the rest of the treasure. Once in the jungle, the villain is in the king's domain and Tarzan thwarts the evil plan as Ballister sinks slowly into quicksand to a most deserved fate.

Back in Palmeria, the queen sentences Boy to die by drinking poison for his part in bringing the defilers to their land. But Tarzan returns the sacred symbols just in time, and the jungle man and his son return home to Jane.

•

Tarzan and the Amazons finally brought Jane back home to the Tarzan treehouse, after an absence of two pictures. On December 3, 1943, Louella Parsons noted in her Hearst gossip column that the original Jane would be returning: "Maureen O'Sullivan to resume her job as Tarzan's mate.... Maureen and John Weissmuller will co-star in *Tarzan and the Amazons* for RKO and Sol Lesser." However, Miss O'Sullivan was pregnant again (with daughter Mia Farrow), and the rumors of her return were finally put to rest in 1944 with the signing of Brenda Joyce as the new Jane.

Discovered by Darryl Zanuck, Joyce (born Betty Leabo) had made a memorable film debut as Fern in the spectacular 20th Century–Fox production of *The Rains Came* (1939). The Missouri-born blonde seemed to fit in nicely with Johnny Weissmuller and Johnny Sheffield, and she did five Tarzan films for Sol Lesser and RKO (the last, *Tarzan's Magic Fountain*, with the new Tarzan, Lex Barker).

Johnny Weissmuller looked like he had really worked himself into shape for this 1945 picture; at age 40 he appeared much closer to his old, trim self. He was also back to his forte: swimming. An exciting scene had Tarzan cutting through the river at top speed to save Boy from a crocodile, "killing" the rubber reptile in a savage battle, as he had done many times before in the MGM pictures.

Johnny Sheffield as Boy completed the Tarzan family once again (along with Cheeta). At age 14, he was playing his sixth Tarzan picture. Young Sheffield was starting to grow quickly, but for the time being he was fine for the part of Boy.

Portraying the wise old queen of the Amazons (who trusted no outsiders except Tarzan) was the diminutive Russian actress Maria Ouspenskaya. The classy Ouspenskaya was twice nominated for Oscars (for *Dodsworth* in 1936 and for *Love Affair* in 1939), but perhaps her most memorable role was as the gypsy woman whose werewolf son bites Lon Chaney, Jr., turning him into a werewolf in *The Wolf Man* (1941). She also appeared in *The Rains Came* with Brenda Joyce.

The rest of the competent cast included perennial villain Barton Mac-Lane as Ballister, who meets a final and justified end by sinking into a quicksand bog; Shirley O'Hara as the lovely Athena, the brave Amazon girl; and Henry Stephenson in another credible performance as Sir Guy, who was a noble chicken in a henhouse full of foxes. Stephenson has an ironic line early in the story, when he is introduced to Tarzan as Sir Guy Henderson: "I'm very glad to meet you Tarzan. Jane has told me so much about you, I almost feel I know you." The veteran actor had a twinkle in his eye when he spoke this line to Tarzan—he had appeared in *Tarzan Finds a Son!* in a similar role.

Brought in to direct the picture was German-born Kurt Neumann, who would direct several other Tarzan pictures for Sol Lesser over the next decade. Neumann was well in command directing action thrillers and kept *Tarzan and the Amazons* moving along at a brisk pace with plenty of excitement. Per usual, the jungle scenes were photographed at the Arboretum.

The screenplay by John Jacoby and Marjorie Pfaelzer returned to the successful Tarzan formula that had worked many times before: greedy white men invading Tarzan's domain to plunder the riches of the land. Making the victims a lost race of beautiful Amazon women was certainly a box-office coup, although the name of the tribe was certainly a misnomer. The screenwriters used poetic license in calling the women "Amazons," for the Amazons of legend were from South America, not from Africa.

There was also no stopping for any real romance between Tarzan and Jane (a little playful fun, perhaps, but none of the steamy love affair that was the trademark of the Weissmuller-O'Sullivan relationship). Once again producer Sol Lesser stuck with his conviction that it was best to keep Tarzan within a limited vocabulary. When the ape-man tries (but fails) to repeat a line from Boy's book: "Swift of foot was Hiawatha," he admits, "Tarzan's mind not so swift!"

The Tarzan motion pictures were now on a regular annual-release schedule. Almost every year for the next two decades, one could count on a new Tarzan adventure. The next one for Johnny Weissmuller, Brenda Joyce, and Johnny Sheffield was *Tarzan and the Leopard Woman.*

Tarzan and the Leopard Woman

Release date: February 1946; Sol Lesser/RKO; *running time:* 72 minutes. *Director and associate producer,* Kurt Neumann; *producer,* Sol Lesser; *story and screenplay by* Carroll Young, *based on the characters created by* Edgar Rice Burroughs; *photography by* Karl Struss; *production designer,* Phil Paradise; *art director,* Lewis Creber; *dance director,* Lester Horton; *film editor,* Robert O. Crandall; *assistant director,* Scott R. Beal; *wardrobe by* Robert Martien; *makeup artist,* Irving Berns; *sound technician,* John R. Carter; *unit manager,* Clem Beauchamp; *musical score by* Paul Sawtell.

Tarzan	Johnny Weissmuller
Jane	Brenda Joyce
Boy	Johnny Sheffield
High Priestess Lea	Acquanetta
Dr. Lazar	Edgar Barrier
Kimba	Tommy Cook
Commissioner	Dennis Hoey
Mongo	Anthony Caruso
Corporal	George J. Lewis
Superintendent	Doris Lloyd

Also featuring King Kong Kashey; Robert Barron; Marek Windheim; Louis Mercier; Georges Renavent; Iris Flores, Lillian Molieri, Helen Gerald, and Kay Salinas as the Zambesi maidens.

Tarzan and family (Jane, Boy and Cheeta) visit Zambesi to shop the bazaars for gifts for Jane's relatives, but the items Jane desires most have been sold and shipped to the new settlement at Bagandi. When the caravan to Bagandi is annihilated, a survivor tells of being attacked by leopards, but Tarzan is suspicious: "Man not killed by leopards. Leopards never kill with claws alone.

Use teeth." Tarzan leads a party to investigate. They are attacked by "savage leopards," but the ape-man is not fooled by the ruse.

Behind the evil doings is the High Priestess Lea, ruler of a deadly cult who worship a leopard god. The men wear leopard skins and claw their victims to death, then cut out their hearts to prove they are men. Lea is aided by the

Weissmuller with Acquanetta (*Tarzan and the Leopard Woman,* 1946).

diabolical Dr. Lazar, a native doctor who resolves to destroy the white men who have invaded his country and to steal their resources.

Lea sends her demented little brother Kimba to spy on the jungle man, who poses a threat to her cult. Feeling sorry for the "lost" boy, Jane invites Kimba to stay with them for a while, but she does not realize the evil in his heart. Tarzan and Boy do not trust the shifty-eyed Kimba (with good reason).

Boy discovers a leopard disguise in a cave and is chased through the jungle by leopard men. Only Tarzan's sharp blade saves his son from death. When Boy returns home, he valiantly defends Jane, just as Kimba is planning to cut her heart out.

Meanwhile, four maidens who are bound for Bagandi to become school-teachers are kidnapped by the leopard men. In trying to free the girls, Tarzan is captured. Soon Jane and Boy are added to the list of prisoners, and all are sentenced to die by sacrifice in a cult ceremony of the leopard people. "We shall fall upon our enemies and enslave them," cries the fanatical Dr. Lazar with Lea by his side. "And this time we will offer our god the hearts of the Zambesi maidens as sacrifice! And Tarzan shall die as well!"

At Tarzan's order, Cheeta cuts the bonds of the captives. When they are safely away, the ape-man explodes. He pulls down the pillars that support their underground temple, and the leopard worshippers are crushed. Dr. Lazar and Kimba survive, but in a bitter struggle fueled by hate, they die at each other's hands.

"Kimba want heart, Kimba get

Weissmuller, Brenda Joyce, Tommy Cook, and Johnny Sheffield (*Tarzan and the Leopard Woman,* 1946).

heart—Lazar's heart. Kimba dead, too," are the wise words of Tarzan. The mystery is solved, and Tarzan has destroyed the leopard woman and her strange, evil cult.

•

Johnny Weissmuller looked his physical best in years for his role as the ape-man in *Tarzan and the Leopard Woman.* Approaching his mid–40s, the trimmed-down Johnny looked like he could continue as Tarzan indefinitely. In an early scene, Tarzan enters a wrestling match with one of the local strongmen (played by a pro wrestler known as King Kong Kashey). Weissmuller easily hoisted the burly 200-pound Kashey over his head like a stuffed doll and tossed him aside. The wrestler takes his defeat in

stride, admitting (as they shake hands), "Again you have defeated Tongolo the Terrible. With Tarzan, Tongolo is not so terrible!"

Returning to the role she had now taken over indefinitely was Brenda Joyce as Jane. Johnny Sheffield as Boy made his seventh film with Weissmuller. Little John (who wasn't quite so little anymore) engages in a serious battle for the first time on screen, fighting Kimba (Tommy Cook) to defend Jane from the young killer who plans to cut her heart out. Proving he wasn't quite ready to step into Tarzan's shoes, Boy needs help from Cheeta, who clubs Kimba over the head at a fortuitous moment.

Effectively portraying Lea, the High Priestess, was an actress who had chosen an unusual name for herself: Acquanetta (born Burnu Davenport). The exotic looks of Acquanetta made her an excellent choice as the villainess, Lea, the ruler of the strange cult of leopard worshippers. Other cast members included Edgar Barrier as her cynical partner in crime, Dr. Lazar; Tommy Cook as Lea's sly, twisted little brother Kimba; and Dennis Hoey as the bumbling commissioner (Hoey had often portrayed the similar character of Inspector Lestrade, in the Basil Rathbone *Sherlock Holmes* thrillers.) In the small role of the school superintendent was Doris Lloyd, who had portrayed Mrs. Cutten in the first Weissmuller Tarzan picture, *Tarzan, the Ape Man*, in 1932.

Director Kurt Neumann once again molded an exciting adventure from Carroll Young's imaginative story and screenplay; he also handled much of the production planning in his dual role as associate producer. *Tarzan and the Leopard Woman* was mostly nonstop action and thrilling drama, with Tarzan usually right in the middle of it all. The ape-man fighting the leopard men in the crocodile infested river and again in the jungle were exciting battles. The scene in which Tarzan's safari is attacked by real leopards was particularly convincing (one realizes that Weissmuller is stabbing a stuffed leopard, but the real leopard footage edited in by Robert Crandall made the entire scene realistic). The Arboretum and the RKO Encino Ranch were used as filming locations for the jungle and city scenes, respectively.

As in all the previous RKO Tarzan pictures, Paul Sawtell wrote the riveting musical score for the picture. The unusual leopard dance numbers were choreographed for the leopard worshippers by dance director Lester Horton. Tarzan's next battle against the forces of evil would be in *Tarzan and the Huntress*, with the sultry Patricia Morison as the woman of the title.

Tarzan and the Huntress

Release date: April 1947; Sol Lesser/RKO; running time: 72 minutes. *Director and associate producer,* Kurt Neumann; *producer,* Sol Lesser; *story and screenplay by* Jerry Gruskin and Rowland Leigh, *based on the characters created by* Edgar Rice Burroughs; *photography,* Archie Stout; *production designer,* Phil Paradise; *art director,* McClure Capps; *film editor,* Merrill White; *associate editor,* John Sheets; *assistant director,* Bert Briskin; *wardrobe by* Harold Clandenning; *makeup artist,* Irving Berns; *sound technician,* Frank McWhorter; *production manager,* Clem Beauchamp; *musical score by* Paul Sawtell.

Tarzan	Johnny Weissmuller
Jane	Brenda Joyce
Boy	Johnny Sheffield
Tanya Rawlins	Patricia Morison
Paul Weir	Barton MacLane
Karl Marley	John Warburton
Smitty	Wallace Scott
King Farrod	Charles Trowbridge

Tarzan in a fight to the death (*Tarzan and the Huntress*, 1947).

Prince Suli .... Maurice Tauzen
Prince Ozira .... Ted Hecht
Monak .... Mickey Simpson

The Tarzan family come bearing gifts when they visit their friend King Farrod on his birthday, which is celebrated by all his subjects and close friends. En route, Tarzan sees an "iron bird" in the sky and knows that the white man's arrival will soon be followed by trouble. "Tarzan hope they keep flying far away," he growls.

Tanya Rawlins and Karl Marley have come to Africa to capture wild animals for zoos. They try to persuade King Farrod to rescind his quota and let them capture as many animals as they want. But the king, a reasonable and generous man, says no; he won't allow his jungles to be depleted to satisfy greedy hunters. "I suggest you take two of each species," he responds.

The king's corrupt nephew Prince Ozira secretly agrees to let the hunters trap animals without a quota—for a bounty, of course. To let them proceed without interference, Ozira has the king murdered, but the murder is made to look like an accident. The killers think the king's son, Prince Suli, has died as well, but he lies unconscious in the jungle, narrowly escaping death.

When Tarzan discovers the hunters trapping without a quota, he issues an angry edict: "Tarzan stay on his side of the river, hunters stay on theirs." The ape-man then calls all the animals to his side of the river with his mighty jungle cry.

Chief hunter Paul Weir ignores Tarzan's order and crosses the river to

Tarzan and family visit the King on his birthday (*Tarzan and the Huntress,* 1947).

trap animals, but Cheeta warns her master. Tarzan and Boy stealthily enter the hunters' camp at night, steal all their guns, and release the caged animals. Without their guns, the hunters are helpless in the jungle. Cheeta finds the guns behind a waterfall where Tarzan has hidden them and trades their location for Tanya's shiny compact.

Meanwhile, Tarzan and Boy discover the wounded prince in an animal trap and save his life. "Boy go home, tell Jane. We go to Teronga. Tell people truth," he barks. The jungle man single-handedly kills three hunters who track them into his viney domain, then calls his ever-faithful elephants to his aid. The hunters' camp is destroyed, and the rest of the animals are released. Ozira and Karl are killed under the crush of Tarzan's mighty pachyderms.

Paul Weir dies a grisly death when

he falls into an occupied lion trap, but Tanya manages to escape Africa in her plane. Tarzan saves Jane and Boy from a perilous trap in a hunter's net, and Prince Suli takes the throne as the rightful king.

•

The "huntress" of the title *Tarzan and the Huntress* was actress Patricia Morison, who was signed by Sol Lesser to be the villainess in his latest Tarzan adventure about ruthless big-game hunters who invade the ape-man's jungle. Morison's character, Tanya Rawlins, was more honorable than her male counterparts (Barton MacLane and John Warburton, who are killed) and she is allowed to "escape" by plane at the end of the picture. Justice seems to have been served without killing off the lovely but misguided Tanya. Morison's motion picture career began with a bang in 1939 with the lead role as the merciless heroine in *Persons in Hiding,* a gangster picture in which she becomes a public enemy. Her 1940s portrayals included the title role in the B-picture *Danger Woman* (1946), which also starred Brenda Joyce (Jane in the RKO Tarzan series).

Bad guy Barton MacLane, who died a nasty death in a quicksand bog in *Tarzan and the Amazons* (1945), was reincarnated to play another villain. This time this unscrupulous big game hunter's most deserved fate was to fall into an occupied lion trap; ironically, hunter Paul Weir had told his men to leave the lion in the trap because "Maybe something else will fall into it." Also helping the picture was a solid supporting cast that included John Warburton as the unprincipled Karl; Wallace Scott as the pilot with the strong comedic accent; Charles Trowbridge as the wise King Farrod; and Ted Hecht as the truly dastardly Prince Ozira.

For once producer Sol Lesser allowed a little romance into the story, when Johnny Weissmuller and Brenda Joyce engaged in a little serious smooching, as well as some playful fun. A nice touch was a smoothly choreographed swimming scene, with Tarzan, Jane, and Boy doing some synchronized swimming à la Esther Williams: crawl, backstroke, crawl, backstroke, all in perfect rhythm and coordinated grace. There was also a stimulating but all too short exotic dance number performed by a female native dancer.

Tarzan and the Huntress was directed by Kurt Neumann, who once again assumed the dual roles of director and associate producer, from a script by Jerry Gruskin and Rowland Leigh. The picture was one of the better RKO Tarzan adventures because of its excellent use of that time-tested formula plot:

greedy white men come to Africa to brazenly plunder, with Tarzan taking exception and rising to battle the forces of evil.

A great deal of fascinating wild animal footage was used to exceptional advantage: aerial shots of huge herds of zebra, elephants, and great flocks of birds; terrestrial shots of savage lions and leopards; and roiling rivers infested with reptiles and hippopotamuses. The native big game hunt was an exciting segment, culminating with the almost grotesque pool of dozens of snapping crocodiles, hungrily awaiting a victim. The climactic scene where Tarzan's elephants come charging to the rescue used some well conceived rear projections to maximum effect; and with the thrilling Paul Sawtell score pounding in the background, it was indeed memorable. As in previous Sol Lesser Tarzan adventures, the Arboretum was used for the location jungle scenes, and the RKO Encino Ranch was the site of the city scenes.

Johnny Sheffield, who as a seven-year-old had made his debut as Boy in the 1939 classic *Tarzan Finds a Son!* was now a solidly built 15-year-old approaching six feet in height. This would be Sheffield's final Tarzan picture; he had simply outgrown the role of Boy. Johnny went on to star in his own series of 12 jungle adventures, beginning with *Bomba, the Jungle Boy* in 1948 and ending in 1955. Having had enough of the jungles by the end of the *Bomba* series, young Sheffield retired from films and entered UCLA, eventually gaining a degree in business administration.

Johnny Weissmuller's long and illustrious career as the cinema Tarzan would conclude after his role in the next Tarzan adventure, *Tarzan and the Mermaids.*

Tarzan and the Mermaids

Release date: March 1948; Sol Lesser/RKO; running time: 68 minutes. *Directed by* Robert Florey; *producer,* Sol Lesser; *story and screenplay by* Carroll Young, *based on the characters created by* Edgar Rice Burroughs; *photography,* Jack Draper; *art director,* McClure Capps; *film editor,* Merrill White; *associate editor,* John Sheets; *assistant director,* Bert Briskin; *costumes by* Norma; *sound supervisor,* James Fields; *production manager,* Ray Heinz; *music composed and directed by* Dimitri Tiomkin.

Tarzan	Johnny Weissmuller
Jane	Brenda Joyce
Mara	Linda Christian
Palanth	George Zucco
Benji	John Laurenz
Varga	Fernando Wagner
Commissioner	Edward Ashley
Tiko	Gustavo Rojo
Luana	Andrea Palma
Inspector general	Matthew Boulton

Many miles beyond Tarzan's jungle home live a cult of strange people called Aquaticans, their forbidden island, Aquatania, secluded by the surly oceans and guarded by the impenetrable African jungles. The Aquaticans fanatically believe in their pagan god Baloo and live in fear of the power-mad high priest, Palanth. The superstitious natives dive for oysters in the dangerous waters and offer the pearls to Baloo (who is really a conspirator of Palanth named Varga).

When the beautiful maiden Mara is ordered by Palanth to marry Baloo, she refuses emphatically: "I'll never marry Baloo. I'll run away to the outside world and find Tiko and die with him." The frightened Mara runs away to find her lover Tiko, who was banished from Aquatania by the high priest for being in love with Mara.

Elsewhere, Tarzan and Jane are expecting a letter from their son Boy, who has gone to England to get a formal education. The messenger who brings the letter is Benji, an absent-minded minstrel who is a friend of the ape-man and his mate. While fishing, Tarzan is surprised to catch a girl in his net like he would a mermaid. It is Mara, who has traveled many miles to escape Palanth and Baloo.

Mara tells the story of her forced marriage to Baloo. Tarzan offers to help, but she is afraid that Tarzan and Jane will be in danger as well. Palanth's deluded followers grab Mara and overpower Tarzan, who rallies to Mara's cause and stalks them back to Aquatania. Meanwhile, Jane and Benji summon the commissioner from Nyaga to investigate the strange happenings at Aquatania. They are guided through the jungle by Tiko, who would die for his beloved Mara.

Tarzan has a sense of humor and dons the costume of Baloo, ordering Palanth to end his evil ways. But the high priest is not amused and threatens to kill the outsider if he interferes anymore. "You mock our God?" asks Palanth. "If our people knew anyone posed as Baloo, they would destroy him." But

Tarzan with the girl Mara, and the false deity (*Tarzan and the Mermaids,* 1948).

Tarzan is hardly afraid of these threats. The equally evil Varga plans to kill Jane and the commissioner before they can uncover his racket of stealing pearls from the natives.

Tarzan makes a perilous dive from the high cliffs only to find Palanth's men and a giant octopus waiting to kill him in the swirling waters. The ape-man battles his enemies and escapes, arriving on the cliff just as Jane and her friends are about to be thrown to their deaths. Tarzan unmasks Varga to reveal an ordinary man, not a god. "Baloo man, not God. High Priest evil!" barks Tarzan. Baloo is no match for Tarzan, who hurls the false deity to his death on the rocks below.

•

Tarzan and the Mermaids was Johnny Weissmuller's final portrayal of Tarzan, ending his 17-year reign as the King of the Jungle. Although the story takes place in Tarzan's Africa it was photographed on location in Acapulco, Mexico. The Acapulco scenery was quite breathtaking at times, and the high dives photographed from various angles above and below were magnificent. A tragic accident occurred when Angel Garcia, doubling for Weissmuller, was killed making Tarzan's climactic dive from the highest cliffs, his body crushed on the rocks.

Weissmuller, at age 43, was still powerfully built, and the scene in which he fights a half-dozen men (hoisting one man over his head like a child) was impressive. He didn't have the lean physique of his younger days, but he still fought his enemies with the heart of a lion. Johnny's swimming and underwater scenes were exciting and demanding.

Weissmuller as Tarzan . . . a final pose (*Tarzan and the Mermaids*, 1948).

Something new for Weissmuller was wearing sandals in his role as Tarzan; he had always previously gone barefoot. Johnny even wore the sandals in the underwater swim scene in which he catches the "mermaid" of the title, who turned out to be Mara (Linda Christian).

Brenda Joyce was by now a fixture in the Tarzan pictures as Jane. Missing was Johnny Sheffield as Boy, who had moved on to do *Bomba, the Jungle Boy* pictures for Walter Mirisch. Boy's absence from the story was explained by a letter from England, where their son had gone to pursue a formal education.

The role of the beautiful maiden Mara went to the relatively unknown Linda Christian, a lovely 24-year-old Mexican actress who later married into European nobility. John Laurenz played the light-hearted minstrel courier who brings Boy's letters to Tarzan and Jane. British actor George Zucco invariably made a diabolical villain; his sinister High Priest Palanth was no exception.

The composer and director of the musical score for *Tarzan and the Mermaids* was Dimitri Tiomkin, who would eventually win several Academy Awards for his music. Tiomkin's score was at times enchanting and usually haunting and powerful, especially the savage vocal choral chants to the false god, Baloo.

The story by Carroll Young was certainly different from previous Tarzan pictures, and at one point in the film you forget you are watching a Tarzan picture. The Acapulco beaches, the young people in swimwear, the playful water jousting, and the romantic ballad sung by Benji displace you into another era (with Tarzan and Jane enjoying the spectacle and sharing a piece of fruit).

But the powerful climax orchestrated by director Robert Florey, with Tarzan battling underwater first with a horde of divers and then with a giant octopus, and finally hurling the evil Baloo onto the rocks below, was a fitting ending for Weissmuller's nearly two decades of action as Tarzan. More than 20 years later, Johnny would return to Acapulco, the scene of his final Tarzan picture, where he would spend the remaining years of his life.

Although Weissmuller was now retired from his role of Tarzan, he would continue to make jungle pictures for years to come as Jungle Jim, beginning almost immediately with the 1948 release of *Jungle Jim*. The new movie Tarzan would be Lex Barker, and Brenda Joyce would join him as Jane in the next RKO picture, *Tarzan's Magic Fountain*, in 1949. For the first time in nearly two decades, Johnny Weissmuller would not be Tarzan; the greatest Tarzan was gone, but the ape-man lives on.

III

More Heroic Tarzans: 1933 to the Present

Tarzan the Fearless

Release date: August 1933; Sol Lesser/Principal Pictures; running time: 85 minutes (feature), 12 chapters. *Directed by* Robert F. Hill; *produced by* Sol Lesser; *based on the characters created by* Edgar Rice Burroughs; *screenplay supervisor,* William Lord Wright; *continuity,* Basil Dickey and George H. Plympton; *dialogue editor,* Walter Anthony; *photography by* Harry Neumann and Joseph Brotherton; *film editor,* Carl Himm; *musical supervision,* Abe Meyer.

Tarzan	Buster Crabbe
Mary Brooks	Jacqueline Wells
Dr. Brooks	E. Alyn Warren
Bob Hall	Edward Woods
Jeff Herbert	Philo McCullough
Nick Moran	Matthew Betz
Abdul	Frank Lackteen
Eltar, High Priest	Mischa Auer
Priestess of Zar	Carlotta Monti
Arab woman	Symonia Boniface
Unga, head bearer	Darby Jones
Warrior	Al Kikume
Guard	George De Normand

Chapter Titles:

1. "The Dive of Death"
2. "The Storm God Strikes"
3. "Thundering Death"
4. "The Pit of Peril"
5. "Blood Money"
6. "Voodoo Vengeance"
7. "Caught by Cannibals"
8. "The Creeping Terror"
9. "Eyes of Evil"
10. "The Death Plunge"
11. "Harvest of Hate"
12. "Jungle Justice"

An African safari winds its way along a trail. Its members include Mary Brooks and her boyfriend, Bob Hall, as well as safari bosses Jeff Herbert and Nick Moran. They are searching for Mary's father, Dr. Brooks, who is a scientist and a friend of Tarzan. Tarzan makes the acquaintance of Mary when he must save her from a crocodile in the river where she is swimming. After the rescue, Tarzan gives Mary a note from her father that he had been asked to deliver, giving directions to his location.

Herbert and Moran also plan to collect a 10,000 pound reward as proof of Tarzan's existence or death, posted

Buster Crabbe as Tarzan, with Jacqueline Wells (*Tarzan the Fearless*, 1933).

by the executors of the Greystoke estate in England. When they find Dr. Brooks' hut, it is empty. He has gone to find a lost temple filled with treasure and has left a map to show the way. Moran attempts to steal the map, but he is outfoxed by Abdul, who memorizes the map and kidnaps Mary.

It's Tarzan to the rescue once again, as he dispatches the Arabs and carries Mary to his jungle lair. They are soon friends, and she teaches him his first words of English. Bob leads a party in search of Mary, and at the first opportunity, Moran steals the map. He doesn't get far before paying for his disloyalty in the bone-crunching jaws of a lion.

Dr. Brooks has been captured by Eltar, the high priest of Zar, and Bob and Herbert are soon added to the list of those to be sacrificed for entering the forbidden city. Tarzan comes to their aid and releases them, but Herbert steals one of the priceless emeralds on the statue of the god of Zar. The unscrupulous Herbert then threatens to

kill Tarzan unless Mary consents to marry him. He still plans to collect the bounty for Tarzan's death.

Meanwhile in Zar, the high priest is enraged when he notices the missing emerald and swears retribution: "I will avenge this blasphemy!" The jungle drums mean trouble as Eltar orders all aliens captured. Tarzan carries Mary safely through the trees to a sanctuary. Tarzan goes for food but never returns. Mary journeys back to her father's hut alone, where Bob, her father, and Herbert are waiting.

Little does Mary know that Tarzan has fallen into a lion trap. His friends Tantor, the elephant, and the ape come to his aid. They lift the unconscious ape-man out of the pit and carry him to a river, where he revives himself. As the safari prepares to leave, Mary doesn't want to leave—she is in love with Tarzan. Bob finally gets a true picture of the villain Herbert, including his coercion of Mary, and exiles him to the jungle.

A mighty ape saves Tarzan's life (*Tarzan the Fearless*, 1933).

As the party trek through the jungle, they are again captured by the guards of Zar. Herbert is also caught, and the stolen emerald is restored to its rightful place. Eltar demands vengeance, proclaiming, "You will not escape again." Bob offers the map to Zar in exchange for their freedom, and Eltar reluctantly agrees.

Later in the jungle, Tarzan fights Herbert to the death. The villain has a gun, but he is no match for the ape-man. Herbert repents with his dying breath. Tarzan is also wounded and crawls into the jungle to recuperate. Mary and her father search in vain for him. Finally returning to their hut, they are greeted by Tarzan. "Tarzan," exclaims Mary, "you're not hurt!" Indeed, the ape-man is alive and well, and the glint in his and Mary's eyes tells the rest of the story.

•

The 1933 Tarzan entry, *Tarzan the Fearless*, once again starred an Olympic swimming champion, this time the newly crowned, Clarence "Buster" Crabbe. Swimming for the United States team in the 1928 Olympics in Amsterdam, Crabbe had finished fourth in the 400-meter freestyle. (Johnny Weissmuller won the 400-meter freestyle at the 1924 games in Paris; he did not compete in the 400-meter in Amsterdam in 1928 but won the gold in the 100-meter freestyle.) The result was not instant fame and fortune. In fact, Crabbe's work as a part-time stuntman was supplemented by working as a stock clerk at Silverwood's clothing store in Los Angeles, at $8 per week.

But after the 1932 Olympics in Los Angeles, where Crabbe won the prestigious 400-meter freestyle in a photo-finish by a mere one-tenth of a second, "Buster" (as he was nicknamed) was soon on his way to Hollywood fame. (Weissmuller, sitting in the front row, hurdled over a fence to get a closer look at the exciting photo-finish.) Crabbe later recalled the momentous change in his life the victory had produced: "That one-tenth of a second changed my life. It was then that [Hollywood] discovered latent histrionic abilities in me."

As a result of his thrilling victory in Los Angeles, Buster Crabbe landed the role of Kaspa, the lion-man in Paramount's production of *King of the Jungle* (1933). The film was obviously a Tarzan imitation, with Kaspa being a child lost in Africa who was raised by lions and growing up to be King of the Jungle. This excellent B+ adventure costarred Frances Dee as his love interest and featured some extremely violent scenes, including one with a bull and a lion fighting in a closed barn.

It wouldn't be long before producer Sol Lesser would call the 26-year-old Crabbe (born Clarence Linden Crabbe) about starring in his new Tarzan production, *Tarzan the Fearless.* Lesser had previously acquired the rights to make a Tarzan picture with the stipulation that Edgar Rice Burroughs' son-in-law James Pierce be cast as Tarzan. Pierce coveted the role of the ape-man, but had neglected his physical training since starring in *Tarzan and the Golden Lion* (1927). Finally realizing he would not be able to get in condition for the strenuous role of Tarzan, Pierce relinquished his rights for a $5,000 payment from Lesser.

With Buster Crabbe now cleared to be the seventh in the long line of Tarzans, the female lead and Tarzan's romantic interest, Mary Brooks, was filled by the petite and lovely blonde Jacqueline Wells (who later changed her name to Julie Bishop). E. Alyn Warren was cast as Mary's father, Dr. Brooks;

and her clean-cut boyfriend, Bob, was Edward Woods. Eltar, the high priest of Zar, was played by Russian-born character actor Mischa Auer.

Sol Lesser had come up with a unique idea for marketing his new Tarzan production: He released the first four chapters of the serial as a 60-minute feature, with the remaining eight chapters to be shown on successive weeks. The only problem was that many theaters didn't show the rest of the chapters, which left the audience hanging and dissatisfied, not knowing what fate had in store for their hero, Tarzan. Today, the feature with added footage (from the serial) that provides a happy ending is apparently all that has survived the years.

Tarzan the Fearless was directed by veteran serial director Robert F. Hill, who had directed the silent Tarzan serial *The Adventures of Tarzan* (1921). The script was written by Basil Dickey, George Plympton, and Walter Anthony, but was not based on any of Edgar Rice Burroughs' novels. The author approved the script with only minor changes, including toning down the "sexual suggestiveness" in certain scenes between Crabbe and Wells. The film also had a complete musical score, supervised by Abe Meyer.

With his handsome looks, smoothly muscled swimmer's physique, and a marvelous athleticism, Crabbe made a respectable screen Tarzan, although he was clearly a clone of Johnny Weissmuller. His character followed the MGM lead in making Tarzan an uneducated savage, who knew not a word of English. Buster sported the skimpy leopard shorts he had worn in *King of the Jungle* and used a new Tarzan yell as the ape-man's victory cry. The studio had originally used three voices for the new Tarzan yell: a baritone, a bass, and a hog caller, but it scrapped that version and settled on one recorded by Tom Held, a film cutter and Buster Crabbe's father-in-law. Location scenes were filmed at Iversen's Movie Ranch, the location of countless Hollywood productions over the years.

There was a great fight between a lion and Tarzan (using a stuntman) early in the film and a fine scene in which Tarzan must rescue Mary from a crocodile. Crabbe showed his Olympic form by cutting through the water with impressive speed. But years later, Crabbe anguished over his role of the ape-man: "The worst Tarzan was me. We had two animals—an elephant that had retired from the circus and a lion with no teeth. But there were a lot of good fights in it, so the kids liked it."

Portraying Tarzan was a one-shot deal for Buster Crabbe, who nevertheless went on to a long and successful film career. The former swimmer made over 80 feature films and several Universal serials, including *Buck Rogers* and his most famous character, Flash Gordon, the dashing space hero. In the early 1950s he starred on television in "Captain Gallant of the Foreign Legion," with his real-life son, "Cuffy" Crabbe, playing his ward.

In semiretirement from the movie business in the 1960s, Crabbe was director of water sports at the Hotel Concord in Kiamesha, New York, and ran his own company, Buster Crabbe Swimming Pools. A fitness expert, and an author of books about exercise, Buster received a special citation in 1981 from the President's Council on Physical Fitness and Sports for his work in promoting better health and fitness for senior citizens. A memorable Tarzan, Clarence "Buster" Crabbe died on April 23, 1983, at age 75.

The New Adventures of Tarzan

Release date: October 1935; Burroughs/Tarzan Enterprises; running time: 75 minutes (feature); 12 chapters. *Directed by* Edward Kull; *produced by* Ashton Dearholt; *screenplay by* Charles F. Royal; *original story by* Edgar Rice Burroughs; *adaptation by* Charles F. Royal and Edwin H. Blum; *photography by* Ernest F. Smith and Edward Kull; *assistant director,* W.F. McGaugh; *art direction,* Charles Clague; *editing,* Edward Schroeder and Harold R. Minter; *special effects,* Ray Mercer; *recording,* Earl N. Crain.

Tarzan	Herman Brix
Ula Vale	Ula Holt
Major Martling	Frank Baker
Alice Martling	Dale Walsh
Gordon Hamilton	Harry Ernest
Raglan	Don Castello
George	Lew Sargent
Bouchart	Merrill McCormick
Mayan queen	Mrs. Gentry

Chapter Titles:

1. "The New Adventures of Tarzan"
2. "Crossed Trails"
3. "The Devil's Noose"
4. "River Perils"
5. "Unseen Hands"

Major Martling and his daughter Alice plan an expedition from Africa to the Dead City in Guatemala in hopes of finding the Lost Goddess, a statue filled with the priceless jewels of ancient Mayan rulers. The larcenous Raglan plans to steal the jewels out of the Goddess and sets sail on the same ship. Tarzan (Lord Greystoke) decides to join Major Martling's venture after he saves the life of a deranged friend of D'Arnot, who tells the ape-man that Tarzan's old mentor is alive but lost in the Guatemalan jungles. Also setting sail is Ula Vale, a British secret agent who hopes to track down a vital formula before Raglan can get his hands on it.

On board ship, Raglan intercepts a telegram addressed to Major Martling that reads: "Document arrived safely. Will guard same carefully until you arrive. *Signed* Padre Muller." Immediately upon landing in Guatemala, Raglan steals from Padre Muller the document that contains instructions for finding the Dead City. It doesn't take Tarzan long to deduce who has stolen the document, and he leads a river safari to intercept Raglan.

Ula Vale watches in horror as Raglan throws one of their men over a cliff. Moments later she too is thrown over the waterfalls to the swirling river. Fortunately, Tarzan quickly comes to Ula's rescue. Later she tells him her purpose in going on the expedition. "I seek to keep the contents of the Goddess from falling into the hands of such vandals as Raglan. My fiancé died following this very same goal."

Tarzan is sympathetic and leaves at once to stop Raglan, who has just killed one of the natives and stirred up trouble. The Martling safari is captured by the angry natives. Tarzan arrives in the nick of time to save Alice Martling from the jaws of a leopard. Soon Tarzan is in pursuit of Raglan, who has discovered the secret entrance to the ancient Mayan city. The ape-man also finds the entrance and leads his friends to it.

Within the walls of the Dead City, strange cult worshippers attack and capture the entire party, including Tarzan (Raglan, however, keeps safely out of sight). Also a long-time prisoner is Tarzan's old friend D'Arnot, who tells his story with bitterness. "I wish they had killed me," says the broken man. "This is worse than death."

The Mayan queen is attracted to Tarzan and wants him as her lover, but he brazenly refuses her offer, knowing that death is the alternative. Before the queen can sacrifice Tarzan, the ceremony is broken by the sight of Raglan stealing the Goddess with a rope from above. In the ensuing riot, Tarzan bravely battles dozens of opponents, but it looks hopeless until Gordon holds off the Mayans with a Gatling gun, and they barely make their escape.

Tarzan catches up with Raglan and defeats him soundly in hand-to-hand combat. At last the Goddess is in safe hands. Major Martling and Alice decide to share the valuable jewels inside the fabled statue with their friends. Tarzan's mission is also accomplished—he has freed his friend D'Arnot.

•

One of the most interesting of all Tarzan productions was *The New Adventures of Tarzan,* which was filmed in the Guatemalan jungles. It starred Herman Brix in the joint role of the savage Tarzan and the civilized Lord Greystoke.

Herman Brix with Ula Holt (*The New Adventures of Tarzan*, 1935).

Brix, who would later be known as Bruce Bennett, had been seriously considered for the MGM lead in *Tarzan, the Ape Man* (1932), but broke his shoulder filming the sports actioner *Touchdown* in 1931.

When Edgar Rice Burroughs was approached by family friend Ashton Dearholt about forming a motion picture company, he jumped at the opportunity to have the final word on a new Tarzan production. The newly formed Burroughs-Tarzan Enterprises (BTE) listed Ashton Dearholt, George Stout, and Ben Cohen as "promoters" and Edgar Rice Burroughs as "owner"; BTE's offices were located on Sunset Boulevard in Hollywood. The expressed mission of BTE was to produce, distribute, and or exhibit talking motion pictures based on the works and characters created by Burroughs. The author of the Tarzan stories made it clear that he was not a movie producer and that he would be a background player only, leaving the production end of things to the professionals.

Burroughs had always wanted motion picture producers to depict his creation Tarzan as he was described in his novels: a savage raised by apes in the jungle, but as an adult, a man who claimed his heritage as Lord Greystoke of England and who was a highly intelligent and educated gentleman. But MGM's Tarzan was an uneducated savage who didn't understand a word of English when he first met Jane Parker and her father in the jungle. This was the negative image that the author hoped to dispel by producing his own Tarzan motion picture. Burroughs also wanted to share in the immense profits that the movie companies had reaped on their earlier Tarzan pictures.

A search for a new Tarzan actor began with requests to MGM and Paramount, respectively, to borrow either Johnny Weissmuller or Buster Crabbe, but neither movie company was interested in lending its star for a dangerous journey into the Guatemalan jungles. So a nationwide search began for the new Tarzan, and many applicants were considered. As Louella Parsons reported in her column of August 16, 1934, "Tarzan's papa" was searching for an "unknown" to play Tarzan in future "jungle operas."

The winner was 25-year-old Herman Brix, a former University of Washington football and track star and an Olympic silver medalist in the shot put at the 1928 games in Amsterdam. (Brix finished with a mark of just under 58 feet; U.S. teammate John Kuck won the gold medal. The 1928 United States Olympic team also featured future Tarzans Johnny Weissmuller and Clarence "Buster" Crabbe.) Burroughs gave Brix the final stamp of approval after hearing from his partners on October 24. According to *The Man Who Created Tarzan* by Irwin Porges, Ashton Dearholt, one of Burroughs' partners, told him: "Herman Brix has outclassed every other applicant, in our opinion." Signed to a movie contract by BTE, Brix was vastly underpaid at $75 per week for a dangerous assignment in the Guatemalan jungles (especially since Jiggs the chimp was "paid" $2,000 for the expedition, which included his trainers). The former shot-putter had acting experience and certainly filled the bill physically, with his muscular athlete's physique, rugged good looks, high level of intelligence, and masculine speaking voice. Brix also came up with his own unique Tarzan yell, with variations for different circumstances.

The rest of the relatively unknown cast included Ula Holt as Ula Vale, who gave a convincing performance as an attractive secret agent who has an occasional pretty smile for Tarzan (there's no Jane in this picture); veteran Australian-born actor Frank Baker, who ably filled the bill as Major Francis Martling, the leader of the expedition; Dale Walsh, who had originally been considered for the female lead, as daughter Alice Martling; Harry Ernest, who played Gordon Hamilton, Alice's boyfriend; Lew Sargent, who humorously acted the bumbling but loyal George (who idolized Tarzan); and Don Castello, who portrayed the deceitful villain Raglan. (Ashton Dearholt's experience as an actor paid off when Castello became too ill partway through production to continue working, and Dearholt took over the role of Raglan.) The woman who played the Mayan queen (who is supposed to be a beautiful, seductive woman) seems to have been miscast, until one finds out that she wasn't an actress at all, but one of the trainers of Jiggs, the chimp who portrayed Nkima.

The new Tarzan picture was filmed in Guatemala, and the new production started out with the working title *Tarzan in Guatemala* (eventually, after much haggling, the final title, *The New Adventures of Tarzan*, was settled on). Edward Kull, who directed serials for Universal in the 1920s, not only handled the director's reins, but worked behind the cameras with Ernest Smith. Producer/actor Ashton Dearholt was to be in charge of production in Guatemala, sending regular reports and rushes to Burroughs in California. The author himself had roughed out an original story for the new Tarzan picture that was adapted by Charles Royal and Edwin Blum.

After filming some of the animal shots at the Selig Zoo in Los Angeles,

Tarzan battles for his life (*The New Adventures of Tarzan*, 1935).

the expedition of 28 people (cast and crew) set sail for Guatemala in late November 1934, aboard the ocean liner *Seattle*. Upon their arrival in San Jose, they were greeted by a tropical storm, and their trip inland to Chichicastenango through rugged jungle required 18 hours to travel barely 100 miles. Locations included the old Spanish capital city of Antigua, the Mayan ruins at Tikal, and Guatemala City (known as "little Paris"). Among the many problems encountered by the production crew, the *New York Times* reported the following on January 12, 1935: "TARZAN: Two cameramen attacked by Guatemalan Indians for disturbing religious ceremonies during filming of picture...."

Production of *The New Adventures of Tarzan* was so difficult and troubled that the film carried this message to movie patrons after the opening credits had rolled:

The production of this film was carried out under conditions of extreme difficulty and hardship, involving personal danger to the actors and technicians, to whom the producers owe a debt of appreciation. The sound recording was occasionally interfered with by the extremely variable atmosphere condition, and your kind indulgence is craved in this direction.

After initial enthusiasm for the early rushes, and despite the noble plan to film on location a genuine Tarzan picture following his fictional character to the letter, Burroughs was extremely disappointed in the reels of footage that the expedition brought back. In a memorandum written on March 5, 1935, Burroughs noted, as quoted in Porges' book:

What we have to work with consists of the story and the Guatemalan background. MGM, with little or no story, made two successful pictures because of the tremendous amount of action injected. We must face the fact that we have little or no action in our picture; and what impressed me last night was the fact that we had sacrificed both the story and the scenic shots in an effort to achieve action that either was not there or not worthwhile, and what action there is, is not particularly thrilling.

Burroughs went on to note further failings of the production:

> Tarzan is unquestionably a subordinate character ... the big climax at the end of the picture features the comedian (Lew Sargent). I should have caught this in the script months ago, but it did not strike me forcibly until I saw it on the screen last night.

When the film was released in October 1935, there was a further, unexpected problem: Movie powerhouse MGM managed to push the independent production of Tarzan out of the major movie houses with its "block booking" policy. At that time MGM was working on its next Tarzan picture, *Tarzan Escapes*, and hoped it would soon be ready for release (actually finished in October, the troubled production would not be released until November 1936 after being completely reworked). So with MGM's strongarm policy of "Book our Tarzan pictures in the future or this Tarzan now," *The New Adventures of Tarzan* was effectively relegated to the smaller independent houses. (The film was, however, quite popular overseas in markets like England and France.)

The critics were mostly unkind to the first BTE project, as this quote from the October 19, 1935, *Variety* review indicates: "Film handicapped here by serial story tempo, acting, plot development and direction. Whole sequences in which hardly a word is spoken. Maybe that's for the best since the dialogue is pretty corny."

Herman Brix certainly could have made a splendid Tarzan/Greystoke if he had been given a professionally produced vehicle to display his considerable talents. Obviously there were times in *The New Adventures of Tarzan* when Brix's inexperience as an actor showed, but that could have been overcome with better direction and dialogue. Brix moved on to play Nioga in the 1938 Republic adventure serial, *Hawk of the Wilderness*. In the 1940s, after changing his name to Bruce Bennett, he went on to a long career with second leads in classic films (coincidentally, all starring Humphrey Bogart), such as *Sahara* (1944), *Dark Passage* (1947), and *Treasure of the Sierra Madre* (1948).

Some credit needs to be given to the producers for going through with the monumental task of filming in the Guatemalan jungles and at last bringing Burroughs' fictional Tarzan character to the screen as his jungle hero had originally been created. It would be almost three decades before further attempts to depict an educated Tarzan/Greystoke were realized. The added depth of character of Tarzan as Lord Greystoke was something Hollywood movie producers never really exploited, and this film should be remembered for this point alone.

The film was released as both a 75-minute feature and a 12-chapter serial; the serial was actually the feature with 11 additional chapters of adventure. Eventually, the whole convoluted mishmash was re-edited, along with added footage, into a second feature, *Tarzan and the Green Goddess*, which was released in 1938. BTE produced only one other film, a 1937 documentary entitled *Tundra*.

Tarzan's Revenge

Release date: January 1938; Principal (Sol Lesser)/20th Century–Fox; running time: 70 minutes. *Directed by* D. Ross Lederman; *produced by* Sol Lesser; *screenplay by* Robert Lee Johnson and Jay Vann, *based on the characters created by* Edgar Rice Burroughs; *photography,* George Meehan; *art direction,* Lewis J. Rachmil; *film editor,* Eugene Milford; *assistant director,* Wilbur McGaugh; *sound engineer,* Terry Kellum; *wardrobe,* Jerry Bos; *musical supervision,* Abe Meyer; *musical score,* Hugo Riesenfeld.

Tarzan	Glenn Morris
Eleanor Reed	Eleanor Holm
Roger Reed	George Barbier
Ben Aley Bey	C. Henry Gordon
Penny Reed	Hedda Hopper
Olaf	Joe Sawyer
Jigger	Corbet Morris
Nevin Potter	George Meeker
Koki	John Lester Johnson

Also featuring Frederick Clarke.

A paddle boat traveling down an African river carries a hunting expedition, whose members are hoping to trap rare animals for their local zoo. The party includes Roger Reed, Mrs. Penny Reed, daughter Eleanor, and her pretentious fiancé, Nevin Potter. Also on board is the wealthy sheik Ben Aley Bey, who has an eye for the beautiful Eleanor and wants to add her to his harem of wives. The sheik lives in a beautiful palace in the jungle and controls the nearby natives; he is used to getting what he wants.

The Reed safari begins, guided by Olaf, who has been secretly hired by Ben Aley Bey to help obtain the girl for him. An interested spectator from the trees above is Tarzan, for this is his jungle. After Eleanor falls into a bog and is rescued by Tarzan, they introduce themselves. Some playful fun lands the girl back in the bog, as Tarzan takes to the trees and Nevin arrives to pull her out. "I was rescued by an ape-man and his monkey," she says (but, of course, no one believes her).

Meanwhile, Olaf plots a trap for the Reed party near the rope bridge that crosses the river. On the other side are Ben Aley Bey's natives, who wait to kidnap the girl. However, this plan will have to wait because Tarzan abducts Eleanor and carries her into the trees. The ape-man offers Eleanor some food, and they become friends, swimming together in a sparkling pool. As night falls they are still together.

The next morning Tarzan is gone, and Eleanor is discovered by her father, who has been searching the jungle. "Oh Eleanor, I thought I'd never see you again," blubbers Roger Reed. The girl admits she was frightened, but somehow she is strongly attracted to Tarzan.

As the plot to kidnap Eleanor advances, the head bearer Koki intends to warn Mr. Reed not to cross the bridge where the trap awaits. Before he can act, Olaf kills Koki with a poison dart. Soon Eleanor is grabbed by natives and brought to Ben Aley Bey's jungle palace. The sheik plies her with hospitality, wine, and native dancers, but the haughty Eleanor is not impressed.

Glenn Morris as Tarzan (*Tarzan's Revenge*, 1938).

A chimp tells Tarzan of Eleanor's plight, and after stopping to save the Reed party from hostiles, Tarzan takes flight to rescue Eleanor. At the palace Tarzan knocks out the guards and scales the gates, then whistles a signal to Eleanor. Moments later he scoops up the girl and escapes, with Ben Aley Bey's men and Olaf in hot pursuit.

Racing through the jungle, Tarzan and Eleanor safely cross the bridge with their pursuers right behind. Tarzan cuts the ropes, the bridge collapses, and Olaf and Ben Aley Bey plunge to their deaths in the crocodile-infested waters below.

Eleanor is unsure of her feelings for Tarzan, but after her jealous fiancé tries to shoot Tarzan and is foiled, she makes up her mind. She decides to stay in the jungle with Tarzan, as her family heads for home on the paddle boat.

•

When Glenn Morris was winning the decathlon at the Berlin Olympics in 1936, probably the farthest thought from his mind was that he would play Tarzan in a movie someday. But in 1937 producer Sol Lesser selected Morris and swimming champion Eleanor Holm (neither with any movie experience) to be Tarzan and Eleanor, the ape-man's love interest, in his production of *Tarzan's Revenge*.

Glenn Morris was born June 18, 1912, the summer that American Jim Thorpe was winning the decathlon in Stockholm; perhaps it was a good omen of things to come. After graduating from high school, Morris went on to All-American status as a member of the Colorado State College of Agriculture

Glenn Morris with Eleanor Holm (*Tarzan's Revenge*, 1938).

football team and starred in track and field. In the 1936 games in Nazi Germany (the Olympics that brought fame to American track star James "Jesse" Owens as well), Glenn Morris won the decathlon with a score of 7900, outdistancing his nearest opponent by 299 points. The winner of the Olympic decathlon is generally considered to be the greatest athlete in the world, competing in 10 track and field events over a two-day period. Morris also won the Sullivan Award in 1936, which was awarded by the Amateur Athletic Union (AAU) to "the athlete who by his or her performance, example or influence as an amateur has done the most during the year to advance the cause of sportsmanship."

Producer Sol Lesser went for sports fame in casting not only Morris as Tarzan, but Eleanor Holm, the 1932 Olym-

pic back-stroke champion, as Eleanor Reed. Holm had won the gold medal in Los Angeles in the 100-meter backstroke and was the favorite to win again as a member of the 1936 American team in Berlin. However, she was expelled from the U.S. team by Avery Brundage, president of the American Olympic Commission for breaking training during the nine-day ocean voyage to Germany; the charges were for "excessive drinking and shooting craps," which she did not deny. Holm later married impresario Billy Rose and resumed her swimming career in "Billy Rose's Aquacade," after her only film role in *Tarzan's Revenge*. Miss Holm did a fine job portraying Eleanor, the wise-cracking ingenue who dumps her creepy boyfriend for the man of her dreams— Tarzan.

"Lightweight vehicle" would

probably best describe this Tarzan picture. The action is kept to a minimum, and in truth it really showcases Holm's swimming talents and sharp wit, rather than Morris' heroics as Tarzan. Although most Tarzans were allotted minimal dialogue, poor Glenn was limited to only four words. In one scene with Holm, he introduces himself as "Tarzan," then learns her name, "Eleanor," and then repeats his own name, "Tarzan." Later, with a mouthful of grapes, he says, "Good!" Except for his Tarzan yell, that was the only dialogue Morris got to speak during the whole picture. For Glenn, it might as well have been a silent movie!

The cast also included a number of good character actors, most of whom were noted for comedy, rather than drama. The blustery but kindly George Barbier was Roger Reed (who wishes to trap rare animals for his local zoo), while Hedda Hopper (who spent most of her time sneezing from allergies) humorously played Reed's wife Penny. George Meeker was the spineless fiancé Nevin; Corbet Morris was Jigger, the family butler; and, of course, the chimpanzee provided plenty of further comedy cutups.

The standard villains included C. Henry Gordon as the sheik, who has his lecherous eyes on the divine Eleanor, and Joe Sawyer as Olaf, the crooked guide with a booze problem and a nervous twitch. Perhaps the best acting in the film came from John Lester Johnson, who effectively portrayed the head bearer, Koki. In his one important scene, Koki is being ordered by Olaf to get the bearers ready to cross the bridge where a trap is waiting for the Reed safari. The loyal and junglewise Koki says to Olaf, "No, you 'little boss.' White-man Reed, him 'Big Boss.' Me

tell him no go cross bridge. Ben Aley Beh, him no good." Before Koki can act on his plan, though, he is murdered by Olaf with a poisonous dart. This was a well-conceived and intensely acted scene; if the entire picture had been written and acted with the emotion that went into this short scene, it could have been a thriller.

Unfortunately, *Tarzan's Revenge* is relegated to B-status, and the best thing that can be said about it is that it's "a pleasant little film." Glenn Morris, who certainly had the physical attributes to play Tarzan, was limited to about 10 minutes of screen time; he fought only one lion (who escaped), had only one major battle (knocking several natives off a rope bridge), and his dialogue was so limited that we are unable to get inside the head of Tarzan and find out anything about him. The romance between Tarzan and Eleanor and their synchronized swimming scenes were nice touches.

After his Tarzan adventure, Morris appeared in *Hold That Coed* (1938) with John Barrymore and Joan Davis, but those two pictures were his only film credits. During World War II, he served as an officer in the U.S. Navy and was wounded in action in the Pacific. Later he worked as an insurance agent, among other jobs. Morris died at the Veterans Administration hospital in Palo Alto, California, on February 1, 1974, at age 61. Certainly, he will be remembered most clearly for winning the decathlon at the 1936 Olympics—a feat that was immortalized in the 1936 sports film biography *Decathlon Champion—The Story of Glenn Morris*. But he will also be remembered as the movies' ninth Tarzan for his only starring role in *Tarzan's Revenge*.

Herman Brix as Tarzan (*Tarzan and the Green Goddess,* **1938).**

Tarzan and the Green Goddess

Release date: March 1938; Burroughs/Tarzan Enterprises; running time: 72 minutes. *Directed by* Edward Kull; *produced by* Ashton Dearholt; *screenplay by* Charles F. Royal; *original story by* Edgar Rice Burroughs; *adaptation by* Charles F. Royal and Edwin H. Blum; *photography by* Ernest F. Smith and Edward Kull; *assistant director,* W.F. McGaugh; *art direction,* Charles Clague; *editing,* Thomas Neff; *special effects,* Ray Mercer and Howard Anderson; *recording,* Earl N. Crain.

Tarzan	Herman Brix
Ula Vale	Ula Holt
Major Martling	Frank Baker
Raglan	Don Castello
George	Lew Sargent
Simon Blade	Jack Mower

Deep in the jungles of Guatemala, the Mayan natives of the Dead City are outraged at the theft of their sacred Green Goddess, which was taken by Tarzan (Lord Greystoke) and the Martling expedition. Unknown to anyone, the sacred statue contains a code book with a secret formula for a new and dangerous explosive, powerful enough to blow whole cities sky-high.

The expedition members are ready to depart for home, when they are attacked by Raglan, who has doggedly followed them from the Dead City. Although Raglan steals the statue, Martling still has the document that contains critical information. "Without this document," says the major, "the thief dare not open it—he'd be blown to Adam by the secret explosive it contains."

Tarzan takes to the trees to follow Raglan, who doubles back and snatches the document from Martling. Later he sends a message to Simon Blade, his accomplice, to pick him up in a schooner at Puerto Barrios. Soon Raglan is on one boat and Tarzan and his friends are following on another boat. Back in the jungles, Tarzan rounds up Raglan's men and sends them packing. He then continues on the trail of their boss.

Tarzan joins up with Martling and George in the jungle and soon must rescue the code book, which has fallen into the river. The ape-man goes over the waterfall but manages to save the book. Ula Holt, who is really a secret agent, has taken the disguise of a native and is also trailing Raglan through the jungles. She pulls Tarzan from the river to return a favor when he saved her life earlier.

Back in the Dead City, Martling and George have been captured and are held hostage for the safe return of the Goddess, or they will die. Tarzan's trail also leads to the Dead City, where he is captured by a hundred warriors. Ula is the next to fall into the hands of the Mayan worshippers.

Ula bravely kills her guard and frees Tarzan from a death trap. The two comrades-in-arms assume the hooded robes of the Mayans as disguises. George is being tortured in the death chamber, but Tarzan breaks in and frees his compatriots. Together with Ula they hasten to leave the Dead City behind.

Back in civilization, Martling discovers that Raglan is in Mantique, so Tarzan starts through the jungle to head him off. When the two men finally meet face to face, Tarzan whips Raglan and again gains control of the Goddess. Soon Tarzan, Martling, George, and Ula are aboard a ship, seemingly headed for safety. But, unknown to them, the ship's captain is Blade, Raglan's partner.

Then Tarzan becomes suspicious. "The captain seems a little too friendly," says the ape-man (who keeps a sharp eye on the situation). Tarzan realizes they are in a trap when Ula spots Raglan on board ship. The captain and Raglan quarrel and struggle. With Raglan taking a bullet in his chest, and dying, justice is finally served.

Moments later a great hurricane hits the seas. Tarzan and Ula take cover with Martling and George in the ship's cabin. They are the sole survivors when Captain Blade and all his crew are drowned in the squall.

Back at Greystoke Manor in England, Tarzan and friends are decorated for saving the Green Goddess. Special agent Ula Vale decides to destroy the dangerous formula, and the threat is finally over.

•

Little can be said about *Tarzan and the Green Goddess* that hasn't already been said about *The New Adventures of Tarzan*. The film was produced by reediting the 12-chapter serial version of *New Adventures* (released in 1935) and adding some footage to compile a "new" feature of 72 minutes. The editing job was accomplished by Thomas Neff, the only change in the technical credits.

Again starring Herman Brix as Tarzan, "the amazing sequel to *The New*

Adventures of Tarzan" (as it was exploited) was simply the further adventures of Tarzan in Guatemala and the Martling expedition to find the Green Goddess. Ula Holt was again the secret agent seeking the formula for a dangerous explosive.

Although *The Green Goddess* did well overseas, it was mostly unappreciated in the United States. *Variety* (May 31, 1938) was particularly cold-blooded in its appraisal of the picture: "*Tarzan and the Green Goddess* falls way short of even the limited possibilities of an independent production ... seldom impresses or even proves exciting...."

An unusual flaw in the film was that the scenery and action involved lions, giraffes, rhinoceroses, and elephants, none of which are indigenous to Guatemala. The obvious inference was that Guatemalan and African wildlife are the same—a major mistake that offended the intelligence of mature moviegoers.

Edgar Rice Burroughs had originally signed a $50,000 loan to finance *The New Adventures of Tarzan* in 1934, and by 1937 Burroughs-Tarzan Enterprises was in serious debt. BTE was saved from further embarrassment (financial and otherwise) by Jesse Goldberg, who, in an agreement with the producers of *Tarzan and the Green Goddess*, was installed as the sole agent for distributing and exploiting the picture, on a 50/50 split. Goldberg did well enough with the picture (especially in England, where it was released in December 1937) to pay off the loan, and BTE was able to clear its books.

By 1939, however, BTE had closed its doors and was officially out of business. The ambitious dream of independently produced Tarzan pictures, featuring Tarzan as Lord Greystoke, the brainchild of author Edgar Rice Burroughs, was shattered.

Tarzan's Magic Fountain

Release date: January 1949; Sol Lesser/RKO; running time: 73 minutes. *Directed by* Lee Sholem; *produced by* Sol Lesser; *screenplay by* Curt Siodmak and Harry Chandlee, *based on the characters created by* Edgar Rice Burroughs; *photography,* Karl Strauss; *art direction,* McClure Capps; *film editor,* Merrill White; *production design,* Phil Paradise; *assistant director,* Bert Briskin; *sound technician,* Franklyn Hansen; *makeup artist,* Norbert Miles; *wardrobe supervisor,* Frank Beetson; *music by* Alexander Laszlo.

Tarzan	Lex Barker
Jane	Brenda Joyce
Gloria James	Evelyn Ankers
Trask	Albert Dekker
Dodd	Charles Drake
Douglas Jessup	Alan Napier
Vredak	Henry Kulky
Siko	Henry Brandon

Lex Barker with Evelyn Ankers and Alan Napier (*Tarzan's Magic Fountain*, 1949).

Pasco .... Ted Hecht
The High One .... David Bond

Also featuring Elmo Lincoln.

Cheeta, the chimp, brings Tarzan a cigarette case and a journal belonging to aviatrix Gloria James, who disappeared some 20 years before. The journal explains the mystery of her disappearance: Her plane had crashed in the African jungles. With Jane prodding his conscience, Tarzan decides to bring the journal to the settlement of Nyaga to be sent to her relatives. While in Nyaga, Tarzan discovers that Gloria James is the only person who can clear Douglas Jessup of a murder charge. Tarzan tells Dodd and Trask, who run the local aviation service, to bring the journal to England. Then he makes a surprising statement: "Tell her people that maybe Gloria James is not dead."

Tarzan is the only one who knows that Gloria has survived and lives with a lost race of people who never grow old, since they have a fountain of youth. When Tarzan goes to the Blue Valley, where the people live, Gloria agrees to return to England to clear Jessup, who already has served many years in prison.

When Tarzan brings Gloria back to the outside world, Jane wants to know how Gloria can still look so young, after so many years. "Soon she will not look so young. She will grow old quickly now," says Tarzan. Meanwhile, Trask and Dodd see the financial rewards in finding a fountain of youth and send Vredak to find the lost valley. Vredak finds the Blue Valley but is killed by a

Tarzan blasts the bully (Henry Kulky) (***Tarzan's Magic Fountain***, 1949).

flaming arrow. The guards are angry and speak out, "Only Tarzan knows the way here. He must be destroyed!"

Later, Gloria writes to Jane that not only has Douglas Jessup been freed, but that they have been married. She and Douglas soon return to Africa and hire Trask and Dodd to fly them into Tarzan's jungle. Gloria asks Tarzan to guide them back to the valley, so they can reclaim their lost youth, but the ape-man adamantly says no to protect the people who live there.

Jane stubbornly decides to lead Gloria and Douglas to the Blue Valley, with Trask and Dodd tagging along to offer their "protection" (naturally, the two profiteers hope to bring the valuable water from the fountain of youth back to civilization and make a fortune). When the party become trapped in a cavern that is rapidly filling with water, Tarzan arrives to save them. (He had been following along to safeguard them.)

That night, while everyone is asleep, Tarzan takes Gloria and Douglas on to the Blue Valley. Realizing they have been tricked, Trask and Dodd force Jane to lead them on. Most of the people of the Blue Valley welcome Tarzan and allow Gloria and Douglas to live among them again. Soon the Jessups have regained their lost youth. Others are not so happy that strangers have entered their valley and want to kill Tarzan to keep their secret safe.

Tarzan is kidnapped and taken to a cave where his kidnappers plot to burn out his eyes, so he can never lead anyone back again. Tarzan bursts his bonds with great strength and rolls a huge boulder onto the men who want to harm him. Meanwhile, Jane, Trask, and Dodd have reached the narrow rocky trail that leads into the valley. The two men are killed by flaming arrows, but Tarzan arrives just in time to save Jane. Tarzan's last enemies are crushed in an avalanche, and he and Jane return to their jungle home. The secret of the Blue Valley is safe forever from the outside world.

•

When Johnny Weissmuller finally "retired" from the role of Tarzan and went on to *Jungle Jim* pictures, it was necessary for producer Sol Lesser to find a new ape-man for the RKO Tarzan series. The man selected was 29-year-old Lex Barker, who was a worthy successor to the crown of the King of the Jungle. Barker was indeed cut out of a mold similar to his predecessor's, with a smoothly muscled physique and a handsome, masculine face. The *New York Times* liked the new Tarzan, as it noted in its February 7, 1949, review of *Tarzan's Magic Fountain:*

> Johnny Weissmuller finally having swung down from his jungle throne after sixteen years, RKO is launching its new muscle king, Lex Barker, in *Tarzan's Magic Fountain*, current[ly] at the Globe. And score one for Mr. Barker. A younger, more streamlined ape-man with a personable grin and a torso guaranteed to make any lion cringe, he seems just what the witchdoctor ordered for this tattered series.

Barker portrayed the role in a fashion similar to Weissmuller's, being a man of action and few words. However, the "Me—Tarzan! You—Jane!" stuff was long in the past, and this modern Tarzan was even occasionally conversant. Sol Lesser saw no reason to replace Brenda Joyce, who had been Jane in the previous four Tarzan films. This was the end of any continuity in the character of Jane, however, because Barker would have five different actresses portray Tarzan's mate in his five jungle adventures. In fact, Brenda Joyce retired from films after *Tarzan's Magic Fountain,* to devote her time to her husband and family.

After finishing high school, Lex

Barker (born Alexander Crichlow Barker, Jr.) had given Princeton University a shot, but found college unrewarding and thus joined a theatrical stock company to get his feet wet in the business. Lex then made his film debut with a small part in *Doll Face* (1945), a musical with Vivian Blaine and Perry Como. He built his career with secondary roles in a series of excellent films like *Crossfire* (1947), *The Farmer's Daughter* (1947), *Mr. Blandings Builds His Dream House* (1948), and *The Velvet Touch* (1948). After toiling at the bottom of credit lists for four years, Lex got his big break and succeeded to the role of Tarzan.

Tarzan's Magic Fountain was directed by Lee Sholem from a screenplay by Curt Siodmak and Harry Chandlee. The theme of greedy white men wasn't new, but the idea of a fountain of youth had not yet been used in a Tarzan picture and was a pleasant twist. By the standards set by the early Weissmuller Tarzan films, this one was a trifle short on action; all in all, however, it was an interesting debut for Barker as Tarzan. Lex looked majestic riding on the head of the elephant through the jungle, and when it was time for some rough stuff, he dispatched the bully Henry Kulky with some judo tricks Johnny Weissmuller had never known. As per custom in the Sol Lesser/RKO Tarzan series, the ape-man's jungle was the Arboretum, with city scenes filmed at the RKO Encino Ranch.

The classy supporting actress Evelyn Ankers convincingly portrayed the lost aviatrix Gloria James, and Alan Napier played her imprisoned husband-to-be Douglas Jessup. A familiar cast of villains included Albert Dekker as one of the all-time great evil-doers, Trask; Charles Drake as Dodd, Trask's cowardly partner (Drake was always playing "spineless" types); Henry Kulky as the bully Vredak (who wore a patch over one eye); and Henry Brandon and Ted Hecht as the Blue Valley guards who attempt to murder Tarzan. In a small role in one of his final pictures was Elmo Lincoln, who had portrayed the jungle man in the first Tarzan picture, *Tarzan of the Apes* (1918).

The next Tarzan picture for Lex Barker would be *Tarzan and the Slave Girl*, which would also feature a new Jane, Vanessa Brown. Incidentally, although Johnny Weissmuller was no longer Tarzan, a recording of his thundering war cry would still be used in many pictures—a subtle reminder of his 17 years as the King of the Jungle.

Tarzan and the Slave Girl

Release date: May 1950; Sol Lesser/RKO; running time: 74 minutes. *Directed by* Lee Sholem; *produced by* Sol Lesser; *screenplay by* Hans Jacoby and Arnold Belgard, *based on the characters created by* Edgar Rice Burroughs; *photography,* Russell Harlan; *production design,* Harry Horner; *production supervisor,* Glenn Cook; *assistant director,* James Casey; *sound technician,* John Tribby; *film editor,* Christian Nyby; *makeup artist,* Gustaf Norin; *wardrobe supervisor,* Frank Beetson; *music by* Paul Sawtell.

Tarzan	Lex Barker
Jane	Vanessa Brown
Neil	Robert Alda
Prince	Hurd Hatfield
Randini Doctor	Arthur Shields
Sengo	Tony Caruso
Lola	Denise Darcel
High Priest	Robert Warwick
Chief's son	Tito Renaldo
Moana	Mary Ellen Kay

Also featuring Shirley Ballard, Rosemary Bertrand, Gwen Caldwell, Martha Clemmons, Mona Knox, Josephine Parra, and Jackee Waldron *as the slave girls.*

Moana is kidnapped from her village, and Tarzan and Jane arrive to investigate. One of the kidnappers is captured by Tarzan, but he is sick with the plague and soon dies. Jane asks Tarzan to go to Randini to get the doctor before the plague spreads out of control.

Soon Tarzan returns with the doctor, nurse Lola, and their safari man, Neil; and many lives are saved with a new serum. Tarzan and company track the kidnappers of Moana, hoping to find the source of the infectious plague and end it. Meanwhile, Sengo, the kidnapper of many girls, whom he treats as slaves, has stolen two more victims in Tarzan's absence—Jane and Lola!

Deep in the jungles Tarzan's safari is threatened by the savage Wadis. They are barely able to escape over a dangerous bridge and suffer heavy losses. Neil is injured and tells Tarzan that he and Cheeta will trail behind and catch up. Meanwhile, Sengo and his enslaved girls

Lex Barker with Vanessa Brown (left) and Denise Darcel (right).

(including Jane and Lola) have arrived in Lyolia, where the people are preparing to entomb their king, who has died of the disease.

The people of Lyolia are also dying from the plague, and Sengo plans to repopulate Lyolia with the captured girls. The prince goes into shock and demands action when his son is infected with the plague. The high priest cannot cure the boy, so the prince (misguided by Sengo) orders him imprisoned. As Tarzan and the doctor approach Lyolia, the all-important medicine is lost along the trail.

Meanwhile, Jane rebuffs Sengo's advances, and she and Lola escape, hiding in the tomb of the king. Sengo sees where they are hiding and orders the crypt sealed; they are trapped. As Tarzan's safari enters Lyolia, Jane screams out. But did Tarzan hear her

muffled cry before the last block was lowered in place?

The doctor promises to cure the prince's son, but without the lost medicine, he is helpless. "Then there is no hope for my people or my son," moans the prince. By this time Tarzan has eluded Sengo's men and entered the tomb, where with brute strength he releases Jane and Lola from the crypt. Tarzan calls his elephants to the rescue with his mighty war cry and the tomb is opened.

Only Tarzan can save the high priest from execution in the lion pit, and he battles Sengo's men valiantly. Tarzan and Sengo fight to the death over the lion pit, and Tarzan wins the battle. By this time Neil has found the serum along the trail and entered the city. The doctor saves the young prince, and the rest of the people will recover as well.

With the crisis over, the new king

Two against Tarzan ... no problem for the ape-man! (*Tarzan and the Slave Girl,* 1950).

frees the slave girls and bids Tarzan, Jane, and everyone else safe passage back to their lands. The king wants Lola to stay on with him to be his queen, but Neil answers with an emphatic No!— Lola is his girl!

•

Lex Barker's second Tarzan picture, *Tarzan and the Slave Girl,* featured the debut of a new Jane, 22-year-old Vanessa Brown (born Smylla Brind), who took the place of Brenda Joyce, who had ably performed as Tarzan's mate in five pictures. A petite, dark-haired beauty, Brown had been a juvenile lead in entertaining films like *Margie* (1947) and *Mother Wore Tights* (1947) before graduating to leading ladies. Years after her role as Jane, she commented to Colin Briggs in an interview in the April 1986 issue of *Hollywood Studio Magazine:*

I looked better in that film than any other I made and received a lot of publicity as being the new Jane. However, I was then wrongly embarrassed about being in it as my intellectual friends considered themselves above escapism like the Tarzan films. Lex Barker was very nice but the director was rather inept and I drove to the studio each day with Denise Darcel, who had a lot of romantic problems she wanted to unload! The producer by then realized I wasn't interested in continuing with the role.

Indeed, this would be Brown's only Tarzan film, but she was effective and played the role with a bit of "spitfire." In one scene Lola (Denise Darcel) has her eye on Tarzan and wants to put in a claim; of course, Jane reacts jealously, and the two are soon fighting like cats. Eventually Lola and Jane become friends and have several scenes together before Tarzan saves them both, trapped in a sealed tomb.

Lee Sholem was directing his second (and last) Tarzan picture for Sol Lesser, from a story by Hans Jacoby and Arnold Belgard. Despite a pretty slim plot (there weren't even any greedy white men in this picture!), it's relatively entertaining. The Arboretum was the site of the jungle locations, with Iversen's Movie Ranch used for additional scenes.

The decent cast included Robert Alda as Lola's laid-back boyfriend Neil. Alda played the role with enough humor to be memorable. He even lets Cheeta finish off his bottle of schnapps, and then they're both stewed! The chief bad guy was Sengo, portrayed by Tony Caruso, whose jagged face was enhanced for this role by a nasty scar across his cheek. As was mentioned, Denise Darcel played Lola, the sexy nurse who swoons when she sees Tarzan; the doctor was Arthur

Shields; and the prince was Hurd Hatfield.

Lex Barker was once again handsome, athletic, and daring, playing Tarzan as sort of a combination of ape-man and Douglas Fairbanks, climbing castle walls, fighting guards with swords, tumbling, and racing his way from one escapade to the next. Naturally, Tarzan survived to fight again. Next time it would be *Tarzan's Peril*, with new mate Virginia Huston.

Edgar Rice Burroughs visited the set of *Tarzan and the Slave Girl* during filming and was photographed with Lex Barker, along with his grandson Mike Pierce and Vernell Coriell, founder-editor of *The Burroughs Bulletin* (a fan newsletter). ERB had often been a welcome spectator on the studio sets of Tarzan pictures, but this was his last visit, for he died on March 19, 1950.

Tarzan's Peril

Release date: March 1951; Sol Lesser/RKO; running time: 79 minutes. *Directed by* Byron Haskin; *produced by* Sol Lesser; *screenplay by* Samuel Newman and Francis Swann, with *additional dialogue by* John Cousins, *based on the characters created by* Edgar Rice Burroughs; *photography,* Karl Struss; *art direction,* John Meehan; *production supervisor,* Fred Ahern; *assistant director,* James Paisley; *sound technician,* Fred Lau; *film editor,* Jack Murray; *makeup artist,* Don Cash; *wardrobe supervisor,* Wesley Jeffries; *music by* Michel Michelet. **African Production Personnel:** *Direction,* Phil Brandon; *photography,* Jack Whitehead; *production assistants,* Tony Dean and Peter Colemore; *white hunter,* Buster Cooke.

Tarzan	Lex Barker
Jane	Virginia Huston
Radijeck	George Macready
Queen Melmendi	Dorothy Dandridge
Peters	Alan Napier
Trask	Douglas Fowley
Bulam	Frederick O'Neal
Andrews	Glenn Anders
Connors	Edward Ashley

Lex Barker with Virginia Huston (*Tarzan's Peril*, 1951).

Nessi .... James Moultrie
Barney .... Walter Kingsford

The beautiful Melmendi has been crowned the new queen of the Ashuba tribe, and the coronation is a gala event. Bulam, king of the Yorango tribe, sends his warriors with a chest full of treasure, but Melmendi rebuffs his proposal. "I'd rather be queen to a herd of swine than marry Bulam!" says the new queen haughtily. The African commissioners Peters and Connors view the ceremony and congratulate Melmendi on her ascension to the throne.

Later in the jungle, Peters and Connors discuss the possibilities that guns confiscated from one of the tribes were supplied by gunrunners, who always mean trouble. Tarzan had been responsible for imprisoning Radijeck, one of the most ruthless slavers and gunrunners. But before Radijeck could

be hanged, the villain escapes and the native drums send the message that echoes all the way to Tarzan's ears. Radijeck, in fact, is already up to his old tricks. He and partners Trask and Andrews are running 200 guns to be sold to Bulam, who would then rule the whole jungle.

Tarzan meets Peters and Connors in the jungle and passes the word that Radijeck has escaped. Everyone agrees that this is bad news. Later, bad news turns to murder as Radijeck guns down the commissioners in cold blood when they discover his gunrunning scheme in the jungle. Along the trail, the ruthless Radijeck causes an "accident" that breaks Andrews' leg and then abandons him to die in the jungle.

Back at the treehouse, Tarzan and

Tarzan in action (*Tarzan's Peril*, 1951).

Jane discover the commissioner's notebook (stolen by Cheeta) and plan to return it the next day to Randini. The river trip is eventful as Tarzan pulls Andrews from the river, who is alive but delirious with fever. With Andrews babbling on about Radijeck and the guns, Tarzan knows it is he who must stop the killer of commissioners Peters and Connors and bring him to justice.

Meanwhile, Radijeck has sold his guns to Bulam, who, in turn, attacks Melmendi's village and enslaves her people. The Ashuba queen refuses Bulam's demand to share his throne, and the whole village is at the mercy of Bulam and his armed warriors.

Traveling at night, Tarzan slips quietly into Melmendi's hut and frees her. With the help of the boy Nessi, Melmendi's people are all released and armed while Bulam's drunken warriors are in a stupor. Tarzan's war cry is the attack signal, and the battle is on as the ape-man duels Bulam to the death. Tarzan is fighting for his life, when Bulam is suddenly thrown to the ground and dies on his own knife blade.

Melmendi thanks Tarzan for saving her people and asks him to stay, but his mission is not finished. "Must find man who started all trouble—Radijeck!" says the determined ape-man. Deep in the jungles, Radijeck has murdered Trask (his last partner), but now Tarzan is rentlessly on his trail.

Radijeck makes it as far as Tarzan's treehouse, where Jane is waiting for her husband to return home. Instead it is Radijeck who bursts in and demands that she guide him safely out of the jungle or die. Jane refuses, and suddenly Tarzan swings in on a vine and knocks the evil Radijeck to his death far below. Tarzan kisses Jane passionately now that she is safely in his arms again.

•

One of the better of Lex Barker's five Tarzan pictures, *Tarzan's Peril* incorporated realistic native and jungle footage photographed in British East Africa. The film opens with jungle drums and genuine African natives dancing and chanting as part of the coronation of the new queen. You get the feeling right away that this will be a *real* Tarzan adventure, and for the most part there is no disappointment.

Lex Barker was part of the expedition that journeyed to Africa, with location sequences directed by Phil Brandon. The African scenery and wild animal footage, including a fascinating hippopotamus "ballet" with dozens of hippos "dancing" in the river and Tarzan swimming nearby, were photographed expertly by Jack Whitehead. White hunter Buster Cooke provided gun protection for the cast and crew. Additional location scenes were filmed in California (at the Arboretum and Iversen's Movie Ranch).

Tarzan's Peril was directed by Byron Haskin, who also directed some outstanding adventure and sci-fi films in his career, including *Treasure Island* (1950) and *War of the Worlds* (1953). Haskin's experience as a cameraman and special effects expert in the 1930s showed in this jungle adventure, with the African footage spliced in effectively and the genuine African drums and chants lending further realism. The swiftly moving story by Samuel Newman and Francis Swann of gunrunning and murder held water, weakened only by some occasionally shaky dialogue; fortunately the action overcame the few lapses.

The cast included a new Jane in the person of Virginia Huston, who made the most of limited screen time and kisses Tarzan passionately when he saves her at the end of the picture. One of the earliest films for the lovely Huston was *The Doolins of Oklahoma* (1949), with Randolph Scott and future Tarzan, Jock Mahoney. Among her other 1950s portrayals were the lead roles in *Woman from Headquarters* (1950), *The Racket* (1951), and *Sudden Fear* (1952).

There was no second-line casting when it came to the villain in *Tarzan's Peril;* marvelous character actor George Macready as Radijeck was truly Tarzan's peril and a cold, remorseless villain. Classy Alan Napier did a superb job as the commissioner Peters, and Dorothy Dandridge was well cast as the proud tribal queen, Melmendi.

Now firmly established as Tarzan, Lex Barker's next jungle adventure would be *Tarzan's Savage Fury*, and once again a new mate—the lovely Dorothy Hart—was selected for the apeman to romance.

Tarzan's Savage Fury

Release date: April 1952; Sol Lesser/RKO; running time: 80 minutes. *Directed by* Cyril Endfield; *produced by* Sol Lesser; *screenplay by* Cyril Hume, Hans Jacoby, and Shirley White, *based on the characters created by* Edgar Rice Burroughs; *photography by* Karl Struss; *art direction,* Walter Keller; *production supervisor,* Glen Cook; *assistant director,* Mack V. Wright; *sound technician,* Don McKay; *film editor,* Frank Sullivan; *makeup artist,* Norbert Miles; *wardrobe supervisor,* Wesley Jeffries; *music by* Paul Sawtell.

Lex Barker with Dorothy Hart (*Tarzan's Savage Fury*, 1952).

Tarzan	Lex Barker
Jane	Dorothy Hart
Edwards	Patric Knowles
Rokov	Charles Korvin
Joey	Tommy Carlton

Tarzan's cousin Oliver (the current Lord Greystoke) is hunting in Africa with Rokov as his white hunter. Rokov murders Greystoke and has Edwards assume his identity, in a scheme to steal a fortune in diamonds that only Tarzan knows where to find.

Elsewhere in the jungle, Tarzan saves an orphan boy, Joey, who is being used as bait for hungry crocodiles, and orders the natives to stop using boys as croc bait. Tarzan decides to bring Joey home to Jane, who is happy to have a "son" in the family. Joey is afraid of lions because his parents were killed by them, but Tarzan teaches the boy to be the master of the beasts and not to fear them.

With Edwards assuming Greystoke's identity, Rokov's safari locates the jungle couple, and Jane is fooled by the deception. "Tarzan, this is your cousin Oliver. He's come all the way from England to see you," says Jane. The visitors explain that they wish to travel to the Waziri country to find the diamonds mentioned in Lord Greystoke's (Tarzan's father's) diary, falsely claiming that England needs the valuable gems for its national security.

At Jane's request, Tarzan reluctantly agrees to guide "Oliver" and Rokov to

Lex Barker with Tommy Carlton (*Tarzan's Savage Fury*, 1952).

the dangerous Waziri country. Indeed, the journey is treacherous: First a hippo attack is provoked by Rokov's itchy trigger finger and then their water supply runs out in the desert. As they near the Waziri land, they are attacked by cannibals. "Oliver" is wounded by an arrow, and Tarzan fights valiantly. Suddenly the brave Waziri appear, and the cannibals retreat with fear in their hearts.

In the Waziri village, the witch doctor wants to kill the intruders. Tarzan explains that he came to the Waziri land many times as a boy with his father. The chief is influenced by an old man who remembers Tarzan. They must find his father's book as proof of their friendship. Meanwhile, Jane has discovered that Edwards is not Greystoke and that he and Rokov plan to steal the diamonds. "You're not Oliver—who are you? I've been a fool to be so taken in," cries an angry Jane. "Tarzan will kill you!"

Rokov not only steals the jewels but murders the witch doctor. Jane is to be sacrificed as retribution for the men's escape. Joey braves the jungle's dangers to find Tarzan, who has found his father's book. The greedy Rokov murders Edwards and then ambushes Tarzan on his return, leaving him for dead. After facing his worst fear—the lion—Joey watches as Tarzan uses superhuman strength to lift a great rock from his back. The boy warns Tarzan of Rokov's treachery, as well as Jane's impending execution.

The ape-man corners Rokov in the jungle, and they fight to the death. Tarzan throws Rokov from the ledge to the lion pit below and races to save Jane. His war cry halts her sacrifice. With the return of the diamonds all is forgiven. The Waziri chief is so impressed by Tarzan and his father's "good book" that he offers Tarzan half his diamonds.

•

One of the most beautiful and physically appropriate actresses in the role of Jane was 28-year-old Dorothy Hart, who costarred with Lex Barker in *Tarzan's Savage Fury*. The long-haired redhead had the right combination of beauty and the necessary "grit" to accompany Tarzan on the dangerous trek to the Waziri land in search of the diamonds. There was some excellent chemistry between Hart and Barker; the playful scenes and serious encounters were more than believable.

Hart had made her film debut in the lighthearted musical fantasy *Down to Earth* (1947) as the Rita Hayworth lookalike, after working as one of New York's most glamorous cover girl models in the 1940s. Dorothy proved herself beyond a shadow of a doubt as a dramatic actress in Mark Hellinger's classic crime thriller *The Naked City* (1948) but was limited to mostly routine programmers for most of her movie career. Later in life she became a spokesperson for the United Nations, proving that she was a woman with depth of character as well as unusual beauty.

Directing *Tarzan's Savage Fury* was Cy Endfield, who later in his career would write the scenario and direct the superb African historical drama *Zulu* (1964), as well as script its excellent prequel, *Zulu Dawn* (1979). Endfield kept the action moving briskly in this Tarzan adventure with the imaginative scenario.

For the scriptwriter, producer Sol Lesser reached back into the past for a screenwriter with superlative credentials: Cyril Hume, who had written the original MGM classic *Tarzan, the Ape Man* (1932), as well as the classic *Tarzan Finds a Son!* (1939). Hume, in collaboration with Hans Jacoby and Shirley White, borrowed important themes from his previous Tarzan scripts and reworked them into his story.

Hume started with the often-used premise of greedy white men seeking Tarzan's help to reach the African interior; of course, Tarzan is opposed to the request, knowing the avaricious ways of the white man, but succumbs to pressure from Jane, who was usually gullible when it came to judging people. Then with the basic plot structure in place, the character of Joey (an orphan boy rescued by Tarzan) was intertwined into the story. There's also a Greystoke in the plot (murdered early by Rokov); a somewhat different version of Tarzan's early years in being raised in the jungle by apes; and the fabled Waziri tribe, all taken, of course, from the novels of Edgar Rice Burroughs.

The cut-and-splice department made good use of the African wildlife footage that had been photographed in British East Africa for the previous Tarzan picture, *Tarzan's Peril*, and reused the native drums and chants for backgrounds. A little trick photography (rear projection) was used to film Lex Barker staring down two cantankerous rhinoceroses and scenes with Tarzan and Joey confronting lions face to face. The Ar-

boretum once again served as the jungle filming location, with additional scenes shot at the Olancha sand dunes and Iversen's Movie Ranch.

The number one villain, Rokov, was portrayed by Charles Korvin as a despicable sort who specialized in cold-blooded murder and perpetually spoke out of both sides of his mouth. Assisting him in his treacheries was Patric Knowles as the backboneless Edwards, who had the guts to be a villain only with Rokov's prodding.

Rounding out the lead characters was Tommy Carlton as Joey, who was a worthy choice to be the "son" of Tarzan. Tommy was athletic and acrobatic (walking on his hands and turning cartwheels, vine swinging, and swimming), as well as an outgoing and dandy young actor.

This is perhaps the most entertaining of the Lex Barker Tarzan pictures. Unfortunately, it was the only Tarzan picture for Hart as Jane, and the character of Joey would not be brought back for the next adventure. *Tarzan and the She-Devil* would be Lex Barker's final Tarzan role, and the new Jane would be Joyce MacKenzie.

Tarzan and the She-Devil

Release date: June 1953; Sol Lesser/RKO; running time: 76 minutes. *Directed by* Kurt Neumann; *produced by* Sol Lesser; *screenplay by* Karl Kamb and Carroll Young, *based on the characters created by* Edgar Rice Burroughs; *associate producer,* Lloyd Richards; *photography,* Karl Struss; *art direction,* Carroll Clark; *assistant director,* Emmett Emerson; *sound technician,* Jean L. Speak; *film editor,* Leon Barsha; *makeup artist,* Gustaf M. Norin; *wardrobe supervisor,* Wesley Jeffries; *music editor,* Audrey Granville; *music by* Paul Sawtell.

Tarzan	Lex Barker
Jane	Joyce MacKenzie
Vargo	Raymond Burr
Lyra	Monique Van Vooren

Fidel .... Tom Conway
M'Tara .... Henry Brandon
Lavar .... Michael Grainger
Maka .... Robert Bice
Selim .... Mike Ross

Greedy ivory hunters Vargo and Lavar have discovered a huge herd of over 100 bull elephants. They see a great profit in the ivory and have only two obstacles—their female employer, Lyra, and the King of the Jungle, Tarzan.

Meanwhile in the city of Dagar, Vargo reports the location of the great herd to Lyra. They decide to capture their ivory bearers from the Lykopo tribe, who are friends of Tarzan. After the raid, the women of the tribe come to Tarzan crying, asking for his help (which he vows to give). Back in Dagar, Lyra asks Vargo, "What about the ape-man?" Vargo smugly replies, "I almost forgot about him. He just didn't seem to be around."

But Tarzan is indeed around, and now he is angry. Under cover of darkness, Tarzan releases the Lykopo men and throws all the rifles into a well. The ape-man battles a dozen men for his own freedom, then pauses long enough to shoot a defiant look at Lyra that seems to say, "In Tarzan's jungle, you cannot hope to succeed with evil."

Lyra and Vargo plan to attack the Lykopo village to capture more bearers and then trap Tarzan when he comes to their aid. Fidel is then assigned to kidnap Jane, to hold her as insurance that Tarzan will call the elephants for them to slaughter. When Tarzan hears gunfire at the Lykopo village, he heads to their rescue. Vargo shoots the ape-man out of the trees. Tarzan falls unconscious to the ground and is captured.

Meanwhile, Fidel has failed to kidnap Jane, who stumbles into the jungle dazed from a fall. Back in their camp, Tarzan hears Fidel's story of an "accident" and breaks free, racing to his jungle home. It is burned to the ground, and he believes that his beloved Jane is dead.

Tarzan's will to fight is gone, and he is easily recaptured by Vargo. He sits in prison and refuses to help the villains, despite Vargo's sharp whip. Unknown to Tarzan, Jane is braving the dangers of the jungle trying to get to her mate, and finally collapses with exhaustion. Tantor, the elephant, picks up Jane and takes her to the Lykopo people, who administer jungle medicine to the feverish woman.

The elephant hunt is about to start, with Tarzan and the Lykopo men in chains. Fidel is unwelcome in the camp after he stampedes the elephants with his carelessness. He reports back to Lyra that Vargo and Lavar are plotting against her.

Jane has now recovered and is searching again for Tarzan, but it is Lyra and Fidel who find her in the jungle. "She wants to see Tarzan," says Lyra with a smirk. "We'll take her there," knowing that Tarzan is imprisoned by Vargo.

Lyra arrives at the camp and orders that Vargo and Lavar be chained for their disloyalty. When Tarzan sees Jane is alive, he can hardly believe his eyes! Lyra warns Tarzan that if he doesn't call all the elephants into the stockade, she will have Jane killed.

With Tarzan's mighty yell, the elephants come, but Tarzan quickly closes the stockade. Tarzan rescues Jane as the stampeding elephants crush everything in sight, including Vargo and the "she-devil" Lyra. Tarzan has saved his elephant friends from slaughter and the Lykopo people as well.

Tarzan with the "she-devil" . . . Monique Van Vooren (*Tarzan and the She-Devil*, 1953).

Tarzan and the evil Vargo ... Raymond Burr (*Tarzan and the She-Devil*, 1953).

•

The final Lex Barker Tarzan picture was *Tarzan and the She-Devil*, with the "she-devil" of the title portrayed diabolically by Monique Van Vooren. The film also featured a new Jane, 29-year-old Joyce MacKenzie, who had made her debut in the Orson Welles' drama *Tomorrow Is Forever* (1946). Joyce was well suited to play Jane, but with Barker bowing out of the series, this was her only opportunity to showcase her considerable talents and beauty.

One of the most recognizable "heavies" of the late 1940s through the mid–1950s was Raymond Burr, who definitely had the build, as well as the powerful voice and dark, menacing looks to play a villain. Burr had built a pretty good Hollywood career playing tough guys and murderers in films like the Hitchcock classic *Rear Window* (1954), the hilarious Martin and Lewis caper *You're Never Too Young* (1955), and many other films. It seemed unlikely at the time that Burr could possibly be cast as an heroic leading man, but, of course, he would eventually gain such billing on television as the brilliant lawyer in Erle Stanley Gardner's "Perry Mason."

Lex Barker as Tarzan had to deal not only with the formidable Burr as Vargo, but with Monique Van Vooren as Lyra, the cold-blooded profiteer who was willing to slaughter elephants and enslave men simply for money. Her coconspirator, Fidel, was played by Tom Conway, who had been a leading man in the 1940s in the enjoyable *The Falcon's Brother* (1942), which had several equally popular sequels. Conway also played a villain in *Tarzan's Secret Treasure* (1941), and once again he was a threat to the ape-man.

To direct the picture, Sol Lesser brought in Kurt Neumann, who had directed two of the better Weissmuller RKO Tarzan adventures, *Tarzan and the Amazons* (1945) and *Tarzan and the Leopard Woman* (1946). Although the story by Karl Kamb and Carroll Young plods along at times, it's pretty typical of the Lex Barker films, enjoyable as long as you don't expect too much or take them too seriously. The Arboretum was the location of Tarzan's jungle, while city scenes were shot at the RKO Encino Ranch. The exciting elephant photography and the realistic stampede were "borrowed" from the 1934 jungle adventure *Wild Cargo*.

Lex Barker did well enough in the role of Tarzan to be remembered favorably, and he probably could have gone on with the Tarzan pictures indefinitely had he not tired of the role. But Barker was indeed ready to expand his acting horizons and next went on to a series of B-westerns, adventure films, and dramas. By the 1960s Lex was doing most of his acting in foreign-produced films, and in 1966 he won Germany's Bambi Award for Best Foreign Actor. In the United States, though, the former Tarzan never really received star status as an actor, and his personal life was often tumultuous; he was married five times, most notably to actresses Arlene Dahl and Lana Turner. Lex Barker died on April 11, 1973, at age 53. After a 25-year career in motion pictures, he is best remembered as the 10th actor to portray Tarzan in the movies.

Tarzan's Hidden Jungle

Release date: February 1955; Sol Lesser/RKO; running time: 73 minutes. *Directed by* Harold Schuster; *produced by* Sol Lesser; *screenplay by* William Lively, *based on the characters created by* Edgar Rice Burroughs; *photography,* William Whitley; *art director,* William Flannery; *assistant director,* Harry Templeton; *sound technician,* Jean L. Speak; *film editor,* Leon Barsha; *makeup artist,* Jack Byron; *wardrobe supervisor,* Henry West; *set continuity,* Winifred K. Thackery; *music by* Paul Sawtell.

Tarzan	Gordon Scott
Jill Hardy	Vera Miles
Dr. Celliers	Peter Van Eyck
Sukulu chief	Rex Ingram
Burger	Jack Elam
DeGroot	Charles Fredericks
Witch doctor	Jester Hairston
Reeves	Richard Reeves
Johnson	Don Beddoe
Malenki	Ike Jones
Suma	Madie Norman

Tarzan is angry when white hunters, DeGroot, Reeves, Burger, and Johnson, invade his jungle, killing the wild beasts wantonly. The ape-man attacks the native beaters and sends a message that the hunters will have trouble from Tarzan. Meanwhile, dissatisfied with the kill, DeGroot sends Reeves across the river to scout for game. The beaters warn that Sukululand is "taboo." The Sukulu treat animals as sacred, and anyone who kills them must die. After killing an elephant in Sukululand, Reeves is indeed put to death for breaking their laws. Back in camp, Burger must report the meager kill to Johnson, who is financing the expedition. Johnson demands that the quotas for ivory, hides, and animal fat be met within 10 days, or else.

Elsewhere in the jungle, Tarzan has been caring for a young elephant, wounded by the hunters. He demands white man's medicine for the elephant from jungle intruders Burger and DeGroot and is advised to go to the hospital on the far side of the jungle. Tarzan takes their guns and sends them packing and then disappears into the trees above.

Arriving at the hospital, Tarzan is impressed by Jill Hardy, the lovely nurse who is swimming in the river. Miss Hardy is the assistant to Dr. Celliers, a United Nations doctor who regularly visits Sukululand, where he is trusted by the natives. The doctor removes the bullet from the elephant, and in turn Celliers asks Tarzan for some of the jungle medicine used on the young pachyderm to stop the bleeding. One of Dr. Celliers' patients is dying, so Tarzan takes to the jungle to get his medicine.

Meanwhile, Burger and DeGroot arrive at the hospital and ingratiate themselves, posing as U.N. photographers. With the doctor leaving for Sukululand, they tag along, planning to round up the animals for the kill. Shortly after they leave, Jill discovers the truth and sets out in her station wagon to warn Dr. Celliers that he's in evil company.

Gordon Scott with future wife, Vera Miles (*Tarzan's Hidden Jungle*, 1955).

Jill's car breaks down in the jungle, and soon she is hopelessly lost. Tarzan arrives just in time to save her from certain death in the jaws of a python. Jill explains the danger Dr. Celliers is in, and Tarzan recognizes the description of Burger and DeGroot. The ruthless hunters have already started driving the animals toward the river, where their beaters are waiting with guns to slaughter them.

When Tarzan and Jill arrive at the Sukulu village, the witch doctor demands death for the intruders. The chief agrees: "When the sun sets and shadow of mountain touches the knife, you shall die. This is your punishment for bringing those into our land who are driving away our animals."

Tarzan escapes into the jungle and calls all the animals back across the river to the safety of Sukululand. Burger and

DeGroot are justifiably killed in the stampede. At the village, the witch doctor has Jill and Celliers thrown into a lion pit, but Tarzan leaps in and shouts, "Umgawa! Umgawa!" and drives the beasts back at their master's command.

The chief once again speaks the truth: "Tarzan call all animals back. Tarzan friend of Sukulu!" The ape-man bids good-bye to Jill and Dr. Celliers and once again disappears into the lofty treetops, with his thundering cry echoing in the distance.

•

The year 1955 brought a new Tarzan actor to the screen in the muscular form of Gordon Scott, who was making his motion picture debut. Born Gordon M. Werschkul in Portland, Oregon, Scott was discovered by a vacationing Hollywood agent at the Sahara Hotel

Tarzan shows off his strength (*Tarzan's Hidden Jungle*, 1955).

in Las Vegas, where he was working as a lifeguard.

A phone call to Sol Lesser halted the interviews in progress for a new apeman, and a screen test was ordered, which Gordon passed with flying colors. Scott had been a drill sergeant during a two-year stint in the army, later worked as a fireman, and gave the cowboy's life a whirl on his brother's ranch in Oregon. Suddenly at age 27, he was a movie actor, soon to star in *Tarzan's Hidden Jungle*.

With a bodybuilder's physique, but not musclebound, the handsome Scott indeed looked like the right choice for the new Tarzan. He turned out to be a decent actor, with naturally quick body movements and athletic skills and a masculine, commanding voice. Scott also had a refreshing viewpoint about how the King of the Jungle should be portrayed as was related in a press

release: "I'm glad I got the role," admitted the actor. "But I just don't want Tarzan turned into a sissy!" Hardly a chance of that happening with the macho Gordon Scott starring as Tarzan for the next half-dozen years.

Although there was no Jane in *Tarzan's Hidden Jungle*, one of the most talented and beautiful female leads in any Tarzan picture was Vera Miles, as nurse Jill Hardy. Miles had made her film debut in *For Men Only* (1952) and then went on to a long career as a Hollywood leading lady. Some of her most important films included the Hitchcock thrillers *The Wrong Man* (1957) and *Psycho* (1960) and two of John Wayne's memorable westerns, *The Searchers* (1956) and *The Man Who Shot Liberty Valance* (1962).

Although Tarzan got an eyeful of Jill Hardy swimming in the river, there was no romantic involvement between him and the lovely nurse. However, Gordon Scott, the man, did marry his lovely costar Vera Miles after the picture was completed.

Lanky, bug-eyed Jack Elam made a good living playing slimy types in movies and was plenty slimy in *Tarzan's Hidden Jungle.* Solid character actor Peter Van Eyck did a nice job as the doctor who is a friend and savior to the natives. Rex Ingram, who appeared in the first silent Tarzan picture, *Tarzan of the Apes* (1918), was effectively cast as the Sukulu chief. A new chimpanzee for Tarzan was played by "Zippy," who had been a regular from the *Howdy Doody* children's television show.

Despite the dynamic new Tarzan, Gordon Scott, and the talented leading lady, Vera Miles, little effort was made to produce a jungle classic; certainly there was nothing new in the unimaginative story written by William Lively. Unfortunately, *Tarzan's Hidden Jungle* had a low budget and was poorly promoted by RKO, which was in the throes of near-extinction.

Sol Lesser continued to reuse jungle and wild animal scenes shot for previous Tarzan pictures, getting maximum mileage from stock footage. He was also still using the less expensive process of black and white photography, while other studios were producing non–Tarzan jungle classics in brilliant Technicolor. *Tarzan's Hidden Jungle* was the 12th and final Tarzan picture for RKO distribution and was one of the last films released by the dying studio, which ceased production of motion pictures around the time this final Tarzan adventure was released.

The first Technicolor Tarzan picture was next for Gordon Scott, *Tarzan and the Lost Safari,* which featured African location photography. The new adventure would be distributed by MGM, which had been out of the Tarzan picture business since 1942 (except for rereleases of old Weissmuller films).

Tarzan and the Lost Safari

Release date: March 1957; Sol Lesser/Metro-Goldwyn-Mayer; running time: 84 minutes; filmed in Technicolor. *Directed by* Bruce Humberstone; *presented by* Sol Lesser; *executive producer,* N. Peter Rathvon; *produced by* John Croydon; *screenplay by* Montgomery Pittman and Lillie Hayward, *based on the characters created by* Edgar Rice Burroughs; *photography,* C.R. Pennington-Richards; *African photography,* Miki Carter; *art director,* Geoffrey Drake; *production designer,* Paul Shuriff; *production manager,* C.R. Foster-Kemp; *assistant director,* F. Stark; *recording director,* Harold King; *film editor,* Bill Lewthwaite; *special effects,* T. Howard and O. Blackwell; *makeup,* L.V. Clark; *music composed by* Clifton Parker; *music director,* Louis Levy.

Tarzan	Gordon Scott
Diana Penrod	Betta St. John
"Tusker" Hawkins	Robert Beatty
Gamage Dean	Yolande Donlan
"Doodles" Fletcher	Wilfrid Hyde White
Dick Penrod	Peter Arne
Carl Kraski	George Coulouris
Chief Ogonooro	Orlando Martins

Gordon Scott with Yolande Donlan and Robert Beatty (*Tarzan and the Lost Safari,* 1957).

Tarzan notices a "sky-bird" in the African skies, which is forced to make a crash landing after hitting a flock of flamingoes. Rushing to the scene of the crash, Tarzan carries the passengers one by one to safety, just before the plane slides off a cliff and into a gorge far below. The stranded passengers include wealthy socialites Diana Penrod and her husband, Dick, the pilot; "Doodles" Fletcher, a writer; an attractive blonde, Gamage Dean; and old friend, Carl Kraski.

Moments after their rescue, Diana is kidnapped by Opar natives. Battling a dozen men, Tarzan is overcome and tossed in the river. Uninjured, he heads to the Opar village, knowing that the chief will sacrifice Diana to the Oparian gods. Meanwhile, the white hunter "Tusker" Hawkins makes a deal with the Opar men to keep the unconscious Diana. He has a better use for her than

sacrifice. Tarzan meets Hawkins and Diana in the jungle, and together they plan to guide the stranded party to the coast.

They must travel through the dangerous Opar country, and Tarzan distrusts Hawkins' intentions. "I can get 'em through, all right," says Hawkins with a smirk. Tarzan eyes Hawkins suspiciously and responds, "I wonder—Hawkins too sure." Indeed, Hawkins is plotting with the Opar men to deliver the stranded members of the safari for sacrifice to Chief Ogonooro (except for Diana, whom he has special plans for). Hawkins' prize for his traitorous actions is the fabulous Tusks of Opar, a fortune in ivory.

The safari moves out, and the bad blood grows between Tarzan and Hawkins, while the Opar drums continue their ominous beat. That night at camp Hawkins relates his loneliness to Diana

Gordon Scott with Betta St. John (*Tarzan and the Lost Safari*, 1957).

(who's having husband problems). He claims he's going to be rich when he finds the Tusks of Opar. The black-hearted white hunter makes a pass at Diana to see if she's interested in his proposition—she's not.

Tarzan knows that the Opar men are watching them from the jungle and suspects a trap. Hawkins claims that they can escape through a gorge ahead, but it is blocked. Tarzan goes on his own to find another escape route. In Tarzan's absence the trap closes as the Opar men take Diana and the rest of the safari through a mountain pass to their village. Later, Tarzan follows and must battle his way through guards waiting to take his life. Instead, Tarzan takes their lives.

At the Opar camp, a savage tribal ceremony is taking place in which the white intruders arc to be sacrificed to the gods. But Tarzan beats out a message on the Opar drums that says Hawkins is a traitor and plans to set their village on fire. Cheeta, under Tarzan's orders, has set the village on fire, using Doodles' cigarette lighter.

In the ensuing confusion, Tarzan and friends escape across a rickety rope bridge, which is also on fire. Tarzan is the last to cross, just behind Hawkins, who is now running for his life. The burning bridge collapses, and the air is thick with Oparian arrows. Tarzan manages to climb to safety as Hawkins falls to his death. Tarzan is now able to lead them back to civilization, and the adversity has brought Diana and Dick back together.

•

With a temporary distribution deal from MGM, producer Sol Lesser was able to spend enough money to inject some much-needed life into the Tarzan series. *Tarzan and the Lost Safari* was photographed in Technicolor, including the location photography by cameraman Miki Carter.

With Gordon Scott now able to perform his Tarzan heroics in color, a whole new dimension was added to the legend of the ape-man. Indeed, black-and-white photography was now a thing of the past, and all future Tarzan pictures would be filmed in color. The African scenery was, of course, the greatest benefactor of the color photography, and the many-colored hues of the flora and fauna now gained life on the screen. Photographer Miki Carter brought a small expedition to Africa to photograph wild animals and jungle backgrounds. Scott was on hand for part of the location production in Kenya and rode on a two-ton rhinoceros for some still camera shots. Miki Carter noted that the white hunters had their big guns trained in case the two powerful beasts got out of hand (a second rhino was right next to the one Gordon rode on).

Scott was proving himself to be a capable Tarzan, performing most of his stunts himself, including playing tug-of-war with Numa, the lion. In an October 1960 interview with Camille "Caz" Cazedessus, Jr., Scott talked about an incident with the "big cat" he worked with:

> In the second picture I made, we used a lion that was raised in captivity by this woman in Tanganyika, and it was a "big baby." It weighed 500 pounds and had a big black mane. I worked with this animal for about a month and I could do almost anything with it. But one day he wasn't feeling too good and as he walked by me I reached out to pat him and he turned around and ripped my pants off!

Scott kept himself in impeccable condition with a rigorous daily workout, and the battles with natives were child's play for him. His ape-man was less of a loner than previous Tarzans and a little more willing to open up to outsiders. In one scene Tarzan recounts his background, telling the tale of his parents' being killed when he was a child and his being raised by apes. At this point, the writers made a slight faux pas: Tarzan calls his ape mother "Kerchak." In Edgar Rice Burroughs' novels, Kerchak was the great ape that Tarzan fought to the death; Tarzan's ape mother was called Kala.

Although there was no Jane for Tarzan to play with, Betta St. John was available for the ape-man to frolic with in the river and to save from natives and hungry crocodiles. St. John was cast as Diana Penrod, a spoiled socialite whose marriage to her husband Dick is on the rocks. (However, after toughing it out in the jungles, Diana and Dick realized they still loved each other.) St. John (born Betty Streidler) had made her debut with a lead role in the Cary Grant comedy *Dream Wife* (1953) and now found herself stranded in Africa. She would return to Africa in a featured role with Gordon Scott in *Tarzan, the Magnificent* in 1960.

The story by Montgomery Pittman and Lillie Hayward had a reasonable premise, with Tarzan forced to lead a stranded group of people to safety after their plane crashes in Africa. The weakest link in the story was the inclusion of the villain "Tusker" Hawkins (ably portrayed by Robert Beatty), who lusts after Diana as much as he does the fabled Tusks of Opar. Hawkins never really had a prayer with Diana, and it is unbelievable that the fierce Oparian warriors would turn over their sacred ivory to a cowardly traitor like him. Brushing this aside, the story is enjoyable and well acted by supporting players, including Wilfred Hyde White as Doodles (a foil for Cheeta); Yolande Donlan as the dumb blonde, Gamage Dean (who also has an eye for the virile Tarzan); and Peter Arne as the foolish husband, Dick

Penrod (foolish for not realizing he had a good woman until it was almost too late).

Directing was Bruce Humberstone (who was in his realm directing action pictures). The story moves briskly along without too many unbelievable detours.

A musical score by Clifton Parker, directed by Louis Levy, added to a thrilling jungle adventure. Scott would soon return in *Tarzan's Fight for Life* and for once he would have a Jane in his life, portrayed by Eve Brent.

Tarzan's Fight for Life

Release date: July 1958; Sol Lesser/Metro-Goldwyn-Mayer; running time: 86 minutes; filmed in Metrocolor. *Directed by* Bruce Humberstone; *produced by* Sol Lesser; *screenplay by* Thomas Hal Phillips, *based on the characters created by* Edgar Rice Burroughs; *photography,* William Snyder; *African photography,* Miki Carter; *art director,* Ernst Fegte; *production supervisor,* Fred Ahern; *film editor,* Aaron Stell; *assistant director,* William Forsyth; *music editor,* Alfred Perry; *sound technician,* Jean L. Speak; *sound editor,* Henry Adams; *script supervisor,* Cora Palmatier; *makeup,* Gustaf Norin; *music by* Ernest Gold.

Tarzan	Gordon Scott
Jane	Eve Brent
Tantu	Rickie Sorensen
Anne Sturdy	Jil Jarmyn
Futa	James Edwards
Dr. Sturdy	Carl Benton Reid
Dr. Ken Warwick	Harry Lauter
Ramo	Woody Strode
High counselor	Roy Glenn

At the hospital at Randini, Dr. Sturdy and his daughter Anne fight an uphill battle. The natives they want to help are influenced by the evil witch doctor Futa, who warns them to stay away from the white doctor. Even the native helpers desert the doctor when they fall under the spell of Futa and his henchman, Ramo.

When Anne goes to meet Dr. Ken Warwick (her fiancé), she and Ken are attacked in the jungle by the Nagasu warriors of Futa. Suddenly Tarzan appears with his thundering war cry and his ferocious assault, and the natives scatter like thieves. Futa is behind the

attack because he is jealous of the hospital doctors. The old chief has died, and the chief's son is too young to rule, so Futa is the tribe's most powerful influence. Dr. Sturdy asks Tarzan to reason with Futa, who used to be Tarzan's friend, although now they are enemies. At the village, Tarzan saves a woman, Toshina, who has been attacked by a crocodile, and against Futa's orders the ape-man takes the wounded Toshina to the hospital.

Dr. Sturdy must amputate the woman's leg. He feels he must save her life or he will lose his dwindling support from the natives. Meanwhile, Tarzan

Gordon Scott with Woody Strode and James Edwards (*Tarzan's Fight for Life*, 1958).

returns to his jungle home to see Jane and his adopted son, Tantu. There is much rejoicing when Tarzan returns home. Later, Tarzan is worried because Jane is suffering from abdominal pains. "I do not worry about things that come and go," says Tarzan. "There will be birds and animals. But there will only be one Jane."

That evening Tarzan's fears are confirmed, and he must rush Jane to the hospital for an appendectomy. Tarzan and Tantu paddle the rivers with urgency, knowing Jane's life is in the balance. At the hospital Jane's operation is successful, but the bad news is that Toshina has died. The medicine man orders Toshina's grieving husband Molo, now under Futa's hypnotic spell, to murder Jane as retribution. "Tarzan's woman must die!" shouts the fanatical Futa.

Meanwhile, the young chief of the Nagasu is dying of the same fever that killed his father. Futa sends Ramo to steal the white man's medicine; then Futa would say that it was his medicine that saved the boy. But Ramo grabs a dangerous viral serum by mistake that will mean instantaneous death if administered.

The vengeful Molo attempts to murder Jane. He is thwarted by Tantu, who surprises the misguided native and runs for help. Rushing to save the young chief, Tarzan enters the land of Nagasu. The ape-man is caught off guard and knocked unconscious. Soon he is tied securely in the dungeon of the golden lion.

The ritual to save the young chief is about to begin, and Futa has decreed that Tarzan must die. "Bring me the warm heart of Tarzan!" he cries, as his warriors depart to kill their victim. Tarzan has managed to free his bonds, and when Ramo comes to cut out his heart,

Tarzan battles as Jane (Eve Brent) watches (*Tarzan's Fight for Life,* 1958).

he battles for his life. As Tarzan escapes, the golden lion cuts Ramo to ribbons with sharp claws and teeth.

With his mighty war cry, Tarzan stops Futa before he can give the "poison" serum to the young chief. To prove himself, Futa drinks the poison himself and dies in seconds. Dr. Sturdy later cures the lad, and the ending is happy as Tarzan kisses Jane passionately.

•

The best things that can be said about *Tarzan's Fight for Life* are that it starred Gordon Scott and featured some fascinating African photography, filmed on location in East Africa. (The African photography is most fascinating if you have the opportunity to view the unedited film shot in Kenya by photographer Miki Carter and his crew. This uncut footage was featured on a 1957

episode of "Bold Journey" entitled "Cartoon King in Africa" with host Jack Douglas.) Beyond those two redeeming factors, this was the last and probably the poorest of Sol Lesser's 16 theatrically released Tarzan pictures. There was a Jane, in the person of blonde Eve Brent and a son in Rickie Sorensen, but the story by Thomas Hal Phillips was pretty thin. Tarzan and his new "family" were also pitched to television, but found no takers. (See the television chapter on "Tarzan and the Trappers.")

There were no greedy white men for Tarzan to match wits with in this story, only superstitious natives who followed the evil witch doctor Futa (James Edwards) and his muscular henchman Ramo (Woody Strode). The theme of Tarzan battling against injustice (cutthroat profiteers who came to plunder the African riches) always worked well in Tarzan pictures, but with only natives and their superstitions to fight, the action at times is barely moving. Indeed, with the story revolving around the jungle hospital at Randini and doctors Sturdy and Warwick (Carl Benton Reid and Harry Lauter), Tarzan must bring Jane through the dangerous jungles for an emergency appendectomy, but this was hardly the kind of action the legend of Tarzan was built upon.

Beyond Gordon Scott, the other redeeming factor in *Tarzan's Fight for Life* was the African photography of Miki Carter. With a crew of only four, plus their white hunters and porters, Carter spent several weeks in Kenya, with a base camp at the foot of Mount Kilimanjaro. Besides the usual wild animals, Carter and company photographed a thundering waterfall, where the whole Zambesi river dumps into a gorge hundreds of feet deep; later they filmed Tarzan swinging over the awesome Murchison Falls, where the mighty Nile roars by. The shots of Tarzan swinging over the falls, riding an adult giraffe, swimming with elephants, conversing with pygmies, and being carried by native warriors spread-eagled between two war dugouts were performed by an unnamed stuntman with a build similar to Gordon Scott's.

Although Scott had not as yet been given a vehicle to leave his mark as the King of the Jungle, his next Tarzan adventure would be one of the most exciting in the long series: *Tarzan's Greatest Adventure*, with a worthy adversary in Anthony Quayle, the beautiful Sara Shane as Tarzan's romantic interest, and the young Sean Connery as a remorseless bully.

Tarzan's Greatest Adventure

Release date: July 1959; Sy Weintraub/Paramount; running time: 90 minutes; filmed in Eastman Color by Pathe. *Directed by* John Guillermin; *presented by* Harvey Hayutin and Sy Weintraub; *produced by* Sy Weintraub; *screenplay by* Berne Giler and John Guillermin; *story by* Les Crutchfield, *based on the characters created by* Edgar Rice Burroughs; *photography,* Ted Scaife; *additional photography,* Skeets Kelly; *art director,* Michael Stringer; *production manager,* John Palmer; *film editor,* Bert Rule; *assistant director,* Peter Bolton; *dubbing editor,* Ted Mason; *sound recording,* Charles Knott and Bob Jones; *sound supervisor,* John Cox; *makeup,* Tony Sforzini; *music composed and conducted by* Douglas Gamley.

Tarzan	Gordon Scott
Slade	Anthony Quayle
Angie	Sara Shane
Kriger	Niall MacGinnis
O'Bannion	Sean Connery
Dino	Al Mulock
Toni	Scilla Gabel

A canoe paddles silently up to the Mantu settlement hospital, and four armed men disembark. With faces darkened by dye, the white men have come to steal the dynamite stored at the hospital. Dr. Quarrels and his assistant

Gordon Scott with Sara Shane (*Tarzan's Greatest Adventure*, 1959).

are murdered, and the dying doctor is able to speak but one word over his radio: "Slade!"

The four armed men, Slade, O'Bannion, Kriger, and Dino, meet Slade's woman, Toni, on board their riverboat. Their destination is a diamond mine only Slade can locate. As they motor upstream, they pass the treehouse of Tarzan, Slade's mortal enemy.

The jungle drums tell Tarzan of the murders, and he travels to Mantu to investigate. There he learns from Colonel Sunley that Slade is responsible. Tarzan is introduced to the pilot, Angie, who perceives Tarzan tracking Slade as some kind of a game—but there is nothing funny in it for the ape-man.

As Tarzan pursues his quarry upriver, the jungle drums give Slade advance warning. Tarzan, alone in his canoe, must save Angie from a crocodile after her plane crashes in the river.

"Thanks, but what do you do for an encore?" she asks glibly. Tarzan only stares back at her because now he must drag this woman along on his manhunt.

Slade's boat has stopped for the night, and the men are getting on each other's nerves—especially since only one man has his beautiful woman along. Tarzan continues to travel at night and soon is close behind. Slade and O'Bannion resolve to finish Tarzan off, but they must settle for sabotaging his canoe. Now Tarzan and Angie must follow the river on foot.

Alone with Angie in a pensive moment, Tarzan explains his hatred for the ruthless Slade. "I would have killed Slade a long time ago, if not for man's law. Now he's broken that law," he grunts. Meanwhile, O'Bannion's twisted sense of humor results in Dino's death by drowning in quicksand, making the odds better for Tarzan.

Camera crew captures Gordon Scott and Anthony Quayle on film (close examination reveals safety wires).

Using a jungle shortcut that puts him upriver of Slade, Tarzan builds a trap that blocks the riverboat from passing. Slade and O'Bannion fight back with dynamite, and Tarzan is badly wounded. Though wounded, the ape-man tracks O'Bannion into the jungle and sends an arrow into his heart.

Slade himself is wounded by dynamite thrown by Kriger, who covets the diamonds and Toni for himself. Slade almost kills Kriger, but knows he needs him to cut the diamonds. When Angie tries to steal medicine for Tarzan's wounds from the boat, she is caught red-handed, and Slade decides to hold his prize as bait for Tarzan.

Back on his feet, though staggering, Tarzan doggedly trails Slade and company. Toni is the next to die, a horrible

death at the bottom of a lion trap. Angie escapes with help from Kriger and finds Tarzan, who is weak and needs sleep. The next morning, Tarzan has recovered. As he and Angie talk, they gain a new respect for each other. Tarzan pulls her close to him and ... (scene fades).

Meanwhile, Slade and Kriger have located the diamond mine and blown open the entrance with dynamite. Inside they find a fortune in diamonds—they will both be rich. But Kriger is greedy and knocks Slade down a shaft. Slade is barely able to save himself with a wire loop he plans to use on Tarzan. Kriger is unaware that Slade is climbing out of his tomb. Slade then sends his attacker plummeting down the shaft to the death meant for him.

Tarzan sends Angie back to the

settlement on Slade's boat. They say their good-byes, and now it is just the two adversaries alone. In the jungle, Slade trains his rifle sights on Tarzan, but the ape-man is as elusive as the wind. Tarzan dodges bullets that whistle by and climbs to Slade's high rocky perch, where Slade waits with his noose.

Finally Tarzan reaches the top of the crag, and the two men battle tooth-and-nail as Slade has his noose around Tarzan's neck and pulls it tighter and tighter. Tarzan finally breaks loose, and Slade is thrown to his death on the boulders below. The ape-man gives his victory cry, and Angie looks back, knowing that Tarzan has won the death struggle.

•

One could easily run out of superlatives in describing *Tarzan's Greatest Adventure,* which was one of the greatest Tarzan motion pictures ever produced. An absolutely riveting adventure-drama would best describe Gordon Scott's fourth film as Tarzan, with a majority of the film being photographed on location in Kenya, lending an air of unmistakable realism to its staging.

Although Scott was still Tarzan, almost everything else would change for the better now that Sol Lesser was out as producer and Sy Weintraub was in. The decision to photograph the picture on location in Africa was the most important factor; in truth only the interiors of a Tarzan adventure should ever be filmed in a studio. The superb cinematography by Ted Scaife authentically captured the African locales, and the rugged scenery in Eastman color was indeed captivating. When an African settlement is seen, it is real; when pygmies surround Tarzan in the jungle, they are authentic.

Competent Britisher John Guillermin was chosen to direct *Tarzan's Greatest Adventure,* and in a career

speckled with excellent films, this was arguably his best (his most celebrated films included *The Blue Max,* 1966, and *The Towering Inferno,* 1974). From the opening precredits scene that sets the stage with Slade (Anthony Quayle) as a ruthless, murdering profiteer, this adventure moves swiftly along without detouring for frivolities. It is not long before the audience is informed that Slade and Tarzan have had a previous encounter and that the blood is so bad between them that it's a boiling rage. When Tarzan is introduced, it is with a sixth sense that he snaps up out of a sound sleep, as if he can *feel* the presence of *something* that disturbs his sleep (in this case, it is Slade drifting by Tarzan's treehouse on his riverboat, motors cut to run silently past his enemy's jungle abode).

Scott portrayed Tarzan in a grim-faced, determined manner that gave new depth to the character of the ape-man. After three previous Tarzan pictures, he had matured and finally mastered the role, so much so that in this particular adventure it's easy to believe that Scott really was the legendary Tarzan. Four years after breaking in as Tarzan, and now at age 31, he had taken on a more hardened set to his features, a wiser look in his eyes. His speech was unbroken, his thoughts were explicitly expressed, and every word spoken by him was clearly understood. Scott barely cracked a smile in this picture, as if to say that this business of murder and manhunting was serious.

The supporting cast all gave superb performances, and perhaps Tarzan's most insidious personal foe was coldly played by Anthony Quayle. The remorseless Slade is driven more by his hatred of Tarzan than by his love of diamonds, which are secondary to him. The multitalented Quayle was well known on the British stage as both an actor and a director and had acted in

The victory cry of Tarzan the ape-man (*Tarzan's Greatest Adventure*, 1959).

films since he made his screen debut in Laurence Olivier's *Hamlet* (1948). Serious acting was Quayle's forte, and he was never more deadly serious than as Slade in *Tarzan's Greatest Adventure*.

The female lead was portrayed zestily by 29-year-old Sara Shane as the sarcastic Angie. At the start of the story, the lovely blonde was impressed by Tarzan's muscles, but by the end of their adventure together, one could guess that the hard-boiled Angie was in love. Shane portrays a pilot who initially is so flippant over the deaths of Tarzan's friends that the ape-man practically loathes her. Later, after they have been through the danger together, they share their deepest thoughts and get to know each other. Suddenly Tarzan gets this "look" in his eyes and pulls her close to him, but then the scene is cut. (A steamy clinch, although used on promotional posters to publicize the film, was unfortunately deleted at the final edit.)

Shane (born Elane Sterling) made her debut in *Easter Parade* (1948) and had acted in films like *Magnificent Obsession* (1954) and *The King and Four Queens* (1956). Although the former model made few films to judge her by, this was probably her finest role; she was totally believable as the beautiful yet gritty aviatrix.

Supporting players included Irish-born Niall MacGinnis as the squinty-eyed Kriger, who not only is as blind as a bat without his glasses, but has a greedy soul as barren as those of his fellow thieves. Al Mulock was Dino, who the audience is told has been recently paroled from prison, where he had been sent for murdering his father 15 years before. The locket he wears around his neck has his mother's picture in it, and he dies a bizarre death in quicksand protecting the keepsake (after first getting his face clawed by a panther).

The provocateur of Dino's grisly demise was a young Scottish-born actor named Sean Connery, who previously had made a half-dozen B-pictures that would never put him in the hall of fame. As the shallow and cutthroat O'Bannion, Connery was competent and formidable, but his long career would not be indelibly etched until he took the role of James Bond three years later in *Dr. No* (1962), the first of his many 007 spy thrillers. Rounding out the cast was Italian beauty Scilla Gabel in her American film debut as Toni, the sexy but not-so-brilliant girlfriend of Slade. And although Cheeta is in this picture, he makes an early exit before Tarzan

begins his manhunt, leaving the chimpanzee shenanigans for another day.

Berne Giler and director John Guillermin wrote the script from a story by Les Crutchfield. Pulling no punches, this was undoubtedly the best Tarzan story ever written; every character was given a personality and a background, every action had a purpose to advance the story, the dramatic moments were absolutely gripping, and the dialogue was thoughtfully planned and worded. An example of well-written dialogue is the macabre scene in which Tarzan and Angie come upon just the arm of Dino, frozen in death, jutting from his sandy grave. Angie is shocked, but not squeamish when Tarzan remarks grimly, "Death is never a pretty sight, and you'll see it again before the hunt is over." Angie's equally grim reply was, "And I thought this would be sport." Her attitude and answers are no longer glib, as she now faces death herself with cold reality.

As the story unfolds, it constantly builds in emotion; there are no wasted or useless encounters. Tarzan didn't have to show his machismo constantly by wrestling wild animals, although he did tangle with one crocodile whose sights were set on Angie after her plane crashed in the river. In one tense scene a deadly spider is crawling up Tarzan's leg, but he can't brush it away because he must remain motionless; one false move would mean death in his cat-and-mouse game with Slade in the jungle. A taut, often haunting musical score by Douglas Gamley added immensely to the absorbing drama of the adventure.

One of the greatest climaxes in any motion picture was Tarzan and Slade, two evenly matched foes, battling to the death on the edge of a jagged cliff. No stuntmen were used for this scene, and only thin safety wires protected the two actors from certain death; if a wire had snapped, the result surely would have been tragic. Suffice it to say, it was probably quite dangerous for Gordon Scott and Anthony Quayle to be grappling so close to the edge of a cliff. The only weapon present was Slade's formidable wire animal noose, which he manages to get around Tarzan's neck. The drama is extremely tense and believable in this well-conceived battle to the death between two powerful adversaries, who were living for this moment when one could destroy the other. When Tarzan manages to knock Slade to his bone-crunching death on the rocks below, there is a collective sigh from the audience that their hero has somehow survived once again. Indeed, Tarzan gives his deafening victory cry in his triumph.

In retrospect, *Tarzan's Greatest Adventure* is a truly great film with an appreciative audience. However, when Paramount released the film in July 1959, it did so without a major advertising campaign and as part of a twin-bill;

in New York it was doubled with Jerry Lewis' wacky comedy, *Don't Give Up the Ship.* The fans that did get to see the film in the summer of '59 loved it, but in most cases it was gone from theaters in only a week. In *Variety's* list of top-grossing films for 1959, *Tarzan's Greatest Adventure* limped in at #80, with anticipated rentals of $1 million. With proper exploitation, the film could have earned several times that amount, but for the most part Paramount wasted a golden opportunity.

Solid critical reviews and the producer's and director's knowledge that they had made an exciting adventure would have to be reward enough. Director John Guillermin's superb staging would not go unrewarded, for he would be at the helm of another ape-man feature, *Tarzan Goes to India* (1962). Gordon Scott would be back for a final encore in *Tarzan, the Magnificent;* this time his adversary would be future Tarzan Jock Mahoney.

Tarzan, the Ape Man

Release date: October 1959; Metro-Goldwyn-Mayer; running time: 82 minutes; filmed in Technicolor. *Directed by* Joseph Newman; *produced by* Al Zimbalist; *screenplay by* Robert Hill, *based on the characters created by* Edgar Rice Burroughs; *photography by* Paul C. Vogel; *film editor,* Gene Ruggiero; *recording supervisor,* Franklin Milton; *art directors,* Hans Peters and Malcolm Brown; *set decorations,* Henry Grace and Robert C. Bradfield; *photographic effects,* Lee LeBlanc and Robert R. Hoag; *assistant director,* William Shanks; *associate producer,* Donald Zimbalist; *makeup,* William Tuttle; *music composed and conducted by* Shorty Rogers.

Tarzan	Denny Miller
Jane	Joanna Barnes
Holt	Cesare Danova
Parker	Robert Douglas
Riano	Thomas Yangha

As the riverboat approaches the African settlement blowing its whistle,

Parker anxiously awaits the return of his daughter Jane, who has been in England for several years. Parker's partner Holt is also on board the boat, as is a Watusi warrior whom Holt rescued from a rival tribe.

Jane's caddish fiancé had deserted her in London when he found that both she and her father were broke. So Jane has decided to join her wandering father in Africa. The Watusi warrior gives Jane a good-luck charm carved from ivory and claims it came from the fabled elephant graveyard.

Holt recalls the legend, "Where the elephants die beyond the great escarpment—the graveyard of a million elephants." Parker is skeptical, but Holt retorts, "I'd rather die rich in the jungle than rot like a pauper." They all agree that since they're completely broke, they will take a longshot gamble to try to find the elephant graveyard.

The members of the safari, including the native guide Riano, the bearers, and the Watusi man, head into the jungle. Watching from the trees is Tarzan, and his strange cry sends a chill up their spines. When a leopard stalks Jane, Tarzan's long knife kills the beast after a vicious fight. The ape-man is swiftly gone, leaving his thundering cry to echo in the night.

The next day Tarzan must save Jane again, this time from a renegade elephant. "Umgawa," shouts Tarzan to halt the charging beast, who then kneels to carry the ape-man and the unconscious girl to Tarzan's jungle home. When Jane awakes, she is deathly afraid to be alone with a savage man who cannot even speak English. Eventually, she learns that this simple man won't harm her, and their playful river frolicking turns into a jungle romance.

Searching desperately, Parker and Holt find Jane in the jungle and she tells them of the jungle man who held her captive. As the safari continues, Tarzan is called upon once again to save them from attacking hostiles. His mighty cry

beckons a herd of zebra to his call, and they trample the natives into the dust. By now Holt is jealous of Jane's attraction to Tarzan, as the girl retorts with a sneer, "He's more of a man than you."

As they climb the steep escarpment, the Watusi man falls to his death, leaving only three, plus Cheeta, who is tagging along. But before they can reach their goal, they are surrounded by pygmies and held captive by a ring of fire. Parker is the first to die, and Jane and Holt are next in line. Suddenly the cry of the ape-man shatters the air, and a rampaging herd of elephants ride to his call. The entire pygmy village is crushed; the flames spread, as Tarzan, Holt, and Jane escape on the back of one of the elephants.

As fate would have it, the beast is wounded by a pygmy spear. With his dying energy, he leads them through a waterfall to the elephant burial grounds. Tarzan cares nothing about the riches of money and turns to leave with Cheeta. However, Jane bids Holt adieu and calls after Tarzan, "Wait!" She realizes money would be nothing without her newfound love, Tarzan, who takes her in his arms and kisses her passionately.

•

The 1959 remake of *Tarzan, the Ape Man* is generally considered to be the second worst Tarzan picture ever made (ahead of only the 1981 MGM remake of this same story). It starred Denny Miller as Tarzan and Joanna Barnes as Jane Parker. Credit for the failings of the film belong to MGM and producer Al Zimbalist, who ordered the special photographic effects boys to butcher one of the all-time great movie originals (the 1932 *Tarzan, the Ape Man*) to save a buck for the studio.

It's hard to comprehend how a studio with the solid reputation of MGM, which was spending $4 million to produce *Ben-Hur* (1959) around the

Denny Miller with Joanna Barnes (*Tarzan, the Ape Man*, 1959).

same time, could stoop to the kinder-garten filmmaking techniques used in this picture. It started with the right idea, borrowing genuine African stock footage from MGM's classic jungle adventure *King Solomon's Mines* (1950); some superb sequences of African na-tives are used from the earlier adventure (in Technicolor), along with the zebra stampede on the veldt, the climb up the escarpment, and additional stock wild animal footage.

If the studio had stopped here, the film might have been all right, but then the vine-swinging scenes from the original 1932 black-and-white classic *Tarzan, the Ape Man* were added. Although the film was tinted to attempt to match the Technicolor photography, the whole technique was patently ar-tificial. Also pilfered were the elephant stampede through the pygmy village (with "flames" crudely superimposed) and the classic scene of Tarzan battling the giant croc from *Tarzan and His Mate* (1934). (You can actually see Johnny Weissmuller's face clearly as he fights the crocodile!)

Probably the most ludicrous "spe-cial effects" were in a Tarzan fight with a leopard and later with Tarzan and Jane swimming underwater with some hippos. In the leopard fight, some de-cent shots of a trainer fighting with a live leopard are mixed with Denny Mil-ler wrestling with a stuffed leopard, which was also passable. But the movie then cut to two separate close-ups of the face of the stuffed animal, resplendent with its plastic fangs and button eyes.

The other riotous scene was of Tar-zan and Jane swimming in the river be-low Tarzan's jungle home, the river bottom thick with hippos. As Tarzan and Jane frolic in the water, they dive down to cavort with the playful beasts (which in reality are extremely danger-ous animals that can chomp a man in half with one bite). This scene was

created by using some washed-out footage of the underwater hippos, with Denny Miller and Joanna Barnes super-imposed "swimming" among the ani-mals; this scene was more hilarious than the cartoons that usually preceded the feature.

This picture starred former UCLA basketball player Denny Miller, as the ape-man. Making his motion picture debut and in his one-and-only starring vehicle, Miller as Tarzan was all right. At six feet three inches and 215 pounds, the blonde-haired Miller had the physi-cal attributes to portray a jungle man, and with his athletic background the minor stunts he was asked to perform were no problem. Tarzan had no spoken dialogue except "Umgawa" and a few simple words he mimics when Jane tries to teach him to converse. In fact, Tar-zan never even speaks his own name, and no mention is made of the ape-man's beginning.

In an interview with the author, Denny Miller recalled how much fun he had making this picture and how much attention and notoriety it has brought him over the years. Miller is a proud member of the Past Tarzans Associa-tion, and said that with all the fun that it's brought him over the years, he wouldn't trade his experience as the ape-man for anything in the world. After the Tarzan film, Miller made his mark in television, most notably as trail hand "Duke" Shannon during his three sea-sons on the classic western *Wagon Train*. Over the years he's often played cow-boys or heavies and occasionally good guys, but his Tarzan starring role led him to a long career in Hollywood.

The cast of *Tarzan, the Ape Man* included frosty actress Joanna Barnes as Jane Parker, who spurns Holt's advances but falls for Tarzan. Barnes made a mighty weak version of Jane; she had been asked to portray Jane as flippant and motivated as much by the potential prize of the ivory hunt as was the greedy Holt. Perhaps her most memorable film role was in her next picture, as the bloodthirsty Claudia in *Spartacus* (1960), starring Kirk Douglas.

Rounding out the lead players were handsome Italian leading man Cesare Danova as Holt and British leading man Robert Douglas as Parker; both performed credible work despite the extreme limitations of plot and dialogue. Another effective actor was the seven-foot Watusi man (unbilled) who por-trayed Wa-tu. The native guide Riano was played by Thomas Yangha.

Tarzan, the Ape Man, 1959 vintage, is definitely not the stuff that legends are made of, but it is part of the Tarzan motion picture history. And if you're in the mood for a few laughs and perhaps even a thrill or two, all tongue in cheek, you can enjoy it if you don't take it too seriously. (As stated in *Unsold Television Pilots* by Lee Goldberg, on February 23, 1968, the feature film was reedited to 60 minutes and shown on ABC television as a pilot for a series.)

Tarzan the Magnificent

Release date: July 1960; Sy Weintraub/Paramount; running time: 88 minutes; filmed in Eastman color by Pathe. *Directed by* Robert Day; *presented by* Harvey Hayutin and Sy Weintraub; *produced by* Sy Weintraub; *screenplay by* Berne Giler and Robert Day, *based on the characters created by* Edgar Rice Burroughs; *photography,* Ted Scaife; *additional photography,* Jack Mills; *art director,* Ray Simm; *production manager,* Roy Parkinson; *film editor,* Bert Rule; *assistant director,* Clive Reed; *sound editor,* Ted Mason; *sound recording,* Buster Amuil and Bob Jones; *sound supervisor,* John Cox; *makeup,* Tony Sforzini; *music by* Ken Jones.

Tarzan	Gordon Scott
Coy Banton	Jock Mahoney
Fay Ames	Betta St. John
Abel Banton	John Carradine
Ames	Lionel Jeffries
Laurie	Alexandra Stewart
Tate	Earl Cameron
Conway	Charles Tingwell
Martin Banton	Al Mulock
Johnny Banton	Gary Cockrell
Warrior leader	Harry Baird
Native chief	Christopher Carlos
Inspector Winters	John Sullivan
Ethan Banton	Ron MacDonnell

Also featuring Ewen Solon, Jacqueline Evans, Thomas Duggan, Peter Howell, John Harrison, and George Taylor.

The Bantons, a clan of renegades, rob the pay office of an African mining settlement, murdering several people in cold blood. A police officer tracks them

Gordon Scott with Betta St. John and tribal members (*Tarzan the Magnificent*, 1960).

Gordon Scott (left) battles Jock Mahoney in quicksand (*Tarzan the Magnificent,* 1960).

into the bush and arrests their leader, Coy Banton. "You make a sound, and I'll slit your throat," he warns while slipping Banton silently out of the clan's night camp.

Before long the Bantons (led by patriarch Abel), free Coy and murder the policeman. Tarzan witnesses this scene, and his arrows kill Ethan Banton and scatter the rest, as he takes charge

of Coy. The dead officer was Tarzan's friend, and he resolves to take the murderer Banton into Mantu himself.

The boat Tarzan must take to Kairobi is ambushed and burned by Abel Banton and his sons, and the captain is murdered. Later, the stranded passengers ask Tarzan to take them on the dangerous journey to Kairobi. With little choice in the matter, Tarzan agrees. At camp that evening, the people tell their stories: Ames is a self-satisfied fool who sees most people as failures; his wife Fay is shallow and is attracted to the vicious Coy Banton; Conway is a failed doctor hoping to start over; Laurie, Conway's girlfriend, believes in him; and Tate, a black man, was the best friend of the murdered boat captain.

The Bantons soon pick up their trail, which leads to a native village where the chief wants to kill Coy Banton himself. Tarzan bargains with his own life, and when Dr. Conway safely delivers the chief's new baby, the group is allowed to go on its way. As the Bantons close in, Tarzan follows the river through swamps and quicksand to throw them off. Fay leaves her handkerchief behind to guide the pursuing Bantons.

Later, Coy Banton jumps Ames, and in the struggle over a gun, Tate is mortally wounded. Tarzan manages to recapture Coy and holds him in a death-lock as they are mired in quicksand, the Bantons searching just inches away from their place of hiding. Eventually, Johnny Banton corners Laurie in the bushes, and Tarzan is forced to kill him in close combat. Tate and Banton are buried side by side.

Martin Banton angrily splits from his father, and now there is only one hunter. That night, Fay foolishly releases Coy and leaves with him. Banton now has little use for her and abandons her to be killed by a lion. Shortly thereafter, Coy and Abel are reunited, and they plot to kill Tarzan, who has sent the others on to Kairobi. "This time I go alone," says the determined ape-man, who is tired of the rising death toll.

The tricky Bantons catch Tarzan in a crossfire, but their strategy backfires when Abel is killed by his own son's bullet. When Coy's rifle is empty, Tarzan throws down his weapons and they fight to the death with their bare hands. Tarzan has almost won the battle, when

Banton slugs Tarzan with his handcuffs, using them like brass knuckles, knocking him unconscious. Tarzan recovers and finally knocks Banton out cold.

Tarzan carries his prisoner back to Kairobi and turns him over to the local police, who will hang the murderer. He bids his comrades—Conway, Laurie, and Ames—good-bye and returns to the jungle, his home. Strangely, Tarzan does not give his triumphant cry. With all the lives it cost, this is a hollow victory for the ape-man.

•

For Tarzan fans, *Tarzan the Magnificent* turned out to be just that, although it didn't quite measure up to the high standards set by the previous Gordon Scott film, *Tarzan's Greatest Adventure*. Nevertheless, it's a realistic, fast-paced, action-packed adventure that contains one of the greatest two-man, hand-to-hand battles in film history. The climax has Tarzan and Coy Banton (Jock Mahoney) throw down their weapons on a crag overlooking a waterfall, as they literally knock each other out. Rugged Scott and former stuntman Mahoney filmed this realistic scene that lasts almost five minutes without stuntmen. They batter each other on craggy rock, dive into the river from a dizzying height, are at each other's throats underwater, claw their way up onto slippery rocks (by this time Banton's shirt is literally ripped off), and are back on land to slug it out once again. Eventually, Tarzan is knocked unconscious when Banton uses his handcuffs like brass knuckles, but the ape-man recovers and finally batters Banton into unconsciousness.

The violent climax is definitely the highlight of the film, in what was possibly the most vicious Tarzan picture ever produced. The murderous Banton clan squeezed their rifle triggers without remorse, shooting people in cold blood.

John Carradine was well cast as the head of this clan of renegades, Abel Banton, his powerful foghorn voice barking out commands like he was born to do so. There was no love in this family, only greed and brutality; it's amazing that one of the sons (played by Al Mulock) is allowed to walk away from the killing before it is all over. You get the feeling that the old patriarch wants to shoot his son Martin in the back as he walks away, but some rare pang of conscience stops him from doing so. Then, in a bitter, ironic twist, Coy Banton shoots his father when the crossfire in which they have caught Tarzan backfires. In the end, Tarzan does not kill the evil Coy Banton, for the gallows is awaiting him in Kairobi—a more fitting end than a merciful quick kill.

Secondary to this compelling main plot is the subplot involving the people who accompany Tarzan on the arduous journey. Lionel Jeffries is convincing as Ames, who is not only a pompous fool but a coward. His wife Fay (Betta St. John) is a frustrated socialite who can no longer stand the sight of her husband, so chooses the sometimes-charming but always deadly Coy Banton as her new lover; after she helps Coy to escape, he kisses her fiercely and then leaves her to die in the jaws of a lion. Charles Tingwell was the former doctor who proves he is still a man of medicine when he delivers a baby to the wife of a tribal chief, and Laurie (Alexandra Stewart) is a beautiful young woman we presume is in love with Dr. Conway.

The purpose of this subplot is primarily to heighten the dramatic effect, for certainly Tarzan would not have taken them along on his dangerous mission. However, this subplot actually takes away from the sheer adventure of the drama. If Tate and perhaps a beautiful woman for Tarzan to become romantically entangled with were

Tarzan's only excess baggage, the story would have worked smoother. The character of Tate (portrayed by Earl Cameron), a man who also wanted to see Coy Banton brought to justice for murdering his best friend, was definitely worthwhile; of course, with his noble purpose, he had to be killed, ironically trying to save the life of the coward Ames.

The screenplay was written by Berne Giler with help from director Robert Day, and although the story works well enough, it's not a classic like Giler's previous collaboration with John Guillermin. There's no love interest for Tarzan, such as the affair with Sara Shane that worked so well in *Tarzan's Greatest Adventure*; instead, Tarzan's human side is shown as a weakness in allowing these people to accompany him.

Jock Mahoney was marvelously cast as Coy Banton, but all you really learn about him is that he is cold, with little regard for human life, even his own. The former TV star was now waiting for perhaps the most important theatrical role of his life—starring as Tarzan in the next two ape-man adventures for producer Sy Weintraub.

Directing the picture was Englishman Robert Day, whose most significant theatrical films were the four Tarzan adventures he directed in the 1960s. The film was staged with a high degree of competence, and the production in Kenya, including several scenes showing the Kikuyu and the Masai tribes, supplied a realism that made this a true Tarzan picture.

Although Scott had now fully realized the character of Tarzan, this would be his final role as the ape-man. Scott had put the hero back in Tarzan, and he had done it in stunning fashion. He performed his own dangerous stunts; worked with wild animals such as lions; and conveyed animal instincts and a cunning intelligence that would have made Edgar

Rice Burroughs, the creator of Tarzan, proud. Scott did not give the Tarzan yell in his last picture, and he would give it no more. He went to Europe the following year to make gladiator and strongman epics, before fading into obscurity in the late 1960s. But Scott gave his fans a good run for their money, for he was one Tarzan who truly believed in the character and fully enjoyed playing the role.

Tarzan Goes to India

Release date: March 1962; Sy Weintraub/Metro-Goldwyn-Mayer; running time: 86 minutes; filmed in Metrocolor and CinemaScope. *Directed by* John Guillermin; *produced by* Sy Weintraub; *screenplay by* Robert Hardy Andrews and John Guillermin, *based on the characters created by* Edgar Rice Burroughs; *photography*, Paul Beeson; *second unit production and photography*, Ellis R. Dungan; *art director*, George Provis; *production supervisor*, Joe Levy; *film editor*, Max Benedict; *assistant director*, Dennis Bertera; *special effects*, Roy Whybrow; *sound recording*, Bill Howell; *makeup*, Stuart Freeborn; *associate producer*, Jesse Corrallo; *music by* Ken Jones, Ravi Shankar, and Panchal Jaikishan.

Tarzan	Jock Mahoney
Jai, the elephant boy	Jai
Bryce	Leo Gordon
O'Hara	Mark Dana
Princess Kamara	Simi
Raju Kumar	Feroz Khan
Maharajah	Murad
Raj	Jagdish Raaj
Chakra	G. Raghaven

Also featuring Aaron Joseph, Abas Khan, Pekelwan Ameer,
K.S. Tripathi, Peter Cooke, Denis Bastian, and Rajendra Presade.

Tarzan arrives in India and is greeted by Princess Kamara. Her father the maharajah has asked his friend Tarzan to save the lives of 300 elephants that will be drowned when the new power plant is completed and the dam that is created will put their jungles under water.

Tarzan meets with the power plant designer, O'Hara, to seek a solution, but O'Hara plans to meet the deadline at all costs. The construction engineer, Bryce, and Tarzan had bumped heads in Africa, in the past, where Bryce had slaughtered elephants for their ivory. Assisting Bryce is Raju, who had been a friend of Princess Kamara but is now alienated from her because of his work on the power plant. Kamara is also helping to get the refugees out of the jungle before the valley is flooded.

The only possible escape route for the elephants is a pass through the mountains that Tarzan plans to use. "Bryce, those elephants aren't going to drown. I'm going to drive them through

Jock Mahoney as Tarzan battling a cobra (*Tarzan Goes to India*, 1962).

Jock Mahoney as Tarzan (*Tarzan Goes to India*, 1962).

the pass," Tarzan warns. Bryce is just as determined to block the pass before the monsoon season hits and angrily responds, "Stay out'ta my way!"

In the jungle Tarzan meets Jai, an orphan boy who rides a mighty elephant called Gajendra. They both want to save the elephant herd and decide to work together. Later they catch sight of the great herd, which is led by a rogue elephant named Bala. Tarzan plans to kill Bala, then use Gajendra to lead the elephants out of the valley through the pass. When Bryce tries to shoot Gajendra to halt the plan, he is stopped by Tarzan's flying drop-kick. But the ape-man is knocked unconscious by a rifle butt and shackled to keep him out of trouble. Chained, Tarzan must fight a leopard barehanded; suddenly Raju shoots the beast in midair. Raju, beginning to see the evil in the ways of his boss, Bryce, releases Tarzan.

Soon, Tarzan and Jai have located the herd and their leader, Bala. Tarzan plans to kill the beast with an arrow to the brain, but he needs help from Gajendra before the old rogue finally dies. Seeing that Tarzan's plan is working, Bryce kidnaps Jai and tries to kill Tarzan. Gajendra again is the hero as the beast rescues Jai and knocks the villain Bryce to his death on the rocks.

Meanwhile, O'Hara refuses to stop the work on the dam and, angrily, Raju quits his job to enlist in Tarzan's "army." Tarzan is warned that O'Hara has a trap rigged with dynamite, but Tarzan has his own dynamite-laden arrow ready to set off the blockade. With Tarzan riding Gajendra, they drive the wild herd toward the stockade built by the refugees. That evening all the elephants are in the stockade, and as Tarzan gives his mighty call, the herd charges toward the pass. Tarzan's dynamite arrow blows open the blockade, and the elephants rumble through to the safety of the other side.

Knowing that the dam is important to the Indian people, Tarzan volunteers the elephants and his "army" to finish the project by the deadline, and O'Hara gratefully accepts. Tarzan bids his friends Jai and Princess Kamara goodbye. His mission in India has been successful.

•

After appearing in *Tarzan the Magnificent* as one of the vilest villains ever, Jock Mahoney became the 13th motion picture Tarzan in *Tarzan Goes to India*. A mutual agreement between Tarzan star Gordon Scott and producer Sy Weintraub to part ways had left the position of the ape-man unfilled. After working in the previous Tarzan picture as the renegade Coy Banton, Mahoney wanted the job of Tarzan and eventually landed the role after various candidates had been screened.

Born Jacques O'Mahoney on February 7, 1919, Jock was the oldest rookie Tarzan ever at age 42 (Weissmuller was 43 when he retired). The handsome and rugged Mahoney was a mixture of Irish, French, and Cherokee Indian heritage, and at six feet four inches and 215 pounds, he had the size and physique to portray the King of the Jungle.

After Jock excelled at the University of Iowa in basketball, football, and swimming, his skills as a pilot landed him a civilian job training U.S. Army pilots at Falcon Field near Phoenix, Arizona. Mahoney later served in the Marine Corps during World War II as a fighter pilot, flying from the USS *Guadalcanal* and chasing submarines in the Atlantic theater.

Raising horses in California after the war, Mahoney got his feet wet in the movie business the hard way by working as a stuntman for five years, doubling for the big stars and taking all the risks while they made all the money. One of his earliest billed roles was in the

Randolph Scott western *The Doolins of Oklahoma* (1949), after which he was on his way to bigger and better things.

Mahoney starred in 78 episodes of the popular TV western series "Range Rider" (for Gene Autry's "Flying A" Productions) from 1951 to 1953, and the series remained in syndication for many years. During the late 1950s, Mahoney was a contract leading man for Universal-International and starred in "Yancy Derringer" for the 1958-59 season as a slick special agent who carried a derringer in his hat.

The lead roles in *Tarzan Goes to India* and *Tarzan's Three Challenges* were possibly the best parts of Mahoney's long career in Hollywood. The first film was photographed in India, and Mahoney did all his own stunts except for the opening scene, in which he dives out of a plane—the Indian government wouldn't allow that stunt, so a dummy was used. Mahoney worked with two live leopards a scene, in which he was chained and attacked by the beasts. The first leopard was not drugged and paced back and forth while Tarzan swung his chains. The second leopard was drugged and sort of leaned on him with his paws around his neck; he was shot by the most welcome Raju. A mongoose was also used to kill a cobra that threatened Tarzan, with Mahoney watching the scene but a few feet away.

Probably the most fascinating aspect of filming in India for Mahoney was working with the elephants. The boy Jai, incidentally, had never worked with elephants until his training for the picture. Both elephants—Jai's Gajendra and Ranga (the rogue elephant)—were over 100 years old. Ranga was nearly 11 feet tall and was used for the distant

sequences like the final charge (the beast was capable of running over 50 miles per hour; they were doing about 45 miles per hour for the final scenes). Mahoney was also in a tree that Ranga pushed down, and he had to keep giving the beast candy to get it to do what it was supposed to do. Mahoney rode Ranga in most of the scenes, and the mighty creature was the state elephant of the maharajah of Mysor.

There was plenty of action in *Tarzan Goes to India,* which was directed by John Guillermin, who had also staged the exciting *Tarzan's Greatest Adventure.* The original story by Robert Hardy Andrews and Guillermin was different from the final script, in that both O'Hara and Bryce (Mark Dana and Leo Gordon) were killed in the final charge of the elephants. In the ending that was actually filmed, Bryce was killed earlier by Gajendra and O'Hara, of course, was not killed. In fact, O'Hara's unselfish intentions were to build the dam needed for power to bolster the poor economy of India. Photographed in Metrocolor by Paul Beeson, *Tarzan Goes to India* was the first Tarzan film to use the widescreen process of CinemaScope.

The chief villain for Tarzan to deal with was Bryce, well portrayed by Leo Gordon, the tough-looking character actor with a square jaw and powerful build. Although there was no love interest for Tarzan during his stay in India, there were the beautiful and compassionate Princess Kamara, played by Indian actress Simi, and the boy, Jai, who played himself. The next adventure for Mahoney as Tarzan would be *Tarzan's Three Challenges*, which was filmed in Thailand and had Woody Strode as his deadly adversary.

Tarzan's Three Challenges

Release date: June 1963; Sy Weintraub/Metro-Goldwyn-Mayer; running time: 92 minutes; filmed in Metrocolor and Dyaliscope. *Directed by* Robert Day; *produced by* Sy Weintraub; *screenplay by* Berne Giler and Robert Day, *based on the characters created by* Edgar Rice Burroughs; *photography,* Ted Scaife; *production design,* Wilfred Shingleton; *film editor,* Fred Burnley; *assistant director,* Clive Reed; *sound editor,* Chris Greenham; *sound mixer,* Wally Milner; *sound supervisor,* Stephen Dalby; *makeup,* Freddie Williamson; *special effects,* Cliff Richardson and Roy Whybrow; *music composed by* Joseph Horovitz and *conducted by* Marcus Dods.

Tarzan	Jock Mahoney
Tarim/Khan	Woody Strode
Cho-San	Tsu Kobayashi
Kashi	Ricky Der
Mang	Earl Cameron
Sechung	Christopher Carlos
Hani	Jimmy Jamal
Tor	Anthony Chinn
Nari	Robert Hu

In a distant oriental land, a successor must be chosen for the ailing ruler Tarim. Opposing Tarim is his brother Khan, who wants his own son Nari to be the new ruler, but Tarim has already made his choice. The man bringing the Chosen One to the Crown City is Tarzan, who accepted the mission as a favor to a friend.

Arriving in this country, Tarzan's guide is killed by pirates; his replacement, Hani, is a spy working for Khan. Tarzan and Hani travel to a village in the hills, where an elder tells Tarzan of the feud between Tarim and Khan. "Khan has always been jealous of his brother, and where there is jealousy there is darkness," the old man says.

At last, they reach the monastery, where Tarim has arranged for Tarzan to meet the Chosen One—a boy named Kashi. To prove himself worthy, Tarzan must pass tests of skill and strength. His archery is perfect to pass the first test, and he resists the pull of two oxen for five sounds of the gong to pass the strength test. Tarzan also passes the test of wisdom and is accepted to escort Kashi to the Crown City through dangerous jungles, along with Kashi's guardians, Cho-San and Mang.

Khan has assigned an assassin to try to kill Kashi, and the spy Hani is still in their midst. On the way to a shrine where Kashi must stop to pray, Hani starts a forest fire that threatens their lives. Tarzan saves Kashi, but Hani is killed.

Tarzan leads Kashi to an underground temple to wait while he throws Khan off their trail. But Khan's assassins have followed them to the temple, and in defending the boy, Mang is fatally wounded. Tarzan fortuitously arrives to kill one of the assassins, but it is left to Cho-San to shoot the other murderer before that assassin can claim the life of Kashi.

Meanwhile in the Crown City, Tarim has died, and the people pay their last respects to their ruler. To succeed to the throne, Kashi must pass certain tests, administered by Sechung. Kashi passes the difficult tests and is

Tarzan's challenge #1 ... the test of strength (*Tarzan's Three Challenges*, 1963).

Jock Mahoney with Tsu Kobayashi and Ricky Der (*Tarzan's Three Challenge*, 1963).

accepted as the new ruler. Sechung announces, "Are there any among our people who would challenge this?" Indeed, the booming voice of Khan echoes out, "I challenge!" The new Tarim calls on Tarzan to be his defender against Khan—a battle to the death.

Tarzan and Khan are tied together and must run a dangerous obstacle course. They drag each other over rough terrain and cross a gorge by rope; if one falls, they both will die. They both survive a high dive into the river, and as they reach the city, the crowd is cheering.

Finally they do battle with swords on a rope net, under which are barrels of boiling oil. The struggle is fierce, when suddenly Khan loses his balance and falls to his instantaneous death in the boiling oil; Tarzan is the victor. His mission accomplished, Tarzan says good-bye to his friends Kashi and Cho-San and heads down the long road back to Africa.

•

Another colorful background was chosen for the new Tarzan adventure, this time the jungles and ancient temples of Thailand. Jock Mahoney returned for his second and final role as Tarzan. Cast as a most worthy adversary for Tarzan was Woody Strode in the dual roles of Khan and Tarim.

Filming began in Thailand around February 10, 1963, and concluded on April 10, with the editing and sound dubbing accomplished later in London. The backdrop was the mountainous jungles of Thailand, only 11 miles from the Chinese border. Although the war in Southeast Asia had not yet escalated, there were snakes and wild animals among the jungle hazards. There was also a hostile hill tribe, the Karim, who harassed the peaceful local villagers, stealing their livestock and even occasionally young women.

At age 44, Jock Mahoney was the oldest Tarzan ever (Johnny Weissmuller had retired at age 43), but the former stuntman still did many dangerous stunts himself in the film. Mahoney and Woody Strode did the first and last 20 feet of a tricky rope dive from a bridge, and dummies did the middle segment. Mahoney also did the fantastic stunt of being run over by a motor boat. The sword fight at the climax is Mahoney and Strode battling on the rope net to the death. In other perilous sequences, they had to set the green jungles on fire with gasoline, and they barely escaped the roaring blazes more than once.

Strode as Khan was truly evenly matched with Mahoney as Tarzan in this adventure, as the two tall athletes fought it out eye-to-eye in the final challenge. Strode's most famous role had been as the black gladiator Draba in *Spartacus* (1960), and again in this film he fought gladiator style in an early scene. Strode portrayed brothers Tarim and Khan, the latter of whom hoped to install his own son as ruler, so he would be the real power behind the throne. Stode was indeed magnificently cast as a villain, and it's a shame that there weren't more roles like this for him while he was in his prime. His role as the cowardly Ramo in *Tarzan's Fight for Life* (1958) simply wasn't effective casting for a man with his commanding presence.

Portraying the Chosen One was Rickey Der, a nephew of Strode. The boy did a convincing job as Kashi, proving that he truly was the rightful heir to the throne. Again there was no romantic interest for Tarzan in this foreign land, but there was Kashi's attractive guardian Cho-San, played by Tsu Kobayashi. It was obvious that producer Sy Weintraub was targeting children as his prime market, with children and cute animals a big part of the newest Tarzan adventures (Jai, the elephant boy in *Tarzan*

Goes to India; and Kashi and Hungry, the baby elephant in this picture).

Director Robert Day kept the abundant action flowing evenly, which together with the intelligent dialogue made the story believable. *Tarzan's Three Challenges* was a well-acted production with few holes in the story; indeed, the script by Berne Giler and Day was one of the most original yet in a Tarzan adventure.

The "three challenges" of the title referred to the tests Tarzan had to pass to prove himself worthy to escort young Kashi to his appointment with destiny: Tarzan against Khan and his assassins in guiding the boy safely to the Crown City; and, finally, the duel to the death against Khan, with Tarzan triumphing as Khan falls to his grisly death. Tarzan, of course, was up to all three deadly challenges as only the ape-man could be.

This was a difficult picture for Mahoney personally; he suffered a severe bout of dysentery, coupled with dengue fever and pneumonia, during production. The actor lost 40 pounds, but even in his weakened condition, he was back in front of the cameras as soon as possible and finished the film. Jock noted that in an early scene with a water buffalo he was 20 pounds overweight, but by the time he accepted Khan's

challenge late in the picture, his physique was gaunt and his face was ashen. It took Jock fully 18 months to recover completely from his illness and to resume working in pictures.

Mahoney turned out to be one of the best Tarzan actors, and it's a shame he didn't get the role until reaching his middle 40s. A 30-year-old Mahoney as Tarzan, with his great skills as a stuntman and the intelligent fire of a Greystoke in his eyes, might truly have been the answer to Edgar Rice Burroughs' quest to film his fictional hero as he had created him.

Although Mahoney was finished as Tarzan, he would appear in several episodes of the Ron Ely Tarzan television series (1966–68) and be cast as Tarzan's adversary, The Colonel, in *Tarzan's Deadly Silence.* Jock would continue to act in films and on television until his death in December 1989. (Mahoney died as the result of injuries sustained in a car wreck, the consequence of a heart attack while driving his vehicle.)

There would be no new Tarzan pictures until fully three years had passed, with a modernized Tarzan, played by former pro-football player Mike Henry, reaching the wide screen in 1966: *Tarzan and the Valley of Gold.*

Tarzan and the Valley of Gold

Release date: May 1966; Sy Weintraub/American International; running time: 90 minutes; filmed in Eastman Color and Panavision. *Directed by* Robert Day; *produced by* Sy Weintraub; *screenplay by* Clair Huffaker, *based on the characters created by* Edgar Rice Burroughs; *photography,* Irving Lippman; *associate producer,* Steve Shagan; *production manager,* Sam Manners; *film editor,* Frank P. Keller; *art director,* Jose Granada; *assistant directors,* Max Stein and Mario Cisneros; *makeup,* Roman Juarez and Elvira Oropeza; *special effects,* Ira Anderson and Ira Anderson, Jr.; *music composed and conducted by* Van Alexander.

Mike Henry as Tarzan with Nancy Kovack (*Tarzan and the Valley of Gold*, 1966).

Tarzan	Mike Henry
Sophia	Nancy Kovack
Ramel	Manuel Padilla, Jr.
Vinero	David Opatoshu
Mr. Train	Don Megowan
Manco the elder	Francisco Riquerio
Talmadge	Edwardo Noriega
Ruiz	Frank Brandstetter

Also featuring Enrique Lucero, John Kelly, Carlos Rivas,
Jorge Beirute, and Oswald Olvera.

Tarzan is summoned to Mexico by his old friend Ruiz for an important mission that is mysteriously unexplained. The chauffeur who is sent to pick him up is one of the assassins who have been assigned to kill the ape-man before he can interfere with the criminal activity of Vinero, an international criminal who takes pleasure in killing people with electronic bombs. At the Plaza de Toros, the most famous bull ring in the world, Tarzan turns the tables on the two men who have been sent to kill him. Soon they both lie dead in the dirt.

Tarzan meets with Professor Talmadge and the police chief, who explain that Vinero and his hired killer, Mr. Train, have located a lost Incan culture and a vast treasure in gold. A small boy named Ramel from the Valley of Tucomy is staying with Tarzan's friend Ruiz, and Tarzan is to meet them at Ruiz's ranch for further details. When Tarzan arrives there, he finds that all the men have been murdered and the boy is gone. Ruiz speaks his last words to Tarzan, who clutches his dying friend in his arms. "It was Vinero's men—they took the boy into the jungle."

It is a personal vendetta for Tarzan now, and he dons a loincloth and prepares to track down Vinero. His "army" consists of two of his old friends, Major, the lion, and Dinky, the chimp, as well as Ramel's leopard Bianco. The leopard trails Ramel's kidnappers into the jungle, and Tarzan's army attacks. Vinero's men are killed, but unfortunately so is the leopard.

Vinero and Mr. Train prepare to take their tank and half-track to the Valley of Tucomy; Tarzan and the boy have the same destination. The twisted Vinero leaves his woman, Sophia, in the jungle to die, setting one of his toys to blow her up if she moves. Tarzan finds Sophia and disarms the device, and she joins his little band.

The way to Tucomy is long and dangerous; several encounters with Vinero's men leave a trail of bodies behind. At last Tarzan, Ramel, and Sophia reach the valley, but Vinero is not far behind with his powerful army and tanks. Tarzan meets with Manco, the leader of Ramel's people, to warn them of the impending danger; but they are a peaceful people and do not understand the coming violence.

Tarzan is imprisoned to keep him from starting any trouble, and soon Vinero and his army roll into Tucomy. The army kills several citizens as a warning, then Vinero demands that the gold be brought to him by morning. Manco releases Tarzan and piles up the gold. "Now you are richer by your hill of gold, and we are poorer by the lives you have taken. Go now," Manco demands.

But Vinero wants more treasure, so Manco leads him to a secret room that has a golden door. Inside, the room begins to fill with gold, and Vinero is soon crushed by the weight of the riches; the greedy man dies surrounded by the gold he sought.

Meanwhile, Tarzan takes command of Vinero's tank and fires on Vinero's men, killing all except Train. The two giants battle hand to hand, and Train strains to break Tarzan's neck. Suddenly, Tarzan wins the battle, and the people of Tucomy are freed from Vinero's tyranny. Tarzan says good-bye to Manco and Ramel, leaving Dinky and Major as new pets for the boy. He and Sophia head back to their respective worlds.

•

Tarzan and the Valley of Gold set the pace for the three Mike Henry Tarzan films; Henry was James Bond in a loincloth. This adventure featured Tarzan jetting to help a friend in Mexico defeat the villain, who is a sadistic international criminal who gets his kicks disintegrating people with his space-age electronic gadgets. Tarzan also has to deal with the bald-pated henchman Mr. Train, who promises to kill the ape-man for his gold-craving boss.

Henry had played linebacker for the Pittsburgh Steelers (1959–61) and the Los Angeles Rams (1962–64) after playing college football at the University of Southern California. While playing defense for the Rams, he also worked for Warner Bros., appearing on TV shows like "77 Sunset Strip," "Hawaiian Eye," and "Surfside Six," as well as the feature film *Spencer's Mountain* (1963).

At six feet four inches and 220 pounds, the muscular ex-jock had the physical requirements to portray the legend of Edgar Rice Burroughs' novels on the big screen, and he was looking forward to the role. In a a press release by Sy Weintraub, Mike Henry noted:

> There's kind of a mystique in Tarzan for me. After all, it's the longest-running single character in the history of motion pictures. And being an L.A. kid, all my life I've been emotionally caught up in movies. The new concept of Tarzan being a contemporary modern who can range all over the world is a special challenge to me.

In the same press release, Weintraub also stated he thought that Mike Henry was the perfect actor to portray Tarzan:

> Mike was really the answer to our dreams. We interviewed over 400 prospective Tarzans until we settled on Mike. You see, Tarzan is no longer the mono-syllabic ape-man; rather he is the embodiment of culture, suavity and style, who is equally at home in a posh night club or the densest jungle. He is the last free soul who seeks adventure and danger, constantly reaching for that last frontier.

The original working title of the film, photographed in and around the jungles surrounding Mexico City in early 1965, was *Tarzan '65* (which would not be appropriate since the film wasn't released until 1966). Henry did his own stunts in the film and worked closely with a not-very-tame leopard named Bianco, as well as a mild-mannered lion called Major and the cute chimp, Dinky (who turned from cute to vicious while filming the next picture and gave Henry a severe bite on the face).

Costarring with Henry as the lost boy Ramel was little Manuel Padilla, who would also costar in the next adventure, *Tarzan and the Great River,* as well as in the Ron Ely television series. The female lead, the sexy blonde, Sophia, was played by sultry leading lady Nancy Kovack; the entourage of villains were led by David Opatoshu as the gold-hungry Vinero and Don Megowan as the nefarious and chrome-domed Mr. Train. An interesting character in the story was Manco, the elder, well played by Mexican actor Francisco Riquerio, who would rather surrender the entire wealth of gold than see a single drop of blood shed.

Directed by Robert Day from a screenplay by Clair Huffaker, *Tarzan and the Valley of Gold* was complete with a trendy 1960s-style musical score by Van Alexander. For Henry, there would be no stopping to rest; before this picture was even released, he was back in the jungles (of Brazil) filming the next adventure, *Tarzan and the Great River.*

Tarzan and the Great River

Release date: 1967; Sy Weintraub/Paramount; running time: 88 minutes; filmed in Eastman Color and Panavision. *Directed by* Robert Day; *produced by* Sy Weintraub; *screenplay by* Bob Barbash; *story by* Lewis Reed and Bob Barbash, *based on the characters created by* Edgar Rice Burroughs; *photography,* Irving Lippman; *associate producer,* Steve Shagan; *production manager,* John Palmer; *film editors,* Anthony Carras, Edward Mann, and James Nelson; *art director,* Herbert Smith; *assistant director,* Mario Cisneros; *special effects,* Ira Anderson; *music composed and conducted by* William Loose.

Mike Henry as Tarzan with Rafer Johnson as Barcuna (*Tarzan and the Great River*, 1967).

Tarzan .... Mike Henry
Captain Sam Bishop .... Jan Murray
Pepe .... Manuel Padilla, Jr.
Dr. Ann Phillips .... Diana Millay
Chief Barcuna .... Rafer Johnson
The Professor .... Paulo Grazindo

A native village is attacked and destroyed by jungle renegades, whose leader is the ruthless Barcuna. These rebels march through the jungles raiding every village, and with each attack Barcuna's power grows. Most of the villagers are taken as recruits or are to be used as slaves in Barcuna's diamond-mining enterprise. Those who oppose him or try to escape are put to death.

Tarzan is called into the situation by his old friend the Professor, who shows the jungle man a vicious poisonous leopard claw used by Barcuna's followers. "It is the symbol of Barcuna, who leads a deadly cult dedicated to the killer instincts of the jaguar," notes the Professor. While Tarzan is visiting Cheeta and some of his other old animal friends at the Professor's animal menagerie, his good friend is killed by the leopard claw. With a heavy heart, Tarzan vows to avenge the Professor's death and to stop Barcuna.

Tarzan soon dons his loincloth and begins his pursuit, with Cheeta and Baron, the lion, as his only army.

Meanwhile, riverboat captain Sam Bishop and his young friend Pepe are attacked by Barcuna's men. When the captain's gun jams, Tarzan comes to the rescue, and the instigators scatter when they are counterattacked by the fierce jungle man.

Tarzan introduces himself to Pepe and Captain Sam, who are delivering medical supplies upriver to Dr. Ann Phillips at her jungle hospital. They decide to join forces and travel together on Sam's boat, but the lion on board makes Sam nervous. Elsewhere in the jungle, Barcuna is warned that Tarzan is coming to destroy him; so he sends men to kill Tarzan first.

As Tarzan and his comrades approach Dr. Phillips' jungle hospital, it is attacked and burned by the leopard men. Barcuna himself has a message for Dr. Phillips, who is stunned at the violence. "Tell your people the jungle belongs to Barcuna," shouts the madman. Ann stumbles into the jungle with her medical bag, and Tarzan is barely in time to save her from a hungry lion.

All with different motives, Tarzan and his party decide to continue on to Marakeet, where there is an epidemic of the plague. The medicine on Sam's boat will cure the natives if they can reach the natives before Barcuna does. An attack by Barcuna's men is repelled by Tarzan, who leaves the river crocodiles to finish the job he started. The group finally arrives in Marakeet, and Tarzan goes to see Chief Monlo, who refuses the doctor's medicine believing it is Barcuna's curse that is killing his people. When young Pepe allows Dr. Ann to inject him with the silver dart (hypodermic needle) as an example, his bravery convinces the chief that the medicine is good.

Now Tarzan must end the threat of Barcuna. He travels through the jungles to Barcuna's slave camp and denounces Barcuna as a fraud. The two challenge each other to fight to the death, and they claw at each other tooth and nail like primitive men. The battle ranges from a dangerous walkway to the river and back to land, as they struggle for life. Finally, Tarzan overcomes his opponent. "The evil is dead—you are free," says the triumphant ape-man.

Baron, the lion, convinces the rest of Barcuna's men that Tarzan's army is indeed the victor. Tarzan says good-bye to Dr. Ann, his young friend Pepe, and Captain Sam. Then he stays on in the jungles to help rebuild what Barcuna has destroyed.

•

With former pro-football player Mike Henry portraying the role of Tarzan, it was only fitting that his adversary in *Tarzan and the Great River* should be former Olympic decathlon champion Rafer Johnson, who was cast as Barcuna, the fanatical leader of the ruthless "leopard cult." The two jungle men were pitted against each other in a battle of wits and muscle; Tarzan would kill the madman in a vicious picture-ending battle to the death.

Historically, great things usually came to the winner of the Olympic decathlon: Past champions, such as Jim Thorpe (1912, Stockholm), Glenn Morris (1936, Berlin), and two-time winner Bob Mathias (1952, Helsinki and 1956, Melbourne), gained great fame from their Olympic feats. In Johnson's case, his victory in the 1960 Olympics in Rome led him to a Hollywood career and a number of starring roles in action features of the 1960s, including the last two Mike Henry Tarzan adventures.

Comedian Jan Murray played the riverboat Captain Sam Bishop, who knew all the angles in conning a buck. His constant comrade was the orphan boy Pepe, played by Manuel Padilla, once again directing this Tarzan adventure to the adolescent market. There were plenty of "cute" scenes with Murray and Padilla engaging in card games and playing with Baron, the lion, and the chimpanzees. The obligatory female lead, Dr. Ann Phillips, was portrayed by Diana Millay. The thanks Tarzan gets from the blonde doctor is a handshake good-bye (not very romantic, this apeman!).

The story by Bob Barbash is unfortunately short in the action department, and not even the overly melodramatic musical score of William Loose could compensate for the lack of true drama. Although there isn't an overabundance of action, there is a great deal of violence; Robert Day had directed the extremely brutal *Tarzan the Magnificent* (1960), and this film followed suit. In fact, this Tarzan was the most cold-blooded ever portrayed on the screen. In one scene a dozen or so of Barcuna's men were torched with a gasoline bomb before they even lifted a finger to attack. (In most Tarzan adventures, as in the novels of Edgar Rice Burroughs, Tarzan rarely took a life unless it was necessary to protect his own life or the lives of others.)

Filming took place in the fall of 1965, and once again, director Robert Day took his camera crews to a distant location, this time, Brazil to capture the magnificent jungles, rivers, and waterfalls. Mike Henry was again asked to work with Baron, the lion, and Dinky, the chimp, as he had done in the

previous picture without any significant problems. This time, however, things weren't as uneventful; in one scene Major was supposed to "attack" some of the hostile natives, but the lion actually chomped down on the leg of an unfortunate fellow, taking the play acting a little too seriously. Although the story is placed in South America, lions and hippopotamuses are used in some of the background scenery, straining credibility. And Tarzan's high dive into the river near the waterfalls was borrowed from *Tarzan's Greatest Adventure*.

The most traumatic event for Henry was when Dinky, the chimp, bit his cheek—a wound that required 18 stitches to close. The chimp was supposed to give his master a smooch on the jaw, but instead he attacked the startled actor. Henry was seriously infected by the monkey bite; after laying in a coma for three days, he developed "monkey fever," which knocked him out of production for three weeks. Dinky, the chimp, also had to be destroyed because he could never be trusted again.

Realistically speaking, this was probably the weakest of Mike Henry's three Tarzan pictures, although none of the trilogy is memorable (not even the use of Johnny Weissmuller's old Tarzan yell could spice this one up). The final Tarzan picture for Henry would be *Tarzan and the Jungle Boy*, and once again his jungle adversary would be portrayed by Rafer Johnson.

Tarzan and the Jungle Boy

Release date: May 1968; Sy Weintraub/Paramount; running time: 90 minutes; filmed in Technicolor and Panavision. *Directed by* Robert Gordon; *produced by* Robert Day; *executive producer,* Sy Weintraub; *screenplay by* Steven Lord, *based on the characters created by* Edgar Rice Burroughs; *photography,* Ozen Sermet; *production supervisor,* John Palmer; *film editors,* Milton Mann and Reg Browne; *art director,* Herbert Smith;

assistant director, Claudio Petraglia; *special effects,* Gabriel Queiroz; *music composed and conducted by* William Loose.

Tarzan	Mike Henry
Nagambi	Rafer Johnson
Myrna Claudel	Alizia Gur
Jukaro (Erik Brunik), the jungle boy	Steve Bond
Buhara	Edward Johnson
Ken Matson	Ronald Gans

A man canoeing down an African river with his young son suddenly encounters rapids that toss the canoe perilously. Moments later the boat capsizes in the swirling waters, and the man and the boy are lost. The man is drowned, but somehow the boy survives.

Six years later, magazine reporter Myrna Claudel and her photographer Ken Matson ask Tarzan for help in finding the lost boy, Erik Brunik, who was spotted in the Zegunda country in the Kenabossa jungle by an aerial photographer. Tarzan agrees to help find the boy, but not for some exclusive magazine story.

As they arrive in a clearing outside the Zegunda country, a great test is under way to choose a successor to the dying chief Otala. The chief's two sons, Nagambi and Buhara, battle through a primitive jungle pentathlon, the winner to become the new chief. The match is even until the last test, when Nagambi dares to cheat to win; he is stopped cold by Tarzan, who saves Buhara's life. The old chief denounces Nagambi and names Buhara his successor, thanking Tarzan for his great service to the Zegundas. Buhara promises Tarzan he will find Jukaro, the jungle boy, but warns Tarzan that he must not follow. "Zegunda country is sacred, and no outsider is allowed to enter and live. Tho' you saved my life, I would have to kill you if I found you there," says the new chief.

Nagambi has sworn to kill Jukaro, so Tarzan journeys alone in spite of Buhara's command, while the stubborn Myrna trails behind with Ken, despite Tarzan's warning to stay put. Meanwhile, the jealous Nagambi and his warriors trap Buhara in the jungle and stake him to die by savage beasts. His death would make Nagambi chief.

Soon a lion attacks the helpless Buhara, but the jungle boy sends his leopard to fight the lion, and Buhara is saved. Jukaro helps the wounded Buhara to his secret hideaway and feeds and nurses him, helping him regain his strength. Eventually, Tarzan finds their hidden jungle; soon the ape-man and Jukaro are fast friends.

When Cheeta suddenly shows up, Tarzan realizes that Myrna and Ken are in mortal danger from the renegade Nagambi. Together, the three warriors (Tarzan, the jungle boy, and Buhara) hit the trail to track down Nagambi. But they are too late; the ruthless Nagambi has killed Ken and their native bearers and has taken Myrna prisoner to sacrifice by fire.

Tarzan goes alone to Nagambi's village to try to save Myrna. On a hill overlooking the village, he gives his mighty war cry, and Nagambi's warriors take after him. But the ape-man is tricky, and he doubles back to free Myrna, amid a hail of spears. Now it is two powerful giants in a battle for supremacy—a fierce fight for life that Tarzan wins. But Tarzan spares the evil one's life. Now Buhara and Nagambi must fight to the death, and the winner will be chief. Buhara's spear finds his brother's

Mike Henry with Steve Bond as the "jungle boy" and Edward Johnson as Buhara (*Tarzan and the Jungle Boy*, 1968).

heart and at last the rightful king assumes the crown of the Zegunda tribe.

After a fatherly talk with Tarzan, Jukaro (Erik) decides to go back to civilization with Myrna and become a geologist like his father. Tarzan bids his friend Buhara good-bye and waves as the plane takes Myrna and Erik back to the other world.

•

The best of the three Mike Henry Tarzan pictures was *Tarzan and the Jungle Boy,* which placed the ape-man back in the African jungles after several years of jetting around the world to exotic places like Brazil, Mexico, Thailand, and India for his adventures. Although photographed once again in Brazil, the setting is Africa, with Tarzan helping to find a lost boy who lives in the jungle on his own, much like Tarzan had done in his youth. Steven Lord's screenplay was an interesting and effective twist on Edgar Rice Burroughs' Tarzan legend, providing a plot with a breath of freshness to it.

Portraying the lost boy Erik Brunik (whose jungle name was Jukaro) was Steve Bond, who did an excellent job with the stunts of vine swinging, climbing, and swimming with Tarzan. Also a touching emotional bond developed between Jukaro and Buhara (Edward Johnson), whom the boy and his leopard save from certain death and then nurse back to health. This relationship was the warm human side to a story that was often filled with gratuitous violence, such as the slaughter of Myrna's entire safari by the vengeful men of Nagambi.

Besides the excellent portrayal by Edward Johnson as Buhara, Rafer Johnson was superb as the evil Nagambi, who is so bloodthirsty he would kill his own brother to be chief of their tribe. After Rafer's one-dimensional role as the heinous madman Barcuna in *Tarzan and the Great River,* his role in this story

gave him an interesting character to develop, although similarly ruthless. The sibling rivalry between the two brothers (one good, the other evil) is well played up, beginning with the primitive pentathlon for the chief's crown, with a slip meaning not only the loss of the crown but certain death.

The chain of command was altered for this picture, with Robert Gordon directing and Robert Day producing (Sy Weintraub was now executive producer). The brutality of the previous Day/Weintraub Tarzan productions was still highly evident, as was the lack of any romance for Tarzan. The inclusion of Myrna Claudel (Alizia Gur) was strictly window dressing, since she and her partner Ken (Ronald Gans) were on the edge of the plot (doing funny things with Cheeta), mostly away from the main action, until her whole safari is wiped out by Nagambi's spearmen, and she is captured. This was Tarzan's hour to shine as he rescues her and defeats Nagambi in a hand-to-hand battle.

The Brazilian jungles again made a brilliantly colored backdrop for a Tarzan adventure (nicely substituting for Africa), and the shooting took place in early 1966; all told, the three Mike Henry films had been produced in less than one year, with the first, *Tarzan and the Valley of Gold,* not having yet been released. This time musical director William Loose came up with a first-rate musical score that added to the drama and was not a noisy melodramatic distraction (as in the previous picture).

The hectic schedule of this production line of Tarzan films precipitated an important decision by Mike Henry: He was through as Tarzan. He told producer Sy Weintraub that he didn't want to portray the jungle man in the upcoming Tarzan television series (the role went instead to Ron Ely). Almost a year in foreign jungles can alter a man's perspectives; the serious animal bites he received and the strain on his health that the poor living conditions had induced made Henry realize that his health was more important to him than his fame as Tarzan. Although Henry looked like he was in the most superb physical condition of his life in the film, it was obviously his mental health that had taken the most serious beating in his strenuous portrayals of Tarzan.

The Mike Henry trilogy of Tarzan adventures will not be classified as great films, but Henry did his best within the parameters of his role. He worked with dangerous animals and did many physically demanding stunts himself. By the end of the third film, his acting and speech were more comfortable and natural; he was becoming an actor in a difficult role. Perhaps it was the lack of any romantic encounters for Tarzan that made these three films weak; the best Tarzan films included a woman for Tarzan to romance as well as rescue from the hazards of the jungle.

The legend of Tarzan had now been on the big screen for 50 years, and it had also taken its share of beatings. For the next 13 years, there would be no new theatrically produced Tarzan adventures until the ill-advised and insulting 1981 remake of *Tarzan, the Ape Man*, with Miles O'Keeffe as Tarzan and Bo Derek as Jane—a film that was hardly what dyed-in-the-wool Tarzan fans had been waiting over a decade for. As a small consolation, Sy Weintraub released two Ron Ely Tarzan adventures in 1970 that were compiled from episodes of the television series.

Tarzan's Deadly Silence

Release date: 1970; Sy Weintraub/National General; running time: 88 minutes; filmed in Deluxe Color. *Directed by* Robert L. Friend and Lawrence Dobkin; *produced by* Leon Benson; *executive producer,* Sy Weintraub; *written by* Lee Irwin, Jack A. Robinson, John Considine, and Tim Considine, *based on the characters created by* Edgar Rice Burroughs; *associate producer,* Vernon E. Clark; *photography,* Abraham Vialla; *production executive,* Steve Shagan; *art director,* Jose Rodriguez Granada; *film editors,* Gabriel Torres and Edward M. Abroms; *special effects,* Laurencio Cordero; *music composed and conducted by* Walter Greene.

Tarzan	Ron Ely
Jai	Manuel Padilla, Jr.
The Colonel	Jock Mahoney
Marshak	Woody Strode
Chico	Gregorio Acosta
Officer	Rudolph Charles
Ruana	Michelle Nicols
Metusa	Robert DoQui
Akaba	Kenneth Washington
Boru	Lupe Garnica
Okala	Jose Chaves
Tabor	Virgil Richardson

Ron Ely and Jock Mahoney fight to the death in *Tarzan's Deadly Silence*, 1970.

Tarzan is stunned when he discovers a friendly jungle village engulfed in flames and learns from a dying native that a man called the Colonel has installed himself as a jungle dictator, forcing the natives to do his bidding. The ape-man swings through the trees to the next village, where he encounters the son of the tribal chief. Tarzan learns that the chief and his brother are being held hostage by the Colonel's native army.

Later Tarzan confronts the Colonel and learns that he is an ex-military expert who has chosen the African jungle to carry on his personal war of oppression and to build a jungle empire. The Colonel is also a master of the bullwhip and shows Tarzan his skills by cutting a man to pieces with the deadly leather "snake."

The Colonel knows that his foe must die or he will endanger his entire operation, so he sends his men to kill the ape-man. Tarzan proves too swift and formidable for the attempts on his life, so the ruthless Colonel has the native boy Jai kidnapped as bait.

Tarzan is forced to face the test of courage by leaping into a pit with Numa, a man-eating lion, but his inherent ability to communicate with the jungle beasts enables him to subdue Numa without a fight. This act of heroism rallies the villagers to attack and overpower the enemy forces and capture the Colonel. The enraged madman angrily vows vengeance against Tarzan.

After Tarzan turns his prisoner over to the Territorial Police, the crafty Colonel escapes into the jungle. Flanked by his two commandos Marshak and Chico, the Colonel begins a military campaign targeted at killing Tarzan.

Trapped in the jungle river, Tarzan dives deep, but is blasted by the shock waves of grenades thrown into the water by the Colonel and his henchmen. Breaking water, Tarzan is shocked to find he has lost his sense of hearing—he's stone deaf.

Even without the precious faculty of hearing, Tarzan is a dangerous opponent. With the aid of his wild animal friends, the ape-man wages his own brand of warfare against the Colonel and his army and destroys his enemies. The jungle tribes are now free from the tyranny of the insane ex-military man, thanks to Tarzan.

•

Tarzan's Deadly Silence starred Ron Ely as the ape-man and was constructed from two episodes of the Sy Weintraub–produced television series that originally aired on October 28 and November 4, 1966; the two-parter was entitled "The Deadly Silence." Former Tarzan actor Jock Mahoney was the deranged Colonel who attempts to conquer the jungle tribes, and his number one henchman was powerful character actor Woody Strode; both actors had played prominent roles in Tarzan adventures in the past. As in the weekly television dramas, Tarzan's young sidekick Jai was played by the diminutive Manuel Padilla, Jr. The film was given theatrical release by National General Pictures in 1970. (For more information on Ron Ely, see the chapter on the 1966–68 television series.)

Tarzan's Jungle Rebellion

Release date: 1970; Sy Weintraub/National General; running time: 92 minutes; filmed in Deluxe Color. *Directed by* William Whitney; *produced by* Leon Benson; *executive producer,* Sy Weintraub; *written by* Jackson Gillis, *based on the characters created by* Edgar Rice Burroughs; *associate producer,* Vernon E. Clark; *photography,* Abraham Vialla; *production executive,* Steve Shagan; *film editor,* Gabriel Torres; *music composed and conducted by* Walter Greene.

Tarzan	Ron Ely
Jai	Manuel Padilla, Jr.
Mary	Ulla Stromstedt
Singleton	Sam Jaffe
Tatakombi	William Marshall
Miller	Harry Lauter
Ramon	Jason Evers
Matto	Lloyd Haynes
Sergeant	Chuck Wood

Tarzan and his young friend Jai often enjoy the peacefulness of the jungle together, but sometimes the jungle can be a deadly place of rebellion. Besides the many dangerous creatures, such as the lion and the

Ron Ely as Tarzan in *Tarzan's Jungle Rebellion*, 1970.

crocodile, there is the deadliest animal of them all—man.

World-renowned archaeologist Dr. Singleton comes to the jungle with his beautiful daughter Mary seeking to find an ancient stone, called the Blue Stone of Heaven, worshipped by the jungle natives. Tarzan agrees to guide the doctor and Mary to a remote area of the jungle to search for the Blue Stone, which had been lost beneath the pyramids in ancient times. Legend has it that whoever stands to the right of the Blue Stone will be endowed with god-like powers.

The power-hungry Colonel Tatakombi also desires the precious Blue Stone for his own reasons and would do anything to obtain it—including destroying anything that gets in his way. When the madman discovers the Blue Stone, he uses the powerful icon to lead the natives into rebellion. Meanwhile, Tarzan unintentionally violates an ancient taboo, which puts him in a precarious position with bloodthirsty natives.

The ruthless Colonel is planning to coerce the jungle tribes to fall in line under his military power. Since his most powerful enemy is Tarzan, Colonel Tatakombi hires Josh Miller to capture the ape-man. No mercy is shown, and the sentence is death for Tarzan.

Mary Singleton has fallen in love with Tarzan and tries to save him from the fate decreed by Tatakombi. In the end, of course, it is Tarzan who calls on his jungle savvy and superhuman strength to defeat Tatakombi and place the Blue Stone where it belongs.

Once again the jungles are tranquil for Tarzan and Jai, as they say good-bye to their new friends Mary and Dr. Singleton, who thank the King of the Jungle for helping them in their quest of the Blue Stone of Heaven.

•

Tarzan's Jungle Rebellion starred Ron Ely as Tarzan and Manuel Padilla as Jai and was compiled from two episodes of the Sy Weintraub–produced television series, which originally aired on October 6 and 13, 1967; the two-parter was entitled "The Blue Stone of Heaven." Leading the guest cast was 70-year-old Sam Jaffe as archaeologist Dr. Singleton. The talented character actor had been in films since the early days of silent films, and his most famous roles were as the High Lama in *Lost Horizon* (1937) and the hero of the classic action adventure *Gunga Din* (1939). Jaffe was also a television star in his own right, as the wise old Dr. Zorba on "Ben Casey" in the 1960s. The villainous Colonel Tatakombi was well portrayed by commanding actor William Marshall, and Tarzan's attractive admirer was played by Ulla Stromstedt.

Tarzan, the Ape Man

Release date: August 1981; Metro-Goldwyn-Mayer; running time: 112 minutes; filmed in Metrocolor. *Directed by* John Derek; *produced by* Bo Derek; *screenplay by* Tom Rowe and Gary Goddard, *based on the characters created by* Edgar Rice Burroughs; *photography,* John Derek; *camera associate,* Wolfgang Dickmann; *film editor,* James B. Ling; *art director,* Alan Roderick-Jones; *sound mixer,* William Randall; *costumes,* Patricia Edwards; *animal trainer,* Paul Reynolds; *stunt coordinator,* Jock O'Mahoney; *music by* Perry Botnik.

Tarzan	Miles O'Keeffe
Jane Parker	Bo Derek
James Parker	Richard Harris
Harry Holt	John Phillip Law
Riano	Maxime Philoe
Africa	Akushula Selayah
Ivory king	Steven Strong
Feathers	Leonard Bailey

Also featuring Wilfrid Hyde-White, Laurie Mains, and Harold Ayer
as the club members.

Jane Parker makes the long journey to Africa to meet the father she has never known, famed explorer James Parker. The hard-boiled father doesn't exactly welcome his daughter, and there's really no love lost between them; he had abandoned Jane's mother when the girl was just a baby.

Parker and his partner Harry Holt plan to safari to beyond the great escarpment to search for the fabled elephants' graveyard. Jane, herself an adventuress, insists on coming along on the dangerous expedition.

Holt has an admiring eye for Jane, but the young woman is as chilly as an icicle. As they talk one night she cools off Mr. Holt with her words, "I don't dislike men, I envy them. I envy your freedom and resent not having the same."

At last they come to the escarpment, an impenetrable sheer cliff. From the treetops comes an eerie cry that Parker says belongs to Tarzan, a white ape-man who, according to legend, is 10 feet tall. The cry terrifies the native bearers, who know that the land of the great white ape-man is taboo.

After completing the perilous climb up the escarpment, Jane relaxes by bathing in the ocean. A hungry lion eyes her from the beach, but Tarzan arrives to call it off. The rifle shots of Parker and Holt chase off the ape-man, but Tarzan has seen what he wants—the beautiful Jane. Parker plans to kill Tarzan, but Jane is convinced he's really a man, not an ape. Parker blames Tarzan for the abduction by natives of Parker's woman. "Ape or man, I'm still going to stuff him on the wall," he shouts bitterly.

As the expedition continues, Jane is kidnapped by Tarzan while she bathes in a stream. The ape-man carries her deep into the jungles, where he is forced to pit his every strength in a life-or-death battle to save her from a mighty python. Exhausted, Tarzan collapses after the fierce struggle. Jane's admiration of Tarzan grows and she realizes that she's falling in love.

Meanwhile, Parker has been searching the jungle for his daughter, who shouts out his name when she hears him approaching. As Jane runs to rejoin her father and Holt, the safari is attacked and surrounded by hostile natives. The three are taken by canoe to their village, where a grim fate awaits them.

As the captors prepare the victims for their strange cult rituals, Cheeta warns Tarzan of Jane's predicament. Tarzan calls his elephant friends, and together they race through the jungle to Jane's rescue. As Tarzan arrives, the cult's bizarrely painted chief stabs Parker with a tusk of ivory, dealing him a mortal wound. As Tarzan swings into battle, the two giants must fight to the death.

An electrifying minute later, the ape-man gives the victory cry of the bull ape.

James Parker, with his dying breath, says good-bye to his daughter, trying to make up for all the lost years in a few moments. Their final words are an expression of regret and love. Jane bids farewell to Holt, who watches in disbelief as Jane and Tarzan walk into the jungle to share their lives.

•

Although it is considered to be the worst Tarzan picture of all time, the blame should not be entirely loaded on the slender shoulders of Bo Derek, the centerpiece of this dismal adventure, or even the brawny shoulders of Miles O'Keeffe, who portrayed the ape-man without uttering a single word beyond his mighty primal scream. The combination of factors that made this film such an unforgivable abomination, are as follows: Director John Derek's self-indulgence in exploiting the Tarzan legend to showcase his young wife, Bo Derek, who was better suited to farces like *10*; a weak script (loosely based on the original 1932 story) that abandoned its primary mission of the search for the elephant graveyard to concentrate on close-ups of a scantily dressed (or naked) Bo Derek and the growing mutual adulation of Tarzan and Jane; and the ridiculous use of slow-motion photography for the only two battles in the picture (Tarzan against the python and the ape-man in his final fight to the death against the hideously painted native chief). In addition, there was the bizarre use of white makeup on the hostile natives and on Jane in the final scenes (which obliterated any compassion the audience might have had for her); and last, but not least, the fact that the number one native villain looked more like a New York punk with his Mohawk haircut, pumped-up physique, and drag

Miles O'Keeffe as Tarzan with Bo Derek as Jane (*Tarzan, the Ape Man*, 1981).

makeup than any jungle enemy that Tarzan had ever faced.

Suffice to say, this is the poorest Tarzan film ever made, for all the reasons just given and more. In reality it should not be classified as a Tarzan picture because the character of Tarzan was totally undeveloped and secondary to the showcasing of Bo Derek. It's a

shame that the name Tarzan was exploited in this way and, in effect, dragged down the entire series.

Not only did Miles O'Keeffe as Tarzan not utter a single word, his Tarzan yell was Johnny Weissmuller's original Tarzan yodel from the 1930s. As a secondary character O'Keeffe didn't get much of a chance for heroics and was mostly around to strut and pose for an admiring Jane. Bo Derek, who can't act, should have been the one without any dialogue. The film was also a waste of the multitalented Richard Harris, who plays an arrogant jerk who at times appears to be almost half-witted in his foolishness. In one scene James Parker quiets a rogue elephant by singing gently to him; for a moment one almost expects him to break into a version of

"MacArthur Park" (Harris's hit song from the 1960s), which would have been no more ludicrous than the film itself.

Tarzan, the Ape Man was filmed entirely on location in Sri Lanka and the Seychelles Islands in the Indian Ocean. Probably the most interesting credit for the picture is that of stunt coordinator Jock O'Mahoney, who had starred in two Tarzan pictures in the early 1960s.

Greystoke: The Legend of Tarzan

Release date: March 1984; Warner Bros.; running time: 129 minutes; filmed in Eastman Color. *Directed by* Hugh Hudson; *produced by* Hugh Hudson and Stanley S. Canter; *screenplay by* P.H. Vazak and Michael Austin, *based on the novel* Tarzan of the Apes *by* Edgar Rice Burroughs; *photography,* John Alcott; *film editor,* Anne V. Coates; *production design,* Stuart Craig; *art directors,* Simon Holland and Norman Dorme; *associate producer,* Garth Thomas; *set decorations,* Ann Mollo; *costumes,* John Mollo; *special visual effects,* Albert J. Whitlock; *special makeup effects,* Rick Baker; *music composed and conducted by* John Scott.

John Clayton, Tarzan, Lord of the Apes	Christopher Lambert
Miss Jane Porter	Andie MacDowell
The Sixth Earl of Greystoke	Ralph Richardson
Capitaine Phillippe D'Arnot	Ian Holm
Lord Esker	James Fox
Jeffson Brown	Ian Charleson
Major Jack Downing	Nigel Davenport
Lord Jack Clayton	Paul Geoffrey
Lady Alice Clayton	Cheryl Campbell

Also featuring Nicholas Farrell *(Sir Hugh Belcher),* Colin Charles *(Olly),* Elaine Collins *(Ruby),* David Endene *(boat captain),* Richard Griffiths *(Captain Billings),* Tristram Jellineck *(White),* Roddy Maude-Roxby *(Olivestone),* Hilton McRae *(Willy),* John Wells *(Sir Evelyn Blount),* Eric Langlois *(Tarzan, age 12),* Daniel Potts *(Tarzan, age five),* Tali McGregor *(baby Tarzan),* Alison Macrae *(Jane, age five),* Ravinder *(Dean),* Harriet Thorpe *(Iris),* David Suchet *(Buller),* Philemon Blake Andhoua *(Aloo),* Paul Brooke *(Reverend Stimson),* Sheila Latimer *(Duchess),* Andrea Miller *(governess),* Jacobin Yarro *(riverbank chief),* Elliot Cane *(Silverbeard),* Alisa Berk *(Kala),* John Alexander *(White Eyes, ape leader),* Christopher Beck *(Droopy Ears, Tarzan's childhood friend),* Max Wilson *(Figs, Tarzan's follower).*

Jack and Alice Clayton (Lord and Lady Greystoke) are shipwrecked on the Ivory Coast of Africa in the year 1885. Clayton builds a rough cabin for shelter from the elements and wild beasts, and Lady Alice soon gives birth to a son.

A jungle fever and the despair of their situation have taken away Alice's mental faculties, and one day she slips into the eternal sleep. Jack is spared continued agony when he is crushed to death in his cabin by a great ape. Meanwhile, the Clayton baby is snatched up by Kala, the she-ape, who abandons her own dead infant on the cabin floor. Kala raises the human babe as her own, calling him Tarzan.

Young Tarzan grows up among the apes, learning their language and living as one of them. One day he and one of his ape friends are cornered by a panther near a stream. As the big cat mauls the ape, Tarzan flogs his way across the stream with his life in the balance, thus learning to swim.

Eventually the young Tarzan finds his father's cabin and wonders at the many strange things he discovers. He also finds Clayton's sharp hunting knife, and after cutting himself realizes he now has a formidable weapon to defend himself against the beasts of prey.

One dark day Kala is wounded by the arrows of pygmies. When the anguished ape-boy carries her to a stream for a mouthful of cool water, a pygmy warrior suddenly deals her a death blow with his spear. The enraged Tarzan kills his first human, snapping his back like a twig. Tarzan screams in agony when he finally realizes Kala is dead.

Years later an expedition arrives in West Africa to collect fauna for the British Museum. Among them is Capitaine Phillippe D'Arnot, a Belgian, who has considerable disdain for his pompous British counterparts. D'Arnot puts the pieces together when he sees a naked white boy in the trees and then later finds the Clayton cabin and the skeletons of John and Alice.

When the expedition is attacked by pygmies, D'Arnot survives his serious wounds by hiding from them in the brush. Eventually Tarzan, a savage who can only grunt the language of the apes, finds the Belgian and nurses him back to health.

By now Tarzan is master of all the beasts through the use of his knife and his superior intellect. When a surly gorilla soundly thrashes his ape "father" Silverbeard, Tarzan issues a challenge— they fight to the death. It is Tarzan's knife that proves the difference. He is now the undisputed Lord of the Apes and is lauded and cheered by his fellow apes for his great victory.

As the days pass, D'Arnot teaches the intelligent Tarzan to speak English, and soon they become close friends. As Tarzan's education progresses, D'Arnot tells him he is really John Clayton and that his parents died in the small cabin. The heir to the title of Greystoke, Tarzan will not believe that he is anything but a white ape, the son of Kala and Silverbeard.

Eventually D'Arnot convinces John that he must go to Scotland with him and discover his roots. The teacher continues the tutelage of the pupil during the long voyage home in preparation for meeting his grandfather, the Earl of Greystoke.

Lord Greystoke is excited when his grandson arrives by carriage, and when John steps down, he *knows* Tarzan is a Greystoke. "My boy—my dear, dear boy!" cries the old man as he embraces Tarzan. A grateful look is in his eyes when he squeezes D'Arnot's hand.

John is introduced to Jane Porter, the American ward of Lord Greystoke, and he is impressed by her beauty. The former ape-man emits a low savage growl when he sees he has a rival for Jane in the stuffy Lord Esker.

Christopher Lambert as Tarzan (*Greystoke: The Legend of Tarzan,* 1984).

John proves to be the hit of his grandfather's dinner party with his animal growls and bird chirps, although Esker looks on with disapproval. Soon, D'Arnot bids John au revoir, leaving Jane to continue John's education. John is overcome with emotion as he races after the carriage of his dearest friend to say good-bye.

This strange new life is often too much for John, who longs to return to Africa again to be Tarzan of the Apes. But Jane is his saving grace, and the two friends grow closer and closer. Soon they fall in love, but their feelings are as yet unspoken. When Esker asks Jane to marry him, she flatly refuses. He blames the "jungle man" for his losing her and storms out of Greystoke Manor in a huff.

At his Christmas banquet, Lord Greystoke warmly introduces his grandson John, the heir to his estates and title. The old man loves him very much. A tragic accident occurs when the elderly Greystoke is killed sliding down the staircase on a serving tray, a childish prank. His dying words to John are a gentle good-bye to the grandson he loves so much.

D'Arnot returns for the Greystoke funeral and to comfort his dear friend. Dressed in black, Jane tells the despondent Johnny she loves him. He enters her room that evening and kisses her passionately (as the scene fades).

John and Jane attend the opening of the Greystoke Gallery, a new wing of the British Museum dedicated to the origin of the species and funded by the late Lord Greystoke. John abruptly rushes out of the close quarters of the gallery and, with a sixth sense, enters a nearby building. Inside he finds the dead carcass of an ape, a poor creature used for experimental research. Many cages are filled with live apes, and to John's surprise, one of them contains his ape "father," Silverbeard.

John reverts to Tarzan, the ape-man, and releases Silverbeard and they fondly embrace. Out on the grounds they run and play. Of course this causes an uncommon disturbance. Together they climb a tree to escape the police, but a rifleman fires and wounds the old ape. The tormented Tarzan holds Silverbeard in his arms until he dies, then screams to the stunned crowd that has gathered, "He was my father!"

Now overcome by civilization's strange ways, John Clayton—Tarzan— speaks of his decision. "I am going home because I know I'm not. Half of me is the Earl of Greystoke, the other half is wild," he somberly tells Jane and D'Arnot. They accompany him back to Africa, but only to say good-bye. Tarzan throws off his clothes and runs into the jungle. Jane watches as Tarzan disappears in the distance, hoping someday they may be together again.

•

The first legitimate Tarzan motion picture in 15 years, *Greystoke: The Legend of Tarzan,* was also the most carefully planned and elaborately produced film of the genre. The result was an absorbing melodrama about the sensitive inner man (Tarzan/John Clayton), rather than the great feats of heroism and sheer physical skill of past Tarzan adventures. To some movie buffs, this film was a disappointment because Tarzan was presented in this light, while many others applauded producer/director Hugh Hudson for his story showing the ape-man's early life before he became the larger-than-life hero of the Johnny Weissmuller/Gordon Scott tradition.

Definitely a thinking man's version of Edgar Rice Burroughs' story, *Greystoke* portrays Tarzan as a sensitive soul who must deal with a series of emotional encounters in his relatively short life, including the death of his ape-mother Kala by pygmy arrows when he was a boy, dying in his arms; nursing the white man D'Arnot back to health after he, too, was wounded by the pygmies; the difficult transformation from a lad born in the jungle and raised by apes to daily life as part of the British aristocracy as the grandson of the sixth Earl of Greystoke; the departure of his comrade D'Arnot, who must return to his homeland, Belgium; the tragic death of his grandfather, who strikes his head after sliding down the staircase on a silver serving tray, the old man dying in his arms; and, finally, his bittersweet reunion with his ape-father Silverbeard in England, only to see him killed in cold blood and to feel the life force ebb away while embracing his last surviving family member. Even his love affair with Jane is tragic, since after he finds his

Tarzan becomes John Clayton, with Lord Greystoke (Ralph Richardson) and D'Arnot (Ian Holm) (*Greystoke: The Legend of Tarzan,* 1984).

true love, he is driven by instinct to return to his African home.

Tarzan's heroism in this story is on a more basic level, such as in his battles for jungle supremacy with the panther and White Eyes (the alpha primate); saving the life of D'Arnot; and standing up for the lad whom Esker plans to whip merely for sitting in his spiffy red automobile. Tarzan never calls in the elephants for a heroic rescue; never saves Jane from certain death; and never saves his beloved Africa from remorseless, plundering white men.

Starring as John Clayton–Tarzan was Christopher Lambert, who fit the role perfectly, but again was a stark departure from the classic physical description of the ape-man. At five feet nine inches tall and with a lean, wiry build, Lambert's Tarzan was built for

climbing trees and jungle survival, not for performing tests of strength with gargantuan animals and humans. Lambert did a superb acting job within the boundaries of his character, truly expressing the deep personal emotions of both the ape-man and John Clayton. Indeed this ape-man was very human, with a fragile psyche, in contrast to Burroughs' fictional Tarzan, who was heroic, emotionally as well as physically.

Other important members of the cast were Ian Holm in a fine supporting performance as D'Arnot, Tarzan's dear friend and mentor. Holm had a great scene of personal fortitude when D'Arnot is shot twice by pygmy arrows and manages to struggle to a hiding place while in intense agony. Moments later he pulls the arrows from his own body and passes out, eventually to be found by Tarzan. Andie MacDowell was charming and beautiful in her film debut as Jane, the love interest of John Clayton. The venerable Sir Ralph Richardson (in his final screen portrayal) was marvelous as Lord Greystoke, the kindly and very human grandfather of, as he warmly called him, Johnny. The highly respected British stage and screen actor died in late 1983 before *Greystoke* was released, and the picture was dedicated to his memory.

The screenplay for *Greystoke* was written in the mid–1970s by Robert Towne (using the pseudonym P.H. Vazak), with Towne also in line to direct and Stanley S. Canter to produce the film for Warner Bros. Towne was well known for his Academy Award–winning screenplay for *Chinatown* (1974), but a combination of Hollywood politics and his devotion of time and energy as writer-director of *Personal Best* (1982) caused the property of *Greystoke* eventually to be passed to Hugh Hudson, who directed the film and coproduced it along with Canter. Michael Austin was brought in to restructure the story as it was now conceived by Hudson, the director of *Chariots of Fire,* winner of the Oscar for Best Picture in 1981.

The scenic African landscape, wide rivers, and majestic waterfalls were superbly photographed by John Alcott in Cameroon (West Africa) in November and December 1982. Only a week before the cast and crew arrived, the slumbering Mount Cameroon (a volcano that is the highest peak in West Africa) had erupted, and the president of the country abdicated his 25-year position under the rumors of a military coup. The film company worked under the difficult conditions of 100-degree heat, torrential rains, sometimes uncooperative and superstitious local native tribes, the almost impenetrable jungles, and the unstable political environment, to ac-

complish their African filming mission with only minor mishaps. Tarzan actor Christopher Lambert recalled the difficult circumstances in a 1984 press release: "We arrived towards the end of the rainy season which lasted longer than usual. You couldn't go anywhere without getting drenched, no matter what kind of protective gear you wore. After a while, it didn't matter. The water was warm—like stepping *out* into a hot shower."

In the dense jungle vegetation lived poisonous snakes and deadly spiders, in addition to the larger carnivorous mammals and primates. Surviving and working under these conditions, Lambert was able to visualize his character of Tarzan clearly: "I imagined what life was like for Tarzan. That he was on a thin edge, between living and dying, from the moment he was born."

The British location settings included Floors Castle, the home of the Duke and Duchess of Roxburghe. The historic castle was built in 1721 and expanded and remodeled in 1821 by renowned British architect W.H. Playfair. Key interiors were filmed at Hatfield House (the stately mansion of the Marquis of Salisbury), which had originally been appropriated from the Catholic church by King Henry VIII as a residence for the royal children. Also used as location spots were Blenheim Palace and the Natural History Musuem.

The realistic ape costumes and makeup were created by Rick Baker. Underneath the elaborate facade, the talented actors portraying the apes were Elliot Cane as Silverbeard, Alisa Berk as Kala, and John Alexander as White Eyes. A marvelous musical score by John Scott complemented the production.

The presentation of the tender alliances between Tarzan and his ape family, as well as John's relationships with D'Arnot and the elderly Greystoke, were warm and enjoyable. Although it does not include the action, adventure, and sheer romance of the 1930s Weissmuller/O'Sullivan classic Tarzan motion pictures, *Greystoke* is an excellent film because of its tender human qualities and its unique (and sometimes humorous) story. A major criticism (if you can call it that) is that *Greystoke* is not a true Tarzan adventure as such, but an elaborately staged drama about an ape-boy who discovers he's really John Clayton, Lord Greystoke, but doesn't want to be. Indeed the name Tarzan is never used in the picture, although the implication is clear enough.

There would be no critical awards for director Hugh Hudson's production of *Greystoke: The Legend of Tarzan*, but the responses from the fans and critics were mostly favorable and applauded his efforts to present the legend of Tarzan from an original viewpoint. The following are some of the reviews:

New York Times **(March 30, 1984)** (Vincent Canby): "From the most unlikely source material comes the season's most unexpected, most invigorating surprise, *Greystoke: The Legend of Tarzan*, a huge, lavishly produced period film that is part adventure, part comedy of manners and part somber melodrama.... Hugh Hudson and his associates have discovered reserves of feeling and beauty in the old Edgar Rice Burroughs' tales that remained unexplored by Burroughs himself and by the dozens of journeymen who have been cranking out Tarzan movies and television serials over the years."

Motion Picture Guide **(Cinebooks, 1985–1987):** "Certainly the most intelligent and probably the best filmic treatment of Edgar Rice Burroughs' classic pulp novels about Tarzan, the white child of noble blood raised by apes in the jungle.... Since Elmo Lincoln first brought Tarzan to the screen in 1918, no film of his exploits has ever been so lovingly based on the fictional character created by Burroughs, and it is unlikely that any film about him after this will reach the same heights."

Movie Home Companion **(Andrews and McMeel, 1985)** (Roger Ebert): "*Greystoke: The Legend of Tarzan* is the most faithful film adaptation of the Tarzan legend ever made.... The obvious challenge for this movie is to convince an audience that it is actually looking at a little human baby being nurtured by wild animals. *Greystoke* passes this test.... But where's the action? Shouldn't there be some sort of pulp subplot about ant men, or the jewels of Opar, or a wild elephant on a rampage? *Greystoke* is the story of the legend of Tarzan, but it doesn't contain an adventure *involving* Tarzan. Who would have guessed there'd ever be a respectable Tarzan movie?"

In addition to these reviews, *Greystoke: The Legend of Tarzan* was also reviewed by the following publications: *America, Commonweal, Macleans, Mademoiselle, N.Y., The Nation, National Review, New Republic, New Yorker, Newsweek, Scholastic Update, Seventeen, Time,* and *Vogue*.

IV.

Tarzan on Television

Tarzan and the Trappers

Copyright: 1958 (unsold TV pilot); Sol Lesser Productions; running time: 74 minutes. *Directed by* Charles Haas and Sandy Howard; *produced by* Sol Lesser; *written by* Frederick Schlick and Robert Leach, *based on the characters created by* Edgar Rice Burroughs; *photography,* William Snyder and Alan Stensvold; *African photography,* Miki Carter; *art directors,* Ernst Fegte and Frank Hotaling; *production supervisor,* Fred Ahern; *film editor,* George Gittens; *assistant director,* Gordon McLean; *set decoration,* Victor Gangelin and Jack Mills; *sound technician,* Jean L. Speak; *music supervision* by Audrey Granville.

Tarzan	Gordon Scott
Jane	Eve Brent
Tantu (Boy)	Rickie Sorensen
Schroeder	Lesley Bradley
René	Maurice Marsac
Sikes	Saul Gorse
Lapin	William Keene
Tyana	Sherman Crothers

Also featuring Bruce Lester, Naaman Brown, Paul Thompson, Carl Christian, Madame Sul-te-wan, Paul Stader, and Don Blackman.

Tarzan hears the restless native drums and knows there is trouble brought by outsiders. He leaves Jane and Boy to investigate and finds that trappers have invaded his jungles, caging his animals. The drums mourn the death of a local villager, and Tarzan speaks with the chief to stop trouble before it starts. "Do not make war on trappers," he says. "Send a message to commissioner in Randini. Tarzan hunt down trappers and free animals."

The troublemakers are Schroeder and the white hunter René, who ruthlessly kill a mother elephant just to capture the baby. Tarzan scares off the two guards (who run like jackals) and frees the baby elephant, snapping its chain with his bare hands. Meanwhile, the two men have captured Cheeta and plan to use Boy as a hostage until they are safely away.

Tarzan calls his elephants to action, and the elephants level the camp and free the animals from their broken cages. Tarzan knocks Schroeder and René out cold; then the commissioner from Randini arrives to take them to jail.

Back home with Jane and Boy,

219

Gordon Scott with Eve Brent and Rickie Sorensen (*Tarzan and the Trappers*, 1958).

Tarzan's friend Tyana brings a message of foreboding: More white men have come to bring trouble for Tarzan. Lapin plans to find the lost city of Zarbo to steal its treasure, while Sikes intends to kill Tarzan for spoiling his brother Schroeder's trapping expedition and sending him to jail.

When Tarzan meets the men face to face, he laughs at Sikes' bold threats. "In the jungle, the hunter becomes the hunted—I go now," warns the ape-man. To escape, he must battle six men, including a giant of a man that Tarzan floors like a punch-drunk fighter.

As Sikes and Lapin trek toward the lost city of Zarbo, it is indeed Tarzan who is the hunter. He gives his mighty war cry, and now they know that he is hunting them. But Lapin decides that the best way to trap Tarzan is with bait—his friend Tyana whom they kidnap from his village.

When he comes to free Tyana, Tarzan is trapped in a hunting net, and both men are tied and prepared for torture. But the warriors of Tyana surround the camp, as Tarzan frees himself and his friend. The barking guns of Sikes save the villains temporarily, but Tarzan is now ready to make war!

Tarzan sets a false trail for Sikes and Lapin to follow that leads them to the lost city of Zarbo. However, Zarbo is deserted, and there is no treasure. Lapin is practically in tears, but Sikes laughs in his face because he still has plans to kill Tarzan.

By now Tarzan has Sikes and Lapin trapped in the empty treasure chamber, and the ape-man flies to the attack. Soon they are all lying unconscious, with the victorious Tarzan standing alone. Tarzan makes arrangements with the natives to turn Sikes and Lapin over to the commissioner and then heads back to his own land. When Tarzan returns, Jane and Boy are anxiously waiting to hear of his adventure.

•

While producing the 1958 theatrical release *Tarzan's Fight for Life,* producer Sol Lesser was also planning to invade the television market with a Tarzan series starring Gordon Scott; Eve Brent as Jane; and Rickie Sorensen as Tantu, their adopted son.

However, Lesser couldn't find a sponsor or network interested in the pilot, so the episodes landed on a shelf collecting dust, unsold. Several years later the three pilots were spliced together to make a 74-minute telefeature, which eventually became part of a syndicated movie package. Originally, the first pilot episode was about Tarzan stopping a ruthless trapper, while the next two episodes had Tarzan dealing with a hunter who plans to kill him and his greedy partner who hopes to find the lost city of Zarbo and its fabulous treasure.

The sets built for *Tarzan's Fight for Life* were reused for the TV pilots, as was the African photography of Miki Carter, including wild animal footage, Tarzan's vine swinging, genuine native tribespeople and dancers, and landscapes and backgrounds. Gordon Scott had been on hand for part of Miki Carter's expedition to Kenya, and in one scene he hopped on the back of a young giraffe (smaller than a horse) and sped off after some villains. Also borrowed were some of the old background music and stock shots of Tarzan's treehouse and more wild animal footage (hippos "dancing" in the river, etc.), from the Lex Barker films.

"Tarzan and the Trappers" was definitely low-grade television melodrama, and it's easy to see why Sol Lesser couldn't find a buyer for the series. Westerns were the raging vogue on television by the late 1950s, and Tarzan riding on the back of a giraffe just didn't qualify as cowboy action. Although Sol Lesser did not find a market for Tarzan on television, Sy Weintraub would bring the ape-man to series TV in 1966, with Ron Ely as Tarzan.

Tarzan Television Series

Date: 1966–1968.

Tarzan . . . . Ron Ely
Jai . . . . Manuel Padilla, Jr.
Jason Flood . . . . Alan Caillou
Rao . . . . Rockne Tarkington
Tall Boy . . . . Stewart Raffill

The ape-man finally came to television for the 1966 season and starred 28-year-old actor Ron Ely. Born Ronald Pierce in Hereford, Texas, Ely had broken into the movies with a small role in *South Pacific* (1958) and a costarring role as a diver in the short-lived TV actioner *The Aquanauts* in 1961. After movie Tarzan Mike Henry turned down the television series, the lanky six feet four inch, 212-pound Ely was cast as Tarzan.

Ron Ely as Tarzan (*Tarzan Television Series*, 1966–1968).

Ely played his character as an educated contemporary Tarzan (living in the 1960s) with perfect diction, yet making his home in the jungle and surviving as a primitive man might do without the conveniences of modern society. Some things never change in Tarzan adventures, and Johnny Weissmuller's Tarzan cry from the 1930s was still in use in these latest jungle episodes. There was no Jane in the life of this Tarzan and, in fact, little room for romance for the jungle man, who was too busy foiling villains in the weekly dramas to chase skirts.

Starring with Ely was diminutive Manuel Padilla, Jr., as Jai, a wiry orphan boy adopted by Tarzan and educated in the ways of the jungle by the crafty former ape-man. Padilla had plenty of experience in the jungles after working with Mike Henry in his first two Tarzan features. The initial five episodes were photographed in the jungles of Brazil, which proved to be too difficult a filming environment for the actors and production crew; thereafter the series was filmed in Mexico. Regular cast members included Jason Flood as Jai's tutor; Rockne Tarkington as the village veterinarian; and Stewart Raffill as Tall Boy, the veterinarian's assistant.

Some of the well-known actors and actresses to appear as guest stars on the series included Jock Mahoney (a former Tarzan), Woody Strode, James Whitmore, Anne Jeffreys, Susan Oliver, Rafer Johnson, Russ Tamblyn, Maurice Evans, Julie Harris, Ruth Roman, Ralph Meeker, Tammy Grimes, George Kennedy, Sam Jaffe, William Marshall, Helen Hayes, James MacArthur, John Dehner, James Earl Jones, Diana Ross, Robert Loggia, Michael Ansara, Fernando Lamas, Malachi Throne, and Neville Brand.

Proving he had the guts and the skills to handle the Tarzan role, Ely insisted on doing all of his own stunts and animal fights and in the first season alone, he suffered 16 wounds and injuries: (1) seven stitches in the head from lion bite, (2) a broken nose in a water fight, (3) a dislocated jaw in a fight, (4) a wrenched neck and disc in a vine-swinging accident, (5) a right shoulder separation in vine-swinging accident, (6) the left shoulder broken from a vine breaking during swing, (7) three broken ribs from the same accident, (8) the right biceps muscle torn in a fight with a lion, (9) claw marks from a fight with a leopard and a puma, (10) the left leg hamstring muscle pulled, (11) the right thigh muscle pulled, (12) bites and claw marks from jungle animals, (13) both ankles sprained from hard landings after leaps, (14) tops of the feet badly scratched in a fall downhill, (15) a cracked left heel, and (16) the bottom of the right foot torn slipping on a rocky

mountain. The broken shoulder incurred while falling from a vine was captured on film and used in the story as if Tarzan had been shot down in an ambush, with Ely wearing his arm in a sling the balance of the episode. This was one tough Tarzan!

Produced by Sy Weintraub, the series included various jungle landscape and wild animal scenes that were borrowed from Weintraub-produced theatrical releases (with Gordon Scott as Tarzan) and spliced into the television adventures. A tragic accident during the first season's production occurred when a rattled elephant grabbed his trainer and hurled him against a wall, killing him.

This television series survived for two seasons on the NBC network with 57 episodes. The premiere, "Eyes of the Lion," aired on September 8, 1966, and the final first-run episode, "Trina," was shown on April 5, 1968. (See Appendix B for a guide to all the episodes.)

Tarzan in Manhattan

Release date: 1989; American First Run Studios; running time: 100 minutes. *Directed by* Michael Schultz; *producer,* Charles Hairston; *executive producers,* Max A. Keller and Micheline H. Keller; *written by* Anna Sandor and William Gough, *based on the characters created by* Edgar Rice Burroughs; *photography by* Laszlo George; *film editor,* Dann Cahn; *production designer,* Vincent J. Cresciman; *casting,* Barbara King; *coproducer,* Gina Scheerer; *music composed and conducted by* Charles Fox.

Tarzan . . . . Joe Lara
Jane Porter . . . . Kim Crosby
Archimedes Porter . . . . Tony Curtis
Brightmore . . . . Jan Michael Vincent
Joseph . . . . Joe Seneca
Juan Lipschitz . . . . Jimmy Medina Taggert

Also featuring Peter Sherayko, Robert Benedetti, Jim Doughan, Oliver Muirhead, Darnelle Gregorio, Joel Carlson, Jerry Queenie, Sloan Fischer, Terry Millines, Rodney Saulisberry, Don McLeod, Buck Young, and Christopher Carroll.

When Tarzan hears rifle shots in his jungle, he races to the scene of a personal tragedy—his ape-mother Kala lies dead from a hunter's bullet. Tarzan screams out Kala's name in agony and moments later is further pained to discover that Cheeta has been abducted by the poachers.

The only clues Tarzan can find are a cigar butt and a matchbook that reads "Beta Noire, 25 East 55th, NY, NY." Tarzan meets his friend Joseph at the trading post. "They killed Kala and took Cheeta," says a sorrowful Tarzan. "I must get to New York to punish Kala's killers and find Cheeta." Joseph bids Tarzan good-bye and wishes him good luck, saying "Now don't you go and get civilized on me."

Arriving in New York wearing jeans and a T-shirt, Tarzan is immediately jailed for failing to pass customs. The ape-man rips out the bars of a window and dives into the river, with bullets from the guards' rifles whizzing by his ears. Now dressed only in his loincloth, Tarzan hails a cabbie, who turns out to be Jane Porter, an educated woman who finds cab driving more to her liking than conventional occupations.

When Tarzan stops a runaway horse and buggy, saving its occupants, Jane is impressed with the courage of the brawny (albeit naïve) jungle man. She offers to help Tarzan find Cheeta. A telephone number inside the matchbook leads to the Brightmore Foundation, owned by wealthy playboy William Brightmore.

Later, Jane enlists the aid of her father, Archimedes Porter, who runs a detective agency. Archie thinks Tarzan is a little strange, running around in a loincloth as he does. But when he learns that Tarzan saved his daughter from a gang of thugs led by Juan Lipschitz, Archie joins in the ape-man's crusade.

Bluffing their way into a costume party given by Brightmore, Tarzan and Archie hope to find Cheeta while Jane keeps their host busy. Brightmore puts his moves on the stunning Jane, while Tarzan's nose leads him and Archie to a dungeon filled with chimps in cages, including Cheeta. Narrowly making their escape, Tarzan is wounded in the ensuing melee.

Archie digs a bullet from Tarzan's shoulder and then heads for the Brightmore Foundation in disguise once again. Snooping in the foundation's secret files, he photographs documents that prove that Brightmore is an international criminal experimenting in protein manipulation and gene splicing, killing hundreds of monkeys used as "guinea pigs" in the process.

The evidence is almost destroyed when Brightmore has Archie's office blown up and the detective is seriously injured. Now it is up to Tarzan and Jane to handle Brightmore, as they head to his estates to get their man. However, the diabolical criminal soon has them trapped on his grounds, and he becomes the hunter. With the odds against him, Tarzan's flaming arrow blows up Brightmore's explosives and jeep, and the ensuing hand-to-hand battle is all ape-man.

Tarzan tells Jane that he must return to his home. "There's less fighting in the jungle—things are at peace." But prompting from a now-recovered Archie and a passionate kiss from Jane have Tarzan and Cheeta staying on in New York indefinitely.

•

"Tarzan in Manhattan," a 1989 CBS telefeature, was a pilot for a proposed weekly series that would have starred Joe Lara as Tarzan. The TV series never got off the ground—Tarzan fans weren't overly enthusiastic about the idea of the ape-man in New York and out of his jungle habitat.

The story had been done before in

Joe Lara as Tarzan with Cheeta (*Tarzan in Manhattan*, 1989).

Tarzan's New York Adventure (1942) with Johnny Weissmuller, except that in that film, the ape-man went to the Big Apple to find his abducted son, Boy. This 1989 updated version had Tarzan heading for New York to find his abducted chimp, Cheeta, and meeting a woman cab driver named Jane Porter. Thus, the story was not exactly original, and the idea of taking Tarzan out of the jungles and transplanting him to civilization simply didn't work. Proving that some things can never be improved upon, the original Johnny Weissmuller Tarzan yell from the 1930s was still being used by the ape-man in 1989.

Twenty-six-year-old Joe Lara beat out 300 other Tarzan hopefuls who auditioned for the part and did a respectable job as the ape-man, considering the limited parameters of his role. Lara was a former photographic model, a far cry from the days when motion picture Tarzans were selected from the ranks of Olympic champions like Weissmuller, Buster Crabbe, Herman Brix, and Glenn Morris.

Kim Crosby also did a nice job as the cute, cab-driving Jane, who was really an intellectual with a college degree in computers. Hamming it up as her father, the private eye, was screen veteran Tony Curtis, while the obligatory villain was played with gusto by Jan Michael Vincent. In the opening scenes, Tarzan's friend Joseph was convincingly played by Joe Seneca.

Certainly, "Tarzan in Manhattan" was directed at the juvenile market because no self-respecting adult Tarzan fan could find much reason to cheer the "misadventures" of this ape-man in New York City. It was pleasant-enough family fare, if you didn't mind a little violence thrown at your kids, but hardly the stuff Edgar Rice Burroughs had in mind when he created Tarzan in 1912.

Tarzan Television Series

Date: 1991–1993.

Tarzan	Wolf Larson
Jane	Lydie Denier
Roger	Sean Roberge
Simon	Malick Bowens (1991–92)
Jack Benton	Errol Slue (1992–93)

The 19th actor to portray Tarzan on the screen was Wolf Larson when Tarzan returned to television in 1991. The 32-year-old actor was born Wolfgang Wyszecki in Berlin, Germany, but was raised in Ontario, Canada. He got his initial break in acting in a few episodes of the TV series "Dynasty" as Joan Collins' secretary, which led to his casting as Tarzan. At six feet, two inches and 200 pounds, Larson played the ape-man with long blonde hair and midcalf leather moccasins protecting his feet.

This modern-day Tarzan was an environmentalist whose primary concern was to protect the wild creatures of the jungle from poachers and polluters. He also had a girlfriend Jane (Lydie Denier), a worldly zoologist with a French

Wolf Larson as Tarzan (*Tarzan Television Series*, 1991).

accent; a native friend Simon (Malick Bowens), a bush pilot who was Tarzan's mentor and contact with the outside world; and a young protégé Roger (Sean Roberge), who lived with him and usually got into more trouble than Cheeta, the chimp. (For the 1992-93 season, the character of Simon was replaced by Jack Benton, portrayed by Errol Slue.)

But the story remained the same; only a few details and names were changed from Edgar Rice Burroughs' legend of Tarzan. One thing that will never change is the use of Johnny Weissmuller's Tarzan yodel from the 1930s, which was used for the umpteenth time as the ape-man's inimitable victory cry.

One of the first season's episodes featured former TV Tarzan Ron Ely as Gordon Shaw, a cunning and remorseless hunter who travels the world over killing big game with his bow and ar-rows; he considers it better sport to give the beasts a chance. When Tarzan foils his hunt for Tantor, the elephant, it is Tarzan who becomes the hunted, the "ultimate trophy," as the hunter puts it. Needless to say, Tarzan wins this battle of wits and jungle skills and has Simon turn Shaw over to the authorities for punishment.

In the series, photographed on location in Yucatan, Mexico, Larson performed most of his own stunts, including several dangerous ones. This new Tarzan series was developed for television by Max Keller and Micheline Keller, who also produced "Tarzan in Manhattan," the 1989 telefeature. (Note: A second syndicated season (1992-93) for the series was not presented on U.S. television, but was successful in over a dozen foreign markets. See Appendix C for a guide to the episodes.)

APPENDIX A:
CHRONOLOGICAL TARZAN
FILMOGRAPHY

1918	*Tarzan of the Apes*	Elmo Lincoln
1918	*The Romance of Tarzan*	Elmo Lincoln
1920	*The Revenge of Tarzan*	Gene Pollar
1920	*The Son of Tarzan*	P. Dempsey Tabler
1921	*The Adventures of Tarzan*	Elmo Lincoln
1927	*Tarzan and the Golden Lion*	James Pierce
1928	*Tarzan the Mighty*	Frank Merrill
1929	*Tarzan the Tiger*	Frank Merrill
1932	*Tarzan, the Ape Man*	Johnny Weissmuller
1933	*Tarzan the Fearless*	Buster Crabbe
1934	*Tarzan and His Mate*	Johnny Weissmuller
1935	*The New Adventures of Tarzan*	Herman Brix
1936	*Tarzan Escapes*	Johnny Weissmuller
1938	*Tarzan's Revenge*	Glenn Morris
1938	*Tarzan and the Green Goddess*	Herman Brix
1939	*Tarzan Finds a Son!*	Johnny Weissmuller
1941	*Tarzan's Secret Treasure*	Johnny Weissmuller
1942	*Tarzan's New York Adventure*	Johnny Weissmuller
1943	*Tarzan Triumphs*	Johnny Weissmuller
1943	*Tarzan's Desert Mystery*	Johnny Weissmuller
1945	*Tarzan and the Amazons*	Johnny Weissmuller
1946	*Tarzan and the Leopard Woman*	Johnny Weissmuller
1947	*Tarzan and the Huntress*	Johnny Weissmuller
1948	*Tarzan and the Mermaids*	Johnny Weissmuller
1949	*Tarzan's Magic Fountain*	Lex Barker
1950	*Tarzan and the Slave Girl*	Lex Barker
1951	*Tarzan's Peril*	Lex Barker
1952	*Tarzan's Savage Fury*	Lex Barker
1953	*Tarzan and the She-Devil*	Lex Barker
1955	*Tarzan's Hidden Jungle*	Gordon Scott

1957	*Tarzan and the Lost Safari*	Gordon Scott
1958	*Tarzan's Fight for Life*	Gordon Scott
1958	*Tarzan and the Trappers*★	Gordon Scott
1959	*Tarzan's Greatest Adventure*	Gordon Scott
1959	*Tarzan, the Ape Man*	Denny Miller
1960	*Tarzan, the Magnificent*	Gordon Scott
1962	*Tarzan Goes to India*	Jock Mahoney
1963	*Tarzan's Three Challenges*	Jock Mahoney
1966	*Tarzan and the Valley of Gold*	Mike Henry
1967	*Tarzan and the Great River*	Mike Henry
1968	*Tarzan and the Jungle Boy*	Mike Henry
1970	*Tarzan's Deadly Silence*	Ron Ely
1970	*Tarzan's Jungle Rebellion*	Ron Ely
1981	*Tarzan, the Ape Man*	Miles O'Keeffe
1984	*Greystoke: The Legend of Tarzan*	Christopher Lambert
1989	*Tarzan in Manhattan*★	Joe Lara

★*A television film—not theatrically released.*

Appendix B:
Ron Ely Television
Episodes (1966–1968)

There were a total of 57 episodes (including five two-part episodes) during the two full broadcast seasons of this series (1966-67 and 1967-68). The original airdates are in parentheses.

First Season

1. "Eyes of the Lion" (September 8, 1966). Revenge and honor motivate young Oringa to stalk the lion called the Red One, a beast that killed his father. Meanwhile, blind jungle princess Nara has trained a lion to be her "seeing eye" guide and protector in the savage wilds. When Oringa and his villagers begin stalking the wrong lion by mistake, it is Tarzan who must intervene and prevent a tragedy from happening. And it is the ape-man who wins the young princess' trust, thus bringing her into the safety of the civilized world. Guest stars: Laurie Sibbald and Ned Romero.

2. "The Ultimate Weapon" (September 16, 1966). Tarzan once killed an ivory poacher named Haines in self-defense; the ape-man and game warden Hoby Wallington had tracked the man and were about to arrest him. But now the poacher's son, Peter Haines, has come to Africa to investigate the circumstances of his father's death and to seek revenge against the murderer. In the course of things, Tarzan must save the life of Peter, who remains unaware that it was actually Tarzan who accidentally took his father's life. Guest stars: Andrew Prine and Jock Mahoney.

3. "Leopard on the Loose" (September 23, 1966). Tarzan's young friend Jai has raised a leopard since it was a cub, but now the full-grown cat must be shipped to a zoo, since it is not trained to live on its own in the jungle. Meanwhile, greedy trading-post worker Bell, preying on Jai's love for his pet, tricks the boy into releasing the beast, so he can recapture the leopard himself and sell it for a profit. It is now up to Tarzan to bring the perpetrator of the scheme to justice and to recapture the leopard, which has been muzzled and would surely die in the jungle. Guest stars: Russ Tamblyn, Ken Scott, and Morgan Jones.

4. "A Life for a Life" (September

231

30, 1966). A jungle crisis occurs when Jai is bitten by a poisonous Mygale spider. The boy will assuredly die unless he receives a blood transfusion within 24 hours. Complicating the matter, the new blood must come from someone who recently survived the Mygale spider's bite. The only two possibilities are a woman photographer and a wanted murderer. Meanwhile, the killer is held captive by a vengeful man who refuses to release him even to save Jai's life. It is left to Tarzan to effect the prisoner's escape and to rush him to Jai's side for the life-saving transfusion. Guest stars: Jon Alvar, Danica d'Hondt, and John Levinston.

5. "The Prisoner" (October 7, 1966). A diamond thief named Spooner attacks and seriously wounds a native policeman, whose tribe demands jungle justice. It is up to Tarzan to get the criminal (who has a fortune in diamonds hidden on his person) to jail before the natives take the law into their own hands. Tarzan, himself wounded in the arm, must fight off the attacks of Spooner's gang, who know the ape-man is the only thing between them and the diamonds. Despite long odds, Tarzan does indeed bring his prisoner to justice. Guest stars: Robert J. Wilke, Charles Maxwell, and Mina Dillard.

6. "The Three Faces of Death" (October 14, 1966). A beautiful tribal queen, Laneen, is challenged by the warrior Jamayo over her right to rule the Nombassa tribe. Laneen's friend Tarzan accepts Jamayo's challenge—three tortuous tests of skill and strength during which the slightest slip would mean death. The two men are tied together and must undergo the Three Faces of Death: a crocodile pool, the Dive of Death, and the Cage of Spears. Tarzan triumphs, and Laneen rightfully remains the ruler of the tribe. Guest stars: Woody Strode and Ena Hartman.

7. "The Prodigal Puma" (October 21, 1966). When a missionary is killed in the jungle by a puma, the doctor's assistant (the beautiful Sheri Kapinski) is left behind in the village; she is angry and cynical. When Tarzan and Rao track and capture the rare puma, the villain Spandrell and his sidekick Hacker carry out a plot to steal the beast and take Sheri as a hostage. Eventually, Tarzan is victorious over Spandrell, freeing Sheri and the puma. Guest stars: Rafer Johnson, Gigi Perreau, and Jan Merlin.

8. "The Deadly Silence: Part I" (October 28, 1966). The Colonel, a deranged ex-military officer, is carrying out a plot to become military ruler of all the jungle tribes. He and his men crush the resistance of tribe after tribe, until Tarzan gets wind of the plot and intervenes. Tarzan, realizing he must rally the natives to fight against the Colonel, bravely leaps into a lion pit to confront the King of the Beasts. The natives, of course, are inspired by Tarzan's bravery, and their courage rises. The crafty Colonel realizes that Tarzan is a threat to his new empire and plots the ape-man's death. Guest stars: Jock Mahoney, Woody Strode, and Nichelle Nichols.

9. "The Deadly Silence: Part II" (November 4, 1966). Tarzan again battles the demented Colonel, who is attempting to rule the jungle tribes by military force. Captured by the territorial police, the Colonel escapes by overpowering his guards and is once more a renegade. Meanwhile, Tarzan is trapped by the Colonel's men and dives into the river to escape, but a grenade thrown into the river causes the ape-man to go stone deaf. Undaunted by his temporary loss of hearing, Tarzan is aided by his jungle friends in eluding the Colonel and his men, eventually defeating them at their own game. Guest stars: Jock Mahoney, Woody Strode, and Nichelle Nichols.

10. "The Figurehead" (November 11, 1966). With the assassination of his father, the spoiled young Prince Sharif is now the ruler of his country. Conspirators are now plotting to kill the young prince, and Sharif escapes from his uncle Karim as he and Jai masquerade as each other to fool the enemies of the Crown. Tarzan steps into the breach to foil the plot of the assassins, as Prince Sharif, now certainly more worldly and less spoiled, is returned to the throne of his country. Guest stars: Ricky Cordell, Anthony Caruso, and Ken Drake.

11. "Village of Fire" (November 18, 1966). When Jai is bitten by an infected jaguar, he is struck with jungle fever and lies near death. The only hope of saving the boy's life is for Tarzan to recover a jungle serum that has been stolen by a native chief, also delirious with the deadly fever. At the village, Tarzan rescues Jai from death by fire, but the boy is still deathly ill. With a feud brewing between the witch doctor and the natives, a woman doctor concocts a serum from the blood of the jaguar and saves Jai's life. Guest stars: Nobu McCarthy, Joel Fluellen, and Chuck Wood.

12. "The Day of the Golden Lion" (December 2, 1966). During the staging of a jungle Olympics, Tarzan enters the games in place of his injured native friend, who must win the golden trophy to win the woman he loves. Also coveting the valuable trophy—the pure-gold statue of a lion—are archaeologist Suzy Parker and her hired henchmen. Despite being attacked by Parker's cutthroat cohorts, Tarzan wins the competition and saves the gold statue. Most important to Tarzan, his friend wins the woman of his heart. Guest stars: Suzy Parker, Curt Lowens, and Rockne Tarkington.

13. "Pearls of Tanga" (December 9, 1966). The Tanga tribe's ocean fishing area is patrolled by a human menace, evil German U-boat commander Admiral Gioco, who covets the pearls hidden in the beds far below. Using his submarine to raid the pearl beds, Gioco poisons the water to kill the fish and the native divers. When Tarzan begins an investigation of the plot, he is captured by the admiral, who sees the ape-man as the only real threat to his plans. But Tarzan escapes the clutches of the admiral and his frogmen and then sends them to their doom. The natives are grateful to Tarzan for solving this deadly dilemma. Guest stars: Carlos Rivas, Pearla Lita, and John Kelly.

14. "The End of the River" (December 16, 1966). When a plane crashes in the jungle, Tarzan rushes to the scene to find a young girl, Suzanne, whose injuries dictate that she must be hospitalized quickly or possibly die. Also surviving the crash are two men handcuffed together—one a policeman, the other a criminal, and both claiming to be the law enforcement official. Tarzan guides them all to the settlement, while a third man lurks in the jungle trying to free the prisoner. Tarzan gets Suzanne to the hospital and gives the wanted man a chance to escape. The man wasn't all bad and had helped the ape-man on the dangerous journey. Guest stars: Jill Donahue, Michael Whitney, and Robert J. Wilke.

15. "The Ultimate Duel" (December 23, 1966). The deranged Dr. Ivor Merrick has set up an electronics lab in the jungle, where he uses a computer to test animal and human behavior. The mad doctor decides that Tarzan would be a good subject for his theories and offers the natives a reward for the ape-man's body. Merrick is guiding the natives, armed with walkie-talkies, with his computer. Tarzan must call on all

his cunning and skill, and finally the betrayal of the doctor's aide, to survive. Tarzan reaches the lab, and with the help of Dr. Merrick's wife, destroys the computer and the threat of the mad doctor. Guest stars: Henry Silva, Gale Kobe, and Don Megowan.

16. "The Fire People" (December 30, 1966). A powerful volcano that is about to erupt threatens the lives of the superstitious tribe who live at the mouth of the roiling cauldron of lava. The tribe's beliefs forbid them to leave their homes under penalty of death. The old prophet strikes fear into the hearts of the natives, while the young king urges them to leave before it is too late. Tragedy strikes when the king's wife and unborn son die, and the king is now convinced that the prophet speaks the truth. When Jai is trapped on a narrow ledge, the king rescues him, and Tarzan must save them both. Finally Tarzan and Dr. Gloria Halverson convince the natives to forsake their beliefs and leave the mountain. Guest stars: Morris Erby, Elsa Cardenas, and Francisco Reyguera.

17. "Track of the Dinosaur" (January 6, 1967). The river water becomes polluted, so the local government sends a team of experts to drill freshwater wells. However, the natives believe the drilling might disturb a prehistoric monster who lives underground, so they ask for Tarzan's help. Meanwhile, a rich vein of minerals has been discovered at the drilling site, and corruption and greed take over the sanity of normally decent people. The villagers are scared away by a mechanical monster, and Tarzan must battle to the death the forces that would kill him and steal the valuable mineral deposit from the native tribe. Guest stars: Lloyd Bochner, Pippa Scott, and Harry Lauter.

18. "The Day the Earth Trembled" (January 13, 1967). A powerful earthquake traps the children and their teacher at a jungle mission school, and Tarzan rushes to their aid. Meanwhile, during the chaos of the earthquake, three convicts escape from the prison farm and try to kill Tarzan. The apeman is too strong for the jailbirds, and he convinces them to help him guide the children through the dangerous jungles to safety. Complicating matters, one of the convicts is the former fiancé of the teacher, Peggy Dean. Despite a stampeding herd of animals, a dangerous river crossing, and the escape attempts of the prisoners, Tarzan leads his merry band to safety. Guest stars: Susan Oliver, John Anderson, and Eugene Evans.

19. "Cap'n Jai" (January 20, 1967). While Tarzan is away, young Jai unwittingly becomes involved with three ruthless sailors who are searching the jungle for a fortune in stolen diamonds. A fourth conspirator who has betrayed the men is murdered by the sailors, and Jai is brought along to help find the jewels. Jai naively believes they are seeking lost "pirate treasure," and he becomes attached to one of the men. Jai and Dutch go off alone together and find the diamonds. But when Jai's life is threatened, the hardened sailor must decide between the boy's life and the stolen treasure. Guest star: Chips Rafferty.

20. "A Pride of Assassins" (January 27, 1967). Gunrunner Albers and his woman partner Diana Lawton have a falling out, and she decides to inform the authorities of their plot to smuggle guns and ammunition into the jungle to sell to renegade natives. Diana is captured by a tribe before she can act, and Tarzan is asked to bring her to safety. While traveling the only path back, Albers and his two cutthroats (one, a knife expert) wait in ambush for their

quarry. Tarzan, as always, is up to the challenge of superior force and defeats his would-be assassins. He also delivers Diana safely to the authorities. Guest stars: Jill Donahue, Gene Evans, and Victor French.

21. "The Golden Runaway" (February 3, 1967). Tarzan agrees to help a young woman, Martha Tolbooth, to search for her lost brother. Deep in the jungle, instead of her brother they find Red McGeehan, a rogue Irishman who escaped the revolution with his life as well as a fortune. McGeehan has a gruff exterior but a heart of gold; he donates a large sum of money to help replace a burned-down orphanage. Meanwhile, Red has his share of problems: Thieves are after his money, the authorities want to know where it came from, and Martha thinks he might have murdered her brother. It is up to Tarzan to straighten out the whole situation; he captures the thieves. McGeehan also wins the heart of Martha, who agrees to be his wife. Guest stars: Gia Scala and Sean McClory.

22. "Basil of the Bulge" (February 10, 1967). A former war hero on the verge of retirement, Sir Basil Bertram, is sent by his government to arrange a tribal treaty governing a river dam needed to halt flooding and provide power for a radar site. Meanwhile, corrupt official Roger Bradley plots to sabotage the treaty for his own gain. Jai overhears the plot and informs Basil, who is disbelieving. Basil is kidnapped by hostile natives, and Bradley plans to force him to lead an attack and thus destroy the government's credibility and ultimately the treaty. Although they don't like each other, Jai and Basil team up to defeat Bradley and save the treaty. Guest stars: Maurice Evans and Warren Stevens.

23. "Mask of Rona" (February 17, 1967). When native masks and shields surface in the art world, Beryl Swann is stunned—they are the unmistakable work of her sister, artist Rona Swann, who is presumed dead. A search party, led by Tarzan, is organized to find the world-renowned artist. Its members include Beryl Swann, art collector Peter Maas, and his sidekick Chambers. Unknown to anyone, Maas and Chambers are gunrunners who plan to steal Rona Swann's art when she is found. The lost artist is indeed found; she lives in a cave and is almost blind. Meanwhile, Tarzan thwarts the gunrunners and destroys the illegal guns. He also convinces Beryl to let her sister live her life in peace and seclusion in the jungle. Guest stars: Jock Mahoney, Leslie Parrish, Martin Gabel, and Nancy Malone.

24. "To Steal the Rising Sun" (February 24, 1967). Accompanied by Tarzan, photographer Lita McKenzie has the permission of Chief Lukumba to film the tribe's religious rituals and a priceless ruby that is used in the ceremonies. Tarzan and the beautiful jet-setter Lita are unwitting accomplices of Lukumba to steal the ruby, duped by the chief's plot to grab the gem for his own during the tribe's yearly ceremony. Tarzan (nobody's fool for long) extricates himself and Lita from the plot and exposes Chief Lukumba as the thief he really is, thus saving the ruby and his own honor. Guest stars: Roy Glenn, Sr., James Earl Jones, Victoria Shaw, and Strother Martin.

25. "Jungle Dragnet" (March 3, 1967). Tarzan agrees to guide a young woman, Mandy Mason, to a mission after her father is killed by a renegade tribe led by native zealots. Meanwhile, Mandy's life is in danger from two men, native revolutionary Kasembi and profiteer Thompson, who plan to silence her knowledge of a priceless oil field

discovered by her late father. Tarzan, Jai, and the girl find themselves in the midst of a jungle dragnet—native warriors ordered by Kasembi and Thompson to kill the interlopers. It is the courage and jungle savvy of Tarzan that extricate the trio and bring the criminals to justice. Guest stars: Victoria Meyerink, Simon Oakland, and William Marshall.

26. "The Perils of Charity Jones: Part I" (March 10, 1967). Spinster missionary Charity Jones forsakes her home in New England to be a missionary in the African jungles, fulfilling her father's dying wish. She brings along the Good Book and a musical organ to help civilize the natives. Upon encountering Tarzan and Jai, she accuses the ape-man of being an unsuitable father for the boy. Charity takes Jai in hand and heads for a mission school. Charity and Jai travel on a riverboat, which is sabotaged by a gunrunner. They are left to pilot a disabled boat; with hostile natives and the gunrunner in hot pursuit, they are soon captured. Although Tarzan is on their trail, will he be in time to save Jai and Charity? Guest stars: Julie Harris, Woody Strode and Bernie Hamilton.

27. "The Perils of Charity Jones: Part II" (March 17, 1967). Charity Jones and Jai are in the clutches of a tribe of hostile natives led by the fierce Chaka, and Tarzan is furiously searching the jungle for the lost duo. With little warning, Tarzan is attacked and seriously injured. Chaka has given Charity and Jai a reprieve from the death sentence, and the two nurse Tarzan back to health. Still, Charity insists on delivering the organ, which causes them to run headlong into the tribe that is scouring the jungle for them. It takes Tarzan at his best to save this unusual trio from the peril intended for them. Guest stars: Julie Harris, Woody Strode, Edward Binns, and Abraham Sofaer.

28. "The Circus" (March 24, 1967). Tarzan is part of a jungle dragnet searching for a convicted murderer, who has disguised himself as a member of a circus troupe touring Africa. Meanwhile, Jai and old friend Dutch Jensen, now employed as a circus roustabout, are the ones who actually uncover the fugitive waiting to escape by crossing the border with the circus. They send an urgent message to Tarzan, knowing they must stall the renegade revolutionary long enough for the ape-man to arrive and capture him. Guest stars: Chips Rafferty, Jack Elam, Sally Kellerman, and Leo Gordon.

29. "The Ultimatum" (March 31, 1967). Tarzan's life is threatened by Madeline Riker, who brings a gang of hired killers to the jungle seeking retribution for the death of her brother—killed by the ape-man. The bloodthirsty woman holds as hostage the entire village that helped Tarzan kill her evil brother, demanding that they surrender the ape-man or forfeit their own lives. Facing the ultimatum of death, the natives deliver Tarzan to Riker and her hired assassins, led by Karnak, to face the wrath of the vengeance-minded woman. Only Tarzan could extricate himself from his death trap and prove his character to be above the crime of murder he is accused of perpetrating. Guest stars: Ruth Roman and Ralph Meeker.

30. "Algie B. for Brave" (April 7, 1967). Tarzan and Jai are visited once again by Sir Basil Bertram, now retired, who is on a secret mission for his government to pinpoint the location of a foreign power's nuclear detection devices. Bertram also takes charge of his nephew Algernon (Algie), a lad who is so unsure of himself that he appears cowardly. Meanwhile, Tarzan seeks the killer of Algie's father—a quest that is one of the most difficult and important

of the ape-man's life. During the trouble that Basil and Algie share, the uncle and nephew become close and discover the real need they have for each other. Guest stars: Maurice Evans and Todd Garrett.

31. "Man Killer" (April 14, 1967). A "bewitching" puzzle for Tarzan begins when riverboat owner Polly Larkin is attacked by what she believes is a leopard. Actually the attack is plotted by a twisted jungle doctor, who hopes to raise money by gaining control of Polly's riverboat. The demented doctor uses psychedelic drugs and murder as proof that a long-dead leopard cult is still alive and that a young boy is the direct descendant of their renegade cult leader — literally a reincarnation of the leopard-man killer. It is up to Tarzan to solve the leopard-man murders. As always the ape-man is up to the arduous and dangerous task. Guest stars: Tammy Grimes, Jeremy Slate, and James Gregory.

Second Season

32. "Tiger, Tiger" (September 15, 1967). Engineer Cliff Stockwell and his wife Melody are in Africa to design and build an important jungle irrigation project. The venture is jeopardized when the native workers are afraid to continue working because of a fierce rogue tiger — a tiger that Stockwell claims does not exist. Tarzan is on hand to warn the engineer that he does not have the experience or the savvy to cope with this potentially dangerous situation. Nevertheless, Stockwell is determined to complete the project on schedule — until he finds there really is a tiger! As always, Tarzan comes to the rescue before trouble gets out of hand. Guest stars: James Whitmore and Anne Jeffreys.

33. "Voice of the Elephant" (September 22, 1967). An unusual jungle law states that working elephants may have a trial if they are accused of a crime. This law comes into play when Jai's elephant is falsely blamed (actually framed) for the tragic trampling of a jungle commissioner. Jai's impassioned plea to vacationing Judge Jim Lawrence to defend the elephant leads to the kidnapping of both the judge and Tarzan. The ape-man pieces together all the facts necessary to solve the mystery and to absolve Jai's elephant. Indeed, the real criminal is caught in his own trap. Guest stars: Murray Matheson, Frederick O'Neal, and Rockne Tarkington.

34. "Thief Catcher" (September 29, 1967). Tarzan is caught in the crossfire of a feud between young native chief N'duma and his rival Kesho. The bad blood is intensified when Jai is kidnapped by Kesho and his henchmen, two escaped convicts named Crandall and Dawkins. Now Tarzan and N'duma are forced to walk into a death trap set by Kesho, in hopes of saving Jai from the sinister chief and his cutthroats. Does Tarzan prove equal to the task of rescuing his young friend Jai and helping chief N'duma to win the feud against his evil counterpart? Naturally! Guest stars: George Kennedy, Don Mitchell, Yaphet Kotto, and Pascual Capote.

35. "The Blue Stone of Heaven: Part I" (October 6, 1967). World-renowned archaeologist Dr. Singleton comes to the jungle with his beautiful daughter Mary to find the Blue Stone of Heaven, an ancient stone worshipped by the jungle natives. Tarzan agrees to guide the doctor and Mary to a remote area of the jungle to search for the Blue Stone, which had been lost beneath the pyramids in ancient times. Legend has it that whoever stands to the right of the Blue Stone will be endowed with God-like powers. In his quest for the stone, Tarzan unintentionally violates an ancient taboo, which puts him in a

precarious position with bloodthirsty natives. Guest stars: Sam Jaffe, Ulla Stromstedt, William Marshall, and Harry Lauter.

36. "The Blue Stone of Heaven: Part II" (October 13, 1967). The power-hungry Colonel Tatakombi desires the precious Blue Stone for his own reasons and would do anything to obtain it—including destroying anything that gets in his way. When the madman discovers the Blue Stone, he uses the powerful icon to lead the natives into rebellion. The ruthless colonel is planning to threaten and coerce the jungle tribes to fall in line under his military power. Seeing that his most powerful enemy is Tarzan, Colonel Tatakombi hires Josh Miller to capture the ape-man. The sentence is death for Tarzan. Mary Singleton has fallen in love with the valiant Tarzan and tries to save him from the fate decreed by Tatakombi. In the end, of course, Tarzan calls on his jungle savvy and superhuman strength to defeat Tatakombi and place the Blue Stone where it belongs. Guest stars: Sam Jaffe, Ulla Stromstedt, William Marshall, and Harry Lauter.

37. "Maguma Curse" (October 20, 1967). Tarzan enters into a battle for justice for a young woman, Frankie McVeigh, who owns a diamond mine that is coveted by unscrupulous promoter Judson Bennett. When a Maguma tree, sacred to the Ebu tribespeople, is cut down, Bennett informs the tribe of the sacrilege. In retribution, N'Gota, the witch doctor, places a curse on Frankie, the daughter of the man believed responsible. With the death curse hanging over Frankie's head, Tarzan battles to defeat the enemies who would end both their lives. Guest stars: Barbara Luna, Simon Oakland, and Ken Renard.

38. "The Fanatics" (October 27, 1967). Crusading reporter Diana Russell enlists Tarzan's aid to prove that a local tribal election is rigged. Native political leader Kimini wants to federate all the tribes in the area under the leadership of one man—himself. Meanwhile, he is actually the pawn of unscrupulous profiteer Brooks, who knows of rich mineral deposits on tribal lands. Tarzan and Diana amass the evidence to expose Kimini and Brooks as frauds, thus restoring integrity to the tribal election process. Guest stars: Diana Hyland, Don Marshall, and William Smithers.

39. "The Last of the Supermen" (November 3, 1967). Though World War II has been over for years, a Nazi invasion strikes Tarzan's part of Africa. Escaped ex–Nazis Von Wolvner and Helge are searching for a fortune in negotiable bonds and securities, buried somewhere in the jungle. Von Wolvner forces Tarzan and the son of a former Nazi, Helmut Stever, to lead them to the buried bonds. The quest becomes even more dangerous when a tribe of angry natives pursue Tarzan and the Nazis. Only the ape-man can extricate himself from this deep trouble and bring the evil Nazis to justice. Guest stars: Alf Kjellin, Antoinette Bower, Michael Burns, and Brock Peters.

40. "Hotel Hurricane" (November 10, 1967). A downed plane in the jungle contains $5 million of syndicate loot—lost money unless someone like Tarzan can locate the plane. Syndicate mobsters hold Jai hostage and force the ape-man to lead them to the downed plane. The life of his young friend is at stake. One of the mobsters whose wife, the hotel owner, left him because of his involvement with the syndicate, cooperates with Tarzan to free Jai and to bring the real criminals to justice. When the ordeal is over, the man and woman decide to reconcile their differences and get back together. Guest stars: Michael Tolan, Bert Freed, and Jean Hale.

41. "The Pride of a Lioness" (November 17, 1967). Dr. Richard Wilson operates a jungle hospital, despite the opposition of native witch doctor Zwengi, who threatens to have him killed. Also hoping the young man will leave Africa is his socialite mother, Mrs. Wilson, whose husband left her alone for many years while he operated his African clinic. She hopes to prevent her son from leading the same life. Tarzan refuses to help Mrs. Wilson coerce her son, so she bands with Zwengi in a bizarre attempt to regain control over Richard and bring him home. Tarzan helps Mrs. Wilson to realize that her husband's cause was noble, as is her son's work, and thus she decides to stay on in the jungle to assist him. Guest stars: James MacArthur, Helen Hayes, and Geoffrey Holder.

42. "Mountains of the Moon: Part I" (November 24, 1967). Tarzan agrees to guide Rosanna McCloud, the leader of a fervent religious group, and her cultists to a "promised land" in Africa. The land was bought and paid for by Rosanna to establish their community, but it really belongs to an African tribe and is part of a forbidden zone. The sad reality is that the group has been cheated by a crooked guide named Whitehead, and the trials of their journey might have been in vain. Guest stars: Ethel Merman, Harry Lauter, and Strother Martin.

43. "Mountains of the Moon: Part II" (December 1, 1967). As Tarzan guides Rosanna McCloud and her religious cultists to the land they hoped would be their new home, they face many perils. The land they purchased from Whitehead is actually owned by King Likui and the Bwala tribe—fierce warriors who don't allow outsiders to trespass on their land. Meanwhile, Tarzan is shot while chasing a crook. Tarzan and the cultists eventually learn

that Whitehead has sold guns to the natives, and they are attacked by warriors led by the young chief. Only one man in Africa can bring this sticky situation to a palpable conclusion—Tarzan. Guest stars: Ethel Merman, William Marshall, and Rockne Tarkington.

44. "Jai's Amnesia" (December 15, 1967). Jai suffers an accident, and the resulting knock on the head leaves him with amnesia. Meanwhile, drifter J.C. Crosby and his band of bullies are plotting to steal a fabulous ruby that is sacred to one of the native tribes. They take advantage of Jai's loss of memory and trick the boy into helping them steal the priceless gem. Tarzan is tracking Jai and Crosby, and in a stunning moment is almost shot. Suddenly Jai's memory returns, the ape-man defeats the crooks, and the jewel is returned to its rightful owners. Guest stars: John Dehner, John Alderson, and Hal Baylor.

45. "Creeping Giants" (December 29, 1967). American engineer Walter Wilson is part of an engineering team hired to build a dam near a mighty mountain range called the Creeping Giants. However, Chief Lwutumba fears that if the men use dynamite, a landslide will bury the villages at the base of the mountain range—and he is right. The villain is engineering team supervisor Colin Yaeger, who plots Tarzan's death when the ape-man is asked to intervene by Lwutumba. Tarzan and Wilson collaborate to expose Yaeger's plot to destroy the villages before it is too late. Guest stars: Robert J. Wilke, Raymond St. Jacques, and Joel Fluellen.

46. "The Professional" (January 5, 1968). Believing he's doing the right thing, Tarzan guides a band of mercenaries, led by Colonel Stone, to locate an isolated tribe. The colonel has been hired by a foreign power to annex some valuable land owned by the tribe—at

any cost. When the tribe refuse to surrender the land peacefully, the colonel takes their chief, Sorda, prisoner. Tarzan now realizes that Colonel Stone is evil and will stop at nothing to gain the land. Using his cunning and jungle tactics, the ape-man rallies the villagers against Stone and his mercenaries and stops them cold. Guest stars: Pat Conway, Jack Colvin, Karl Swenson, and Clarence Williams.

47. "The Convert" (January 12, 1968). Three nuns—Sister Terese, Sister Ann, and Sister Martha—are planning to build a jungle hospital to care for sick and wounded native villagers. The local natives, who don't trust the motives of the nuns and want them to leave, are led by Chief Nerlan. Meanwhile, greedy land developer Larson uses the nuns as pawns in a plot to make himself rich, exploiting the hostility between the two factions for his own purposes. But Tarzan sees through Larson's plot, defeats the villain, and makes the villagers realize the good that the nuns and the hospital will bring them. Guest stars: Malachi Throne, James Earl Jones, and Diana Ross.

48. "King of the Dwsari" (January 26, 1968). An American expatriate, "King" Brown, has managed to install himself as ruler of a tribe of jungle natives. The cunning Brown used a simple trick to win over the natives: They had never seen a camera, and when he took their pictures, he claimed to have control of their souls. Meanwhile, Tarzan has been taken prisoner by Zwaka, the bodyguard of King Brown. While ambushers try to steal Brown's gold, Tarzan escapes and cooks up a little superstition of his own. The ape-man defeats Brown with his own black magic and returns control of the tribe to themselves. Guest stars: Robert Loggia, Morgan Woodward, and Ernie Terrell.

49. "A Gun for Jai" (February 2, 1968). A jungle feud is brewing between a group of trigger-happy hunters and a native tribe, who resent the intrusion of interlopers in their homeland. Tarzan and Jai run into the safari. While Tarzan goes to hear the natives' side of the story, Jai makes friends with Mulvaney, who gives the lad a gun for target practice. Jai accidentally shoots Cheeta, who races off into the jungle with the boy crying out in pursuit. Tarzan's investigation reveals that the hunters have stolen valuable treasures from the natives. It is up to the ape-man to recover the stolen items and return them, as well as teach Jai a little lesson about the danger of guns. Guest stars: Peter Whitney, Geoffrey Holder, and Ed Baker.

50. "Trek to Terror" (February 9, 1968). Dr. Kenneth Kiley, friend to Tarzan and loved by the natives, is wrongly accused of murder by a vindictive and corrupt police inspector, Regis. Tarzan is tricked into revealing the whereabouts of the doctor, and Regis plots with his accomplices to murder Dr. Kiley "accidentally" on the long trek through the jungle back to the city. Law or no law, Tarzan sides with right—he knows his friend is not guilty of murder and battles Regis to learn the truth and save the doctor from an undeserved fate. Guest stars: Michael Ansara and Booker T. Bradshaw.

51. "End of a Challenge" (February 16, 1968). Two longtime rivals, Tarzan and Chief Bangu of the Masai, must form a temporary truce when Jai and the chief's son, Ubi, are kidnapped by Montroso, the thief. Jai and Ubi think it is lots of fun to steal a ride on the elephant safari, but change their minds when the safari is raided by ruthless mercenaries. Meanwhile, Tarzan and Bangu are in pursuit of the safari, and despite the distrust between the old enemies, they succeed in rescuing the

boys. Still, old wounds heal slowly—the two men refuse to bury the hatchet in spite of their trials together. Guest stars: Chill Wills, Woody Strode, and Henry Jones.

52. "Jungle Ransom" (February 23, 1968). Tarzan tracks and captures outlaw leader Ramon Cortinez and plans to bring him in to the authorities. But Tarzan's plans are waylaid when a young woman, Phyllis Fraser, asks the ape-man to help save her husband Larry, who is held for $250,000 ransom in the outlaw's camp. There is trouble for Tarzan in the form of a strongman named Sampson, but, as always, the ape-man is up to the challenge. Later, Phyllis is shattered when she discovers that Ramon and her husband were in cahoots, in an elaborate plot to dupe her out of a quarter of a million dollars. Guest stars: Fernando Lamas, Barbara Bouchet, Jack Hogan, and Ted Cassidy.

53. "Four O'Clock Army: Part I" (March 1, 1968). Tarzan enlists the aid of Sir Basil Bertram, a retired general, to raise and train a native militia. The goal is for the Waziri natives to protect themselves from marauding slave traders. Meanwhile, missionary Charity Jones, who is against all forms of violence, tries to persuade the slavers to give up their illegal and immoral pursuit of slaves. But it is up to Tarzan and Sir Basil to motivate the villagers to defend themselves from the marauders. Guest stars: Maurice Evans, Julie Harris, and Bruce Gordon.

54. "Four O'Clock Army: Part II" (March 8, 1968). When slave traders burn the Waziri village and capture prisoners, including Jai, Sir Basil Bertram and Charity Jones form a truce to work for a common cause. Tarzan and Sir Basil are captured by the slavers, but Sir Basil manages to escape. With Charity's help, he frees Tarzan and Jai. De-

spite past differences, Charity and Sir Basil, along with Tarzan, defeat the slavers who were threatening the Waziri tribes. Guest stars: Maurice Evans, Julie Harris, and Bernie Hamilton.

55. "Rendezvous for Revenge" (March 15, 1968). Tarzan believes that in the past he killed a man—Dan Burton, an African-style rustler—when the man fell from a cliff where the two were struggling. It turns out that Burton was only crippled from his fall. Now, to gain revenge, Burton's girlfriend Doria has set a trap for Tarzan. Doria, along with two of Burton's men, plans to throw Tarzan off the same cliff, to render him a cripple as Burton is now. But Tarzan escapes the trap and vainly attempts to capture Burton, who makes his getaway with Doria across the border, tossing grenades in Tarzan's path to halt his pursuit. Guest stars: John Vernon and Laraine Stephens.

56. "Alex the Great" (March 22, 1968). Tarzan is called to a local village to protect it from savage, man-eating cats that have been lured to the area by Kamal Amir, a pint-sized villain with plans to steal a priceless cat idol that the villagers worship. The ape-man also meets Alex Spense, a former Olympic athlete who challenges Tarzan to a test of strength so he can show off his superiority. Meanwhile, Kamal sets a trap for Tarzan and Alex and abducts Stacey, Alex's fiancée. The ape-man and Alex halt their battle of strength to join forces and rescue Stacey from the small but powerful evil one, Kamal. Guest stars: Neville Brand, Michael Dunn, and Diane Williams.

57. "Trina" (April 5, 1968). Tarzan is surprised to find an all-girl safari stranded in the jungle. Although reluctant, Tarzan agrees to lead the mini-skirted females in search of Trina's long lost uncle, Ben MacKenzie. Unknown

to Trina, her uncle has spent the past 20 years unifying the upriver tribes and is now known as Chembe Kunji, Lord of the Earth. When Tarzan locates him, MacKenzie is unwilling to release his hold on the tribes or relinquish his power; thus a confrontation with the ape-man is inevitable. Guest stars: Stacey Maxwell and Nehemiah Persoff.

APPENDIX C:
WOLF LARSON
TELEVISION EPISODES

First Season

1. "Tarzan and the Poisoned Waters" (October 6, 1991). Tarzan discovers that many of the jungle animals are sick and dying, and he traces the problem to greedy gold distillers, who use deadly mercury in their process and then let the PCB-saturated sludge run into the river, where the animals drink. Confronting the interlopers, Tarzan is shot at and tumbles down a waterfall; he appears to be grievously injured. Although he is wounded and his adversaries have guns, Tarzan and his small army overcome the intruders. Guest star: Jorge Rivero.

2. "Tarzan and the Silent Child" (October 13, 1991). When a plane crashes in the jungle, Tarzan must deal with a cocaine smuggler who has duped the pilot into carrying the illegal cargo without his knowledge. The true villain is Hauser, whom Tarzan defeats in a battle of strength. The young daughter of the pilot is traumatized and unable to speak, but after her jungle ordeal with Tarzan and Jane, she regains her power of speech. Guest stars: James Healy, Gregory Paul Jackson, and Olia Deneuve Ougrik.

3. "Tarzan Tames the Bronx" (October 20, 1991). When Simon's teenage godson Carlos—a tough kid from the Bronx—comes to the jungle for a visit, Tarzan takes the boy under his wing. The boy is bitter and afraid of heights because his father was killed in a fall from a construction site. Tarzan's wisdom and guidance help to straighten out the young man, before his character is permanently damaged. When Simon is trapped in his vehicle by a fallen burning tree, Carlos overcomes his fear of heights to help Tarzan rescue Simon. Guest star: Leonardo Garcia.

4. "Tarzan and the Picture of Death" (October 27, 1991). An internationally famous model and her photographer visit the jungle for a fashion shoot. Tarzan, Jane, and Roger are outraged that part of her wardrobe is a full-length leopard coat. When Jane explains that a photo shoot would further exploit the jungle animals and kill more creatures, Tarzan demands that the unwelcome visitors leave the jungle at once. Kendra and Blake recklessly commandeer a jeep and careen toward a washed-out road, and Tarzan is forced

to save their lives—teaching them a valuable lesson in the process. Guest stars: Richard Eden and Claire Cellucci.

5. "Tarzan and the Unwelcome Guest" (November 3, 1991). Roger's father (Taft) visits his son in the jungle and is not impressed by his progress as a researcher. He decides to pull the plug on the funding for the research that Jane and Roger are conducting. Later, when Taft suffers chest pains in the jungle and has forgotten his heart medicine, it is Tarzan to the rescue with his own herbal potion. Of course, Taft has a change of heart and offers to continue the funding, allowing Roger to remain in the jungle. Guest star: Chuck Shamata.

6. "Tarzan and the Caves of Darkness" (November 10, 1991). Tarzan must match wits with a greedy ivory poacher named Cordell Winslow, and his gang, who are slaughtering elephants for their tusks. The vicious poachers throw Roger into a crocodile-infested river and set a death trap for Jane, but with Tantor's help, Tarzan rescues them both. The corrupt Winslow is captured by Tarzan and is on his way to jail, but offers a warning to the ape-man: "I will be back!" Guest star: Gavin O'Herlihy.

7. "Tarzan and the Woman of Steel" (November 17, 1991). Jane's once-frail cousin Patrice comes for a visit, and Jane is amazed to find her now a robust, muscular bodybuilder (who, of course, is smitten with Tarzan). When Tarzan and Jane discover that Patrice is taking steroids, she storms angrily into the jungle, only to run face to face with a savage cougar. Tarzan comes to her rescue and must risk his own life to save Patrice. Guest star: Marisa Pare.

8. "Tarzan and the River of Death" (December 1, 1991). When Tarzan discovers former drug dealer Karl Hauser dumping barrels of toxic waste

into the river, there is a violent confrontation. With his mighty war cry, Tarzan calls his elephants to trample the camp of the polluters and then with the help of some parrots, tracks Hauser through the jungle. When Hauser attempts to bury Tarzan in the toxic sludge, it is he who buries himself as he accidentally slides into the river. Guest star: James Healy.

9. "Tarzan and the Killer Lion" (December 8, 1991). A beautiful woman named Nikki Carlson crash-lands her plane in the jungle and is rescued from the burning wreckage by Tarzan. Her mission: to kill Tarzan's lion Juma, whom she has mistakenly identified as the lion that killed her father years before. When Nikki finally confronts Juma in the jungle, it is her life that is threatened. It is up to Tarzan to save her and then explain the truth. Guest star: Joanne Vannicola.

10. "Tarzan's Christmas" (December 15, 1991). Tarzan's chimpanzee friend Maya is wounded defending Cheeta from a cougar, and Tarzan brings the ancient chimp to his compound in hopes of saving its life. When the old chimp dies, Tarzan is devastated. Jane decides to postpone her trip home for Christmas to see her sister and instead spends the holiday with Tarzan. Everyone finally gets into the Christmas spirit, and Tarzan and Cheeta drop white flower petals from the roof to simulate snow falling for Jane.

11. "Tarzan and the Orphan" (January 19, 1992). Jane finds a lion cub in the jungle that has strayed from its pride. Later, Jane accidentally touches the cub, giving it a human scent, so when they try to place the cub with a pride of lions, it is rejected because of Jane's scent. Tarzan finds the solution: He rubs the cub with a plant that removes the human scent, and the cub is

then accepted by the pride. Jane is ecstatic at the success of their rescue mission.

12. "Tarzan and the Mystic Cavern" (January 26, 1992). Roger's self-esteem is at a low ebb, and he goes to the Paxton caves to find some rare leaves needed in Jane's research. As the cave starts to flood, Roger becomes trapped, and Tarzan arrives in the nick of time to save him. On the way out of the cave, Roger spies some ancient cave paintings and believes he has made an important discovery. Despite the fact that this is not a great historical find, Tarzan lets Roger believe it is, to help boost the young man's sagging confidence.

13. "Tarzan and the Pirate Treasure" (February 2, 1992). Jane's former fiancé, Jack Traverse, arrives at Jane's compound, hoping to rekindle their former romance. But instead of love, Traverse is actually after a pirate's treasure that only Cheeta can locate. With Tarzan blocking his every effort to gain the treasure, Traverse takes Jane hostage to force Tarzan to help him. But Tarzan leaps to action and frees Jane and with lightning speed disarms Traverse. Tarzan then makes sure the treasure will remain hidden forever. Guest star: Adrian Paul.

14. "Tarzan in the Sacred Cave" (February 9, 1992). When the evil Cordell Winslow returns to the jungle to steal priceless artifacts, Tarzan thwarts his plan and returns to the Sacred Cave to replace the stolen items. However, Winslow follows him and shoots Tarzan's rope. The ape-man falls to the ground and strikes his head, causing him to revert to a beast. Eventually, Tarzan regains his faculties through a second blow to the head and battles and defeats Winslow. Tarzan seals the Sacred Cave forever, with plans to

donate the artifacts to a museum. Guest star: Gavin O'Herlihy.

15. "Tarzan and the Killer's Revenge" (February 16, 1992). Rhino poacher Bruno Valletti, whom Tarzan sent to prison years before, escapes and returns to the jungle. He shows up at the compound and overpowers Roger and Simon, leaving them tied next to a bomb with a burning fuse. The vengeful Valletti next goes after Tarzan and Jane, who with Cheeta's help, manage to win the battle with the brute. Moments later, Tarzan cuts the fuse to the bomb just in time to save Roger and Simon, who breathe a sigh of relief. Guest star: Lorenzo Caccialanza.

16. "Tarzan's Journey to Danger" (February 23, 1992). Jane is bitten by a poisonous spider. After capturing it in a jar, she falls to the ground unconscious. The only man who could possibly prepare an antidote for such a bite is an old tribal healer named Tubuto. Tarzan and Cheeta brave the treacherous journey to find Tubuto, who directs them to the last source of the healing plant. The old man instructs Tarzan how to prepare the antidote, and the ape-man rushes back to administer the medicine. Jane's life is saved. Guest star: Norman Beaton.

17. "Tarzan and the Extra-Terrestrials" (March 1, 1992). Edmund Hampton, a retired schoolteacher, wants to view an upcoming lunar eclipse. He had a dream that during the eclipse he was destined to meet extra-terrestrials (who he hopes will save the Earth from travesty). Hampton even believes that Tarzan is one of the aliens. But when Tarzan saves Hampton from a rogue leopard and bleeds like an ordinary man Hampton's dream is shattered. Even though there is a strange happening during the eclipse, Tarzan tells Hampton that it is himself,

not aliens, who must work to save the Earth. Guest star: Aubrey Morris.

18. "Tarzan, the Hunted" (March 8, 1992). Tarzan must match wits with Gordon Shaw, a world-renowned bow hunter who comes to Africa to kill an elephant. When Tarzan stops Shaw just as he is about to kill Tantor, Shaw decides that a much greater prize would be Tarzan himself. Using Simon's life as bait, Shaw offers Tarzan a deal: If he can survive 24 hours or until Shaw's arrows are exhausted, Simon will live. As the game of cat-and-mouse continues, the ape-man is quicker than Shaw's arrows. Finally, Tarzan dodges Shaw's last arrow, and the two adversaries struggle on the edge of a cliff. Tarzan is victorious when Shaw tumbles over the cliff, barely grabbing a branch and crying out for Tarzan's help. Guest star: Ron Ely.

19. "Tarzan and the Enemy Within" (March 15, 1992). Tarzan is haunted by a recurring nightmare—a small plane crashes, and he is unable to save the lives of the passengers. Simon helps Tarzan to understand that he is dreaming about the crash that killed his parents and that his guilt feelings are unwarranted. Returning to the site of the crash, Jane helps Tarzan exorcise the old ghosts that are haunting him and realize that there was nothing he could have done to save their lives. Amid the wreckage of the plane, Tarzan finds a locket containing photos of his parents and with his precious memento in hand, he returns to his home, at long last at peace with his memories.

20. "Tarzan's Eleventh Hour" (April 12, 1992). A misbehaving Cheeta is slapped by Roger, and the chimp reacts angrily, running away into the jungle. Meanwhile, the bond of friendship between Cheeta and Tantor, the elephant, is so strong that the mighty beast refuses to eat or drink in the absence of his diminutive friend. As Tantor's condition becomes serious, Roger searches the jungle for Cheeta. When Roger finds the chimp, they both fall into a hunter's pit and are threatened by a powerful python. Tarzan arrives in the nick of time to vanquish the reptile and free Roger and Cheeta. Back in camp, Tantor quickly recovers from his funk when he sees his tiny simian friend.

21. "Tarzan and the Deadly Gift" (April 19, 1992). Hoping to spark a romance with Jane, photographer Blake Evans brings her a gift from Mexico—a ferret. However, the ferret is carrying a deadly virus that threatens all the jungle creatures. The threat becomes imminent when a jealous Cheeta knocks over its cage, allowing the infected animal to escape. Tarzan tracks the ferret to a ravine blocked by a landslide and eventually recaptures the rodent. He vaccinates it to eliminate the potential menace. When Blake prepares to leave the jungle, his exit is bittersweet because he has been rejected by Jane (who, of course, loves Tarzan). Guest star: Richard Eden.

22. "Tarzan and the Savage Storm" (April 26, 1992). In the midst of a savage jungle storm, Tarzan and friends (gathered around a fire telling ghost stories) are surprised by a visitor—Jane's ex-fiancé Jack Traverse, whose plane was forced down by the storm. The unscrupulous Traverse plans to steal a rare panther cub, and when the storm subsides grabs his prey and escapes in Simon's vehicle. After subduing the ferocious mother cat, Tarzan uses a shortcut to intercept Traverse in the moving vehicle. The battle is over in moments because Tarzan is too strong for the poacher. Tarzan returns the cub to its mother and deals with Traverse accordingly. Guest star: Adrian Paul.

23. "Tarzan and the Golden Egg" (May 3, 1992). When the rare goshawk is threatened with extinction by the spraying of pesticides, Jane enlists Tarzan's help to prevent the tragedy. Together they must journey to the Varunga Cliffs, where the eggs of a single female goshawk will soon be threatened by further spraying. After a long journey, they reach the cliffs, and Tarzan climbs toward his goal. Just as he reaches the nest, the plane approaches carrying the deadly pesticides. Calming the frightened female with his jungle call, Tarzan scoops up the eggs just in time. Later, their mission of mercy complete, Tarzan, Jane, and Roger watch the male and female goshawks circle the sky in a mating ritual.

24. "Tarzan and the Test of Friendship" (May 10, 1992). Roger Taft, Sr., arrives in the jungle and offers Jane a stunning promotion: running his multi-million-dollar foundation dedicated to saving the environment. The job would force her to move to New York. Jane takes a walk to think it over and gets lost in the jungle. Tarzan and Tantor, searching for Jane, arrive just as her campfire is about to burn out of control. Back in camp, Jane dreams of kissing Tarzan, but confused by her emotions, she accepts Taft's job offer. Meanwhile, malaria-stricken Simon is wandering the jungle, and after Tarzan and Jane rescue him from a deadly snake, Jane decides to stay on in the jungle with her good friends. Guest star: Chuck Shamata.

25. "Tarzan in the Eye of the Hurricane" (May 17, 1992). As a hurricane approaches the jungle, Roger delivers a mysterious briefcase to Simon to be sent out with the next mail. It turns out that the briefcase contains a manuscript that Roger has written, detailing his jungle adventures and making Roger the disproportionate hero of these adventures.

When Simon and Roger argue over the merits of the book, Tarzan reminds them of their bitter argument at Christmas, in an attempt to bring them together. Simon agrees to fly the manuscript out the next day, but a mighty gust of wind carries away the pages. Everyone is secretly relieved at this turn of events, until Roger reveals that he has another copy of the manuscript.

Second Season (not presented on U.S. television)

26. "Tarzan and the Missile of Doom." Tarzan battles a renegade Navy Seal who has rerouted a nuclear missile to land in the jungle.

27. "Tarzan and the Forbidden Jewels." A hunter comes to the jungle, and hearing of a secret stash of jewels, forces Tarzan to take him to where it is hidden.

28. "Tarzan and the Broken Promise." An old acquaintance of Tarzan's shows up ostensibly to renew their friendship, but is actually intent on recovering buried cash.

29. "Tarzan and the Amazon Women." Tarzan must rescue a journalist who is captured by fierce "Amazon" female warriors.

30. "Tarzan and the Karate Warriors." Tarzan matches wits and skills with two unscrupulous karate champions who are in the jungle to pick up illegal rhino powder.

31. "Tarzan and the Lion Girl." Tarzan and his friends try to help a girl who has been raised by lions make the transition back to civilization when they discover she is ill.

32. "Tarzan and the Deadly Delusion." Jane goes temporarily insane when she accidentally ingests a plant made poisonous by toxic waste. Tarzan must rescue her.

33. "Tarzan and the Primitive Urge." When Tarzan tries to head off a dangerous junglewide spraying of pesticides, he loses his memory and returns to his primitive ape-man roots.

34. "Tarzan and the Mysterious Sheik." A sheik comes to the jungle intent on finding oil and kidnaps Jane. Tarzan must save her and expel the sheik from the jungle.

35. "Tarzan and the Runaways." Tantor, the elephant, and Cheeta, the chimp, feeling ignored, run away together and get into deep trouble.

36. "Tarzan Meets Jane." On the eve of Jane's first anniversary in the jungle, she remembers her initial meeting with Tarzan.

37. "Tarzan and the Wayward Balloon." When Jack and Roger's hot-air balloon crashes, Tarzan and Jane must rescue them.

38. "Tarzan and the Fugitive's Revenge." A dangerous prisoner escapes, intent on wreaking revenge on his archenemy, Tarzan.

39. "Tarzan and the Mutant Creature." Jane is kidnapped and taken to an underwater cave by the lagoon's "sea creature." Tarzan must rescue Jane and free the strange creature so it can return to the ocean.

40. "Tarzan Rescues the Songbird." Jane's old flame (a successful blues singer) arrives in the jungle to rekindle their old romance and to escape from a problem.

41. "Tarzan and the Fire Field." When Roger tries to reaffirm his manhood by single-handedly recovering a fossil, he stumbles on to a field of ex-

ploding fire geysers. Only Tarzan can save him.

42. "Tarzan and the Movie Star." A movie star comes to the jungle to do research and ends up learning a lesson in humility from Tarzan.

43. "Tarzan and the Fountain of Youth." Tarzan must stop a deadly cosmetics queen from murdering monkeys for her "secret" formula.

44. "Tarzan and the Law of the Jungle." Fearing that he has turned Cheeta into a house pet, Tarzan releases him to the wild, so the chimp can make his own choice.

45. "Tarzan and the Shaft of Death." When Tarzan is nearly killed in the collapse of an old mine shaft, the tables are turned and Jane must rescue him.

46. "Tarzan and the Polluted River." Tarzan faces off with a greedy prospector who returns to the jungle to mine uranium.

47. "Tarzan's Dangerous Journey." Tarzan helps a young doctor face the tribal test that will enable him to become chief of his people.

48. "Tarzan and the Toxic Terror." Roger's brush with death leads Tarzan on a collision course with a chemical dumper who threatens to destroy the ocean.

49. "Tarzan and the Earthly Challenge." When Roger decides to return home to an old girlfriend, Tarzan and friends use an environmental challenge to change his mind.

50. "Tarzan and the Mysterious Fog." Tarzan must stop a duplicitous chemist from destroying the jungle with tests of a new poison gas.

INDEX